Philosophy of Religion

Philosophy of Religion: An Introduction with Readings provides an introduction to philosophical thinking about some of the central aspects of religion.

With the entry-level student in mind, Stuart Brown guides the reader through three main topics: whether or not there is life after death; whether or not there is a powerful, beneficent intelligence controlling the universe; and the nature and appropriate defence of religious belief or faith. A concise discussion of the classical arguments in philosophy of religion is combined with an emphasis on its relationship to contemporary science (especially Darwinism) and philosophy of mind.

Philosophy of Religion: An Introduction with Readings is a superb philosophical introduction to religion. It will be of equal interest to students of philosophy and religion.

Stuart Brown is professor of philosophy at the Open University.

Philosophy of Religion

An introduction with readings

Stuart Brown

London and New York

First published 2001
by Routledge
11 New Fetter Lane, London EC4P 4EE

Simultaneously published in the USA and Canada
by Routledge
29 West 35th Street, New York, NY 10001

Routledge is an imprint of the Taylor & Francis Group

© 2001 The Open University

This updated and revised version is based on a coursebook previously published by the Open University

Typeset in Perpetua and Grotesque Monotype by Taylor & Francis Books Ltd
Printed and bound in Great Britain by TJ International Ltd, Padstow, Cornwall

British Library Cataloguing in Publication Data
A catalogue record for this book is available from the British Library

Library of Congress Cataloging in Publication Data
Brown, Stuart C.
Philosophy of Religion: An Introduction with Readings / Stuart Brown.
1. Religion – philosophy. I. Title.
BL51 .B778 2000
210–dc21 00-030516

ISBN 0–415–21237–5 (hbk)
ISBN 0–415–21238–3 (pbk)

Contents

Preface

ACKNOWLEDGEMENTS

I am grateful to colleagues at the Open University for comments on various drafts of this book and for suggestions as to what should be included in it.

Grateful acknowledgement is also made to the following sources for permission to reproduce material in this book: Badham, L. 'Problems with accounts of life after death', in Badham, P. and Badham, L. 1987, *Death and Immortality in the Religions of the World*, New Era Books, by permission of the author (for Reading 1). Dawkins, R. 1986, *The Blind Watchmaker*, Addison Wesley Longman, by permission of the author (for Reading 2). Stannard, R. 1989, *Grounds for Reasonable Belief*, Scottish Academic Press, by permission of the author (for Reading 3). Hick, J. 1966, *Evil and the God of Love*, Macmillan (for Readings 5 and 6).

HOW TO USE THIS BOOK

This book is divided into three parts, which are subdivided further into a total of seven chapters. As you read through it you will find there are a number of places where you are asked to stop and do something. At many of these places there are straightforward exercises which give you the opportunity to use and develop skills you should already have acquired. The answers given at the back of the book should give you useful feedback on how you are doing. There are also exercises which consist of activities and questions to give you the opportunity to develop some of the less routine skills involved in doing philosophy, which may involve using your experience of the subject in an imaginative way in the attempt to think up criticisms or articulate a position of your own. Here you should not expect to have anticipated what I was about to say. None the less, in order to achieve the study objectives that are suggested for the book and for each chapter, you are advised to attempt all the activities and questions as well as the other exercises.

STUDY OBJECTIVES

By the end of your study of this book you should:

- Be able to offer arguments for and against the main positions discussed.
- Be able to recognize some of the interconnections between theories of the mind and beliefs about mortality or immortality.
- Be able to assess some of the claimed implications of Darwinism for religious belief.
- Have had practice in a range of reasoning techniques.
- Have broadened your knowledge of philosophy.
- Have gained in expertise and confidence in reading and evaluating the philosophical writings of others.
- Have gained in expertise and confidence in articulating and arguing for a point of view of your own.

This book will have achieved its objectives if it encourages you to read and think further about some of the topics discussed. At the end of each chapter, further reading is suggested, often of works that themselves have a full bibliography. Some important figures from the history of philosophy have contributed to debates in the philosophy of religion and, where appropriate, I have given some attention to their contributions. There are references here not only to the original works but also, in the notes, to recent writings on the thought of these philosophers which should be helpful if you choose to follow them up.

Introduction

This book aims to introduce some of the central questions in the philosophy of religion. It does not presuppose prior knowledge of philosophy. On the contrary, it aims, where appropriate, to introduce some of the techniques and vocabulary of the subject and to provide the reader who wishes it with the opportunity to acquire or consolidate knowledge of general philosophical skills.

Philosophy of religion has always been closely interconnected with other areas of philosophy. For instance, discussions of the mortality or immortality of the soul turn in large measure on questions about the nature of the soul or mind. Since these questions belong to philosophy of mind, we will be drawn into discussion of some of the theories about the nature of mind and of its relation to the body. Moreover, philosophy of religion, and indeed philosophy generally, is not an isolated branch of enquiry but is connected in various ways with other branches of enquiry, including the natural sciences. So, for instance, questions about the implications of modern biology for how we think about humans and other animals are of importance in discussing religious views of humankind. For this reason, questions about the implications of Darwinism for such views are included in this book.

The first part is concerned with arguments for or against belief in an afterlife. In Chapter 1 we will consider an argument for immortality which assumes that we are essentially souls or minds that happen to be located in or united to a body. This argument is associated particularly with the ancient Greek philosopher Plato (c. 428–347 BC), though it may be even older. Plato wrote about the soul finally escaping from the prison-house of the body but he often referred with approval to the doctrine of the *transmigration of souls*,[1] according to which souls (at least at a lower stage of moral development) go (migrate) from one body to another. We will consider the philosophical difficulties that arise for both of these ideas. Some of Plato's arguments for immortality have often been favoured by subsequent philosophers, who have thought of immortality as involving the continuous existence, for ever, of disembodied minds or souls. But there are, as we will see, many problems with this conception of immortality.

In view of these problems, it has become more common for philosophers to consider that survival of persons after death is possible, if at all, where they retain bodies. This tendency has run in parallel with a tendency to reject views in the philosophy of mind that treat the mind as a subsistent entity separate from the body and to favour some form of materialism, the view that everything is fundamentally material. The result has been a revival of philosophical interest in the possibility of what, in the Judaeo-Christian tradition, is called 'the resurrection of the dead', which involves survival in a bodily form. We will be considering (in Chapter 2) some of the philosophical difficulties for belief in the resurrection as well as a materialist theory of the resurrection which promises to meet some of them. At the end of the first part we will consider the implications of Darwinism for belief in immortality.

Belief in immortality has commonly rested largely on the belief that there exists a designer of the universe whose purposes are suited by human survival. In the second part of the book we will be looking at both traditional and very modern arguments for believing that the universe has a designer. We will also look at some of the arguments for the existence of God based on considerations to do with morality. Finally, we will look at the strongest arguments *against* believing that there is a good purpose in the universe, namely those drawn from the existence of evil.

Epistemology, or the theory of knowledge,[2] provides a thread of argument that runs through this book. The strongest argument for immortality, for example, is one that seeks to demonstrate it on the basis of logical deduction from premises we already know. Such an argument, if successful, would put the claim to knowledge about immortality on the highest possible footing. But there is a weaker sense in which we might be said to know certain things which, though not absolutely demonstrable, are overwhelmingly or at least highly probable. We will be considering an argument for the existence of God for which this has been claimed, which is based on observation of the world around us. Although the word 'epistemology' strictly means 'theory of knowledge' – *episteme* is the ancient Greek word for knowledge – it is extended in practice to include the theory of belief, especially rational belief.

The arguments seeking to establish religious knowledge or at least rational belief on the basis of premises we are all expected to accept or upon observations about the world we are all capable of making are a part of what is commonly called *natural religion*. But much of what is believed (for instance, in Judaism, Christianity and Islam) is based upon *revelation*, i.e. it is believed because it has been revealed by God to a chosen prophet (and, often, then written down). The question whether anything should be believed on the basis of revelation belongs to the epistemology of religion. Christian apologists in particular have claimed that it can reasonably be, since prophets show themselves to be chosen by God by successfully performing miracles. The historical evidence of the miracles related in the Gospels was in this way appealed to as a good reason for recognizing Jesus as chosen by God and therefore his sayings as divinely inspired. Miracles were thus seen as providing the very foundation of the Christian religion. We will be examining one of the classical criticisms of this line of argument in the final part of the book.

Supposing, however, that religious belief is not based on demonstrations or on convincing evidence of one kind or another, should it be regarded as a bad thing? In religion faith is commonly a virtue, but some philosophers have regarded it as a vice. This issue about 'the ethics of belief' is one we will explore in the final chapter, where we will consider arguments on both sides.

NOTES

1 This doctrine is discussed in Chapter 1.
2 Epistemology is usually taken to include the theory of belief because of the important question about the relation between knowledge and belief.

I Life after death

The question whether we survive our deaths is one philosophers have discussed since antiquity. The positions they have adopted have been affected, in large measure, by which of three theories about mind and matter they have adopted. The three theories are:

1 The view that there are *two* essentially distinct kinds of thing or, in philosophical parlance, 'substance' in the world — namely, minds and bodies. This view is particularly associated with the seventeenth-century French philosopher René Descartes[1] and it is commonly referred to as *Cartesian dualism*.

   Dualism is contrasted with views according to which there is only *one* kind of fundamental thing in the universe. These latter views — which are forms of what is called *monism* — differ amongst themselves as to what kind of entity they take to be fundamental. The other two major metaphysical theories we will be concerned with are both forms of monism.

2 The first form of monism we will consider holds that the fundamental entities in the universe are all mind-like. They are either actually souls or minds, or are at least analogous with minds, souls or spirits. This is the view referred to as idealistic monism or simply as *idealism*.

3 The second form of monism we will consider holds that everything in the universe is fundamentally material. This is the view referred to as materialistic monism or simply as *materialism*.

We will consider the implications of the first two theories (dualism and idealism) in Chapter 1 and the third (materialism) in Chapter 2.

Dualist theories of the relation of mind and body are the ones most commonly associated with arguments for immortality. Many religious views about survival and arguments for believing in it presuppose the possibility of a disembodied existence. Dualism allows this. But so does idealism. These two theories and the question whether they provide a philosophical underpinning for belief in immortality are the topic of Chapter 1.

NOTE

1   Descartes (1596–1650) argued for a radical distinction between mind and body in his *Meditations on the First Philosophy* (1641). The doctrines associated with his name are usually referred to as 'Cartesianism'. For an introduction to Descartes's philosophy, see the entry in Craig (1998) and Cottingham (1986).

1 Disembodied existence

DESCARTES ON IMMORTALITY

In the seventeenth century many people saw the new mechanistic science as a threat to religious belief because it seemed to encourage a wholly materialistic view of the world. Defenders of the mechanistic approach, including Descartes, were suspected of materialism, which was seen as fundamentally irreligious. Once it became clear, however, that Descartes himself had adopted a radical dualism of mind and body which enabled him to reject materialism and assert the existence of non-material substances (such as God and human souls), his philosophy came to be seen in an entirely different light. Descartes's dualism became the basis on which many have reconciled their religious beliefs with their acceptance of modern mechanistic science.

Descartes is, then, particularly important, not only for the philosophy of mind but for that part of the philosophy of religion that is concerned with the soul. Both 'soul' and the now unfashionable word 'spirit' have a religious aura about them. But there are no philosophically important distinctions drawn between them in present-day discussions about immortality.

Descartes initially intended to offer a rigorous demonstration of the immortality of the soul and advertised it in the subtitle he gave to the first edition. And, although in the end he decided not to offer a demonstration of immortality at this point, he thought the demonstration he had given of 'the distinction between the human soul and the body' prepared the ground in the best possible way. He insisted[1] that 'one cannot think of any opinion on this subject [the relation between mind and body] that is more congenial to theology'. Although, as we will see, the argument Descartes had in mind is one that goes back at least to Plato, Descartes added to it a modern (mechanistic) view of the world and therefore of the workings of the human body which has retained a particular credibility and relevance.

Although Descartes had advertised that in his *Meditations* there 'are demonstrated the existence of God and the immortality of the soul', and although the work does indeed contain two arguments for the existence of God, there is not a comparable argument for the immortality of the human soul. In his synopsis of the *Meditations*, however, he explains why it was not appropriate to attempt to produce a demonstration at that stage. We need not concern ourselves here with his reasons in detail. It is sufficient to note that they have to do with the kind of clarity and rigour he was aspiring to in that work and with the fact that he would have had to use assumptions he could not have justified until a later stage. None the less, he did at least offer a sketch of how the argument would go. The nature of a mind, he claimed, is very different from that of a material body (any piece of matter) for the following reason:

> We cannot understand a body except as being divisible, while by contrast we cannot understand a mind except as being indivisible. For we cannot conceive of half a mind, while we can always conceive of half of a body, however small.
>
> (*Philosophical Writings* II, 9, in Cottingham (1992))

Descartes claims that 'these arguments are enough to show that the decay of the [human] body does not imply the destruction of the mind, and hence to give mortals the hope of an after-life'. What he seems to have intended is that the destructibility of material bodies follows from the fact that they are inherently divisible, whereas minds, being indivisible, are not destructible for this reason and indeed might not be destructible at all. If we suppose that the natural processes of decay and destruction always involve breaking things down into their parts, then only things that are by nature divisible into parts are liable to such processes. Descartes was aware that such an argument could only proceed on the basis of assumptions taken from the natural sciences. In a reply to criticisms he qualified his conclusion that the mind is immortal by adding 'in so far as it can be known by natural philosophy' (*Philosophical Writings* II, 109). There may be processes of annihilation unknown to physics (natural philosophy) and, for all Descartes claimed to have proved to the contrary, it is possible that 'God gave it [the soul] such a nature that its duration comes to an end simultaneously with the end of the body's life'.

Descartes did not claim that his argument for the immortality of the soul was an original one. It is likely that he knew there was a very similar argument in Plato, whose argument is perhaps the classical a priori argument for immortality. Plato's argument, which is based on a premise about the 'simplicity' of the soul, has been used again and again by other philosophers and is worth considering in more detail.

THE PLATONIC ARGUMENT FROM THE SIMPLICITY OF THE SOUL

Plato's most important discussion of immortality is in his dialogue *Phaedo*, which is a dramatized account of the last days of his teacher, Socrates. Socrates has been condemned to death and, surrounded in prison by his friends, he seeks to reassure them that, when he takes the poison as required by law, his soul will not be dispersed at death, as they feared. One of the arguments he uses[2] is that the things that are liable to be dispersed are composite things, whose parts are liable to be scattered. Anything that is *non-composite* or simple is immune to being dispersed in this way since it does not have parts. The soul is a 'non-composite' or simple thing. Therefore, when the body is dispersed after death, the soul will live on. For souls are not liable to be dispersed.

Plato did not amplify this argument. But it has seemed to many philosophers since to be intuitively plausible. It is easy to construct a list of things which, if you were asked to destroy them, you would destroy by breaking them down into parts. A confidential manuscript can be destroyed by being torn into sufficiently tiny bits (or, nowadays, shredded); a wooden table can be destroyed by chopping it up for firewood; a statue by smashing it in pieces; and so on. The thought is that all material things are like this. But a soul, on the other hand, is different. You can easily imagine half a manuscript, half a table or half a statue. But, as Descartes pointed out, it is not possible to imagine half a soul. That is what is meant by saying that the soul is indivisible, simple or non-composite. Plato's argument appears to be that destroying something is always a matter of breaking it into parts. Destroying can only be done to things that are composite. It cannot be done to things that are indivisible or simple. It cannot, therefore, be done to souls. Souls are therefore indestructible. Thus, though the body is destroyed through death, the soul remains and is immortal.

EXERCISE 1.1

ARGUMENT FROM THE SIMPLICITY OF THE SOUL

Try to state this argument so that it is clearly *valid*, i.e. try to spell out the premises (starting-points of arguments) so that the conclusion really does follow from them. The main conclusion is going to be 'Therefore, the soul is immortal' and (just to get you started) you could begin with the premise 'Anything that cannot be dispersed is immortal'. To reach the main conclusion you will often, as in this case, need to have sub-conclusions, which complete one stage of the argument and serve as premises for a further stage of the argument. In setting out the argument you should indicate which are your premises and which are your sub-conclusions. What you should produce will look something like this:

1   Anything that cannot be dispersed is immortal;
2   (To be supplied by you.)
3   (To be supplied by you.)

Therefore,

The soul is immortal.

Check your answer against the one at the back of the book before reading on.

DISCUSSION

The argument to the sub-conclusion is valid by a basic rule of inference[3] known as *affirming the antecedent*. This rule states that any argument of the form:

1   If p (the antecedent) then q:
2   p

Therefore, q is valid.

Here the argument, put in this form, begins:

1   If something does not have parts, it cannot be dispersed.
2   The soul does not have parts.

Therefore, the soul cannot be dispersed.

The conclusion is validly inferred by repetition of the same rule. The argument is, then, *valid*. We must, that is to say, accept the conclusion *if* we accept the premises. But that does not mean we must accept the conclusion full stop. For we may have good reason to refuse to accept one or more of the premises. An argument may, as this is sometimes put, be valid but that does not necessarily mean it is *sound*. For an argument to be sound it is necessary not only that it is valid, but also that the premises from which its conclusion is derived are themselves all true. In other words, if we have good reason to reject any one of the premises we have good reason to reject the argument as unsound. Let us, then, consider the bases on which some of the premises of the above argument are put forward.[4]

There is, behind premises 1 and 2, a general observation about the world, namely that the way material things are naturally destroyed is by their being broken into parts. The assumption is that this is the *only* way things naturally get destroyed. That assumption needs to be made for the argument to be valid, for us to be able to conclude that anything without parts is indestructible. For, if there are other ways things can naturally get destroyed, then it may be, after all, that things without parts can be destroyed. So, is the general observation about the way things are naturally destroyed correct?

R. G. Swinburne has made this objection to Plato's argument:

Now certainly the normal way by which most material objects cease to exist is that they are broken up into parts. The normal end of a table is to be broken up; likewise for chairs, houses, and pens. But this need not be the way in which a material object ceases to exist. Things cease to exist when they lose their essential properties. The essential properties of a table include being solid. If a table was suddenly liquefied, then, even if its constituent molecules remained arranged in the shape of a table by being arranged in a table-shaped mould, the table would have ceased to exist. So if even material objects can cease to exist without being broken into parts, souls surely can cease to exist by some other route than by being broken into parts.

(Swinburne (1997), pp. 305f.)

Swinburne is here using a common philosophical method of objection – the counter-example. He is, that is to say, trying to show that the general observation that things are only destroyed by being broken into their parts is false because there are exceptions or counter-examples. A table reduced to liquefied form is no longer a table, he thinks, because it has lost the properties that are essential to its being a table. He does not say what these are, but they would presumably include those properties like solidity in virtue of which it can be used as a table.

Even if there were only one way for *material* things to be destroyed, however, that does not show that the soul, if it lacks parts, is immortal. For, as Descartes admitted, there might be ways for the soul to go out of existence which are quite natural to it and quite different from the ways in which material things go out of existence. The eighteenth-century German philosopher Moses Mendelssohn (1729–86) pursued this line of thought by suggesting that, for all Plato or others had shown, the soul might be subject to a process of vanishing. In a work he also called *Phaedo* (1767) Mendelssohn sought to strengthen Plato's argument by showing that the soul cannot merely vanish since that would mean gradually losing its substance and this would not be possible for a simple thing. However, Immanuel Kant (1724–1804) argued in his *Critique of Pure Reason*[5] that it was an illusion to think of the soul as a simple substance.

THE SOUL AS AN ILLUSORY ENTITY

The Platonic argument for the immortality of the soul makes use of the premise that the soul does not have parts, i.e. it is a simple thing. This premise was rejected by Kant. The soul is not, according to Kant, a thing at all. There is, none the less, a deep temptation to think that it is. And Plato's argument for immortality supposes that the soul is a separate thing – what later philosophers have called a *substance*. But, or so Kant sought to show,[6] if we engage in this kind of a priori metaphysics or general theory about the nature of reality, we find ourselves led into all manner of contradictory conclusions and irresolvable disputes. Kant's approach has in some respects been taken up again in the twentieth century, when a number of philosophers have diagnosed the mistake as arising from a misunderstanding of the way our language works. More specifically it has been suggested that a characteristic mistake of the metaphysician is to assume too readily that noun phrases (such as 'my soul') stand for entities.

This assumption is not confined to the specialized world of philosophy. A knowing play on the way nouns and noun phrases (like 'the number one') can appear to stand for actual things is to be found in Lewis Carroll's *Through the Looking Glass*. Here is a conversation that takes place:

> 'Who did you pass on the road?' the King went on, holding out his hand to the Messenger for some more hay.
>
> 'Nobody,' said the Messenger.
>
> 'Quite right,' said the King: 'this young lady saw him too. So of course Nobody walks slower than you.'
>
> 'I do my best,' the Messenger said in a sullen tone, 'I'm sure nobody walks much faster than I do!'
>
> 'He can't do that,' said the King, 'or else he'd have been here first …'
>
> (Carroll (1960), pp. 281f.)

This is an example – not uncommon in Lewis Carroll's writings – of a philosophical joke. To enjoy the joke we need to be philosophers enough to realize that the King is actually talking nonsense but doing so with a kind of consistency that gives the interchange with the Messenger an appearance of sense. The King is guilty of falsely representing nothing as a special kind of entity when it is not an entity at all. 'Nobody', as the word is normally used, is not the name of an individual. 'Nobody came this way' is really short for 'It is not true that any person came this way'.

In a similar way it might be argued that, just as 'nobody' is not (as normally used) the name of an individual, so phrases like 'my soul' and 'my mind' do not refer to a special entity which can be thought of as existing apart from other entities. Hence where these phrases look as if they might refer to something substantial it is possible to replace them with phrases which do not encourage this illusion. For example, if I say 'I will keep your problem in my mind' it is possible to hear this as analogous to 'I will keep your money in my safe', as if my mind (like my safe) was a container where special kinds of things can be kept (such as problems and ideas). But whereas the point of telling you that I will keep your problem in my mind is just to assure you that I will not forget it, the point of telling you that I will keep your money in my safe is in part to tell you where it will be, and not just to assure you that I will look after it. If I do not forget your problem then it follows that I have kept it in my mind. On the other hand, I can look after your money in many other ways than keeping it in my safe. That the mind can seem an entity analogous to a safe is an illusion of language encouraged by phrases like 'I will keep it in my mind'.

One recent philosopher, Gilbert Ryle (1900–76),[7] referred to Descartes's substantial mind as 'the ghost in the machine', using the word 'ghost' exactly to call in question whether there are such entities as minds, as has been supposed in much metaphysics. In his *The Concept of Mind* (1949), Ryle sought to argue that we can say everything we want to say about our mental life without having to assume that the mind is an entity at all. Ryle sought to show that when we talk about our states of mind we are not describing a ghostly theatre but referring to how we are likely to behave. Ryle's approach assumes that the roots of the temptation to believe that minds are substances lie in language: for instance, in the way the word 'I' might appear to designate a non-physical entity, especially when used in phrases like 'I think'; or again the noun phrase 'the mind' as in phrases like 'I am keeping it in my mind', which appears to suggest that I am storing something in some non-physical container; and there are many other examples. The method is to show that all these turns of language, that tempt the unwary to assume that souls or minds are entities, need not and should not be taken in that way. The thought is that, through a careful examination of how these phrases are actually used, we will find ourselves no more tempted to think of the mind as an entity than we are to take 'Nobody' to be the name of somebody.

The suggestion that the apparent substantiality of minds or souls is an illusion which is fostered by the existence of noun phrases is not one we can explore in full here. But we should note one limitation of this objection. Let us grant, for the sake of argument, that, in everyday contexts, our use of the words 'mind' and 'soul' in noun phrases never requires us to suppose that a separate entity is being referred to. The question remains whether there is anything wrong with those religious and philosophical uses of the words which *do* imply that there are substantial minds and souls. The objection might have rhetorical force for those who, unlike Platonists and Cartesians, are not wedded to such special uses of these words. But Platonists and Cartesians will take some persuading that they have used the words 'mind' and 'soul' in ways that, if they understood everyday language properly, they would not use them.

This line of objection is a deep one and neither easy to clinch nor shrug off. It has influenced the decline of dualism amongst British philosophers in recent decades. It is one way of arguing that there is no need to assume the existence of souls or minds as separate entities. But there is another way of arguing that to do so is to make an unwarranted assumption.

THE SOUL AS AN UNWARRANTED ASSUMPTION

There is a principle named after the great English mediaeval philosopher and logician William of Occam (*c.* 1285–1349),[8] which has been widely used in scientific and philosophical arguments for many centuries and has been an important critical tool in metaphysics as well as the sciences. The principle, stated baldly, is that *Entities should not be multiplied beyond necessity*. It is known as *Occam's Razor*, because it is used to eliminate superfluous entities. The principle is not without problems – and we will consider one of these at a later stage. But a bias towards ontological simplicity is deeply embedded in scientific thinking and has significantly affected philosophical thinking.[9]

One way of presenting the principle involved in Occam's Razor is to say that if one person believes there are more kinds of entity in the world than it is necessary to assume then the *onus of proof* lies with them to establish their existence. The phrase 'onus of proof' is used here in the sense in which it is in a court of criminal law, where the onus lies on the prosecution to prove the guilt of the accused. There is no onus of proof on the accused to prove they are not guilty. They are presumed innocent until they are proved otherwise. Likewise the onus lies on those who claim there are extra kinds of entity in the world to prove their case. The rest of us are entitled to *presume* these extra entities do not exist until it has been shown that they do.

The list of these extra entities is very long: it includes extraterrestrials and abominable snowmen, witches and demons, angels and deities, as well as a host of theoretical entities that have littered the history of science and philosophy. The point is *not* that none of these entities exists, still less that we *know* they do not. The point is rather that we are entitled to presume that they do not until those who claim they do give us positive reasons for supposing they do.

Applying this principle to the case of souls and minds, the question is whether it is necessary to assume that they are existing things or, in the philosopher's special jargon, *substances*. Descartes thought he could demonstrate the existence of at least his own mind. As he pointed out in his *Meditations*, whatever else I can doubt I cannot doubt that I am doubting. *Cogito, ergo sum* – I think, therefore I exist. And Descartes certainly thought he was entitled to infer that he was a *thinking thing*. But, if we apply his method of doubt strictly, it would seem that all he was entitled to infer from the existence of his doubts was that doubting went on and not that he was a substantial mind. It is quite possible to accept that people have doubts etc. without believing in such entities as minds. Descartes's argument does not establish that we need to assume a substantial mind. If we accept the use of Occam's Razor in this context we will presume that there are no substantial minds or souls in the absence of some other, better argument to convince us.

We have been considering a particular argument for immortality based on the assumption that the soul is a simple, indivisible, thing. We have noted the objection that, even if the soul were simple (indivisible), it would not follow that it could not cease to exist, since there are other ways for things to cease to exist than for them to be broken into constituent parts. We have also noted two more general objections which would also apply to other arguments for the immortality of the soul. Both objections are to suppose that there are such entities as souls (or minds).

CARTESIAN DUALISM AND IMMORTALITY

As we have already seen, Descartes claimed that it was impossible to think of any account of mind and body that was 'more congenial to theology' than his own. Even if it was impossible to prove the immortality of the soul – and Descartes was modest in his claims about this matter – dualism seems to be particularly congenial to belief in a future state. To this extent Descartes's thought has affinities with that of Plato. According to one of his devoted followers, his dying words were reminiscent of Socrates. Whether true or not, Claude Clerselier's account puts into Descartes's mouth words that are very apt, considering his philosophy:

> And so, my soul, you have been a captive for a long time. This is the hour at which you must
> go out of prison and leave the encumbrance of this body behind you.
>
> (Translated from Descartes (1964–76), V, p. 482)

This image of the body as a prison-house of the soul from which it escapes when a person dies derives from Socrates, who is reported by his pupil Plato in the *Phaedo* as presenting this view of the relation of the soul to its body. Descartes's view about bodies being mere machines adds an element unfamiliar in Plato. But in many respects their views about the mind–body relation fit together well. Descartes could easily have thought of his own death as an escape of his soul from the prison-house of his body.

Even if no proof of immortality were possible and even if belief in immortality were largely a matter of religious faith, it might be argued that dualism helped to make immortality credible in a way it would not otherwise be. It is arguable, in Descartes's phrase, that dualism is 'congenial' to religious belief in an afterlife, i.e. makes it more likely that such a belief is true. There are a number of serious difficulties, one of which is discussed briefly later,[10] for Cartesian dualism as an account of the relation between mind and body. And these difficulties are compounded by arguments that suggest there is no reason to suppose that there are such entities as minds at all. But even if these difficulties could be overcome and Cartesian dualism is assumed to be in itself a plausible position, there are further problems about considering it as congenial to belief in immortality.

Two of these difficulties are worth highlighting. One is that his dualism leads to a serious dilemma about the nature of animals. Another is that immortality requires the survival of the same person and that a Cartesian account of persons as essentially disembodied minds does not provide an adequate basis for talking about the survival of the same person. Let us look at each of the difficulties in turn.

THE ANIMALS DILEMMA

Descartes, who did not draw a distinction between the mind and the soul, believed that whether or not a creature had a mind or soul was an all or nothing matter. For Descartes animals were just like machines, or 'automata', operating like elaborate clockwork without any consciousness. They did not have minds or souls at all.

This *all or nothing* position is a source of difficulty for the Cartesian account, for either

1 animals are granted minds, in which case they get *everything* associated with minds;

or

2 animals are denied minds, in which case they get *none* of the things associated with minds.

The dilemma for Cartesians, briefly stated, is as follows. In the first case, animals are too much like humans, being naturally immortal; this is contrary to orthodox Christianity. In the second case, animals are not sufficiently like humans, being mere machines; this is contrary to common sense. Descartes himself opted for offering animals nothing in the way of a mind. This seemed implausible to most of his contemporaries, who wanted to place animals somewhere in the middle: capable of feeling pain and so in some respects like humans but, unlike humans, lacking an immortal soul. And that middle position remains the one most likely to be adopted by religious people, who may be expected to insist that some consideration must be shown for animals, since they are capable of suffering, but not the same consideration as should be shown for humans, since animals do not have immortal souls. The dilemma that faces Cartesian dualism about animals arises because the Cartesian dualist cannot adopt this middle position and is forced to one or other of two unpalatable extremes: either claiming that animals have no feeling and are mere machines; or granting animals immortal souls on the same terms as humans.

A dilemma is a very powerful kind of argument. It begins by stating that one and only one of two propositions must be true, in this case either 'Animals have minds' is true or 'Animals do not have minds' is true. A dilemma then claims that unacceptable consequences follow whichever of these propositions is supposed to be true. Those who are allegedly caught in the dilemma – in this case the Cartesians – may be caught on one or other of its 'horns'. This is the dilemma the Cartesians were thought by their critics to face:

First horn: If animals, like humans, have souls, then these souls are also indivis-
                    ible and hence are also naturally immortal.
Second horn: If animals do not have souls, then they are mere machines and do not
                    feel pain.

One way out would be to 'grasp' the first horn and allow that animals are immortal, as did a few critics who believed in a doctrine known as the transmigration of souls (discussed later in this chapter). Another option would be to admit the indivisibility and indestructibility of animal souls but claim that more is required for immortality.

What Descartes did was to 'grasp' the second horn of the dilemma by denying that animals have souls. The Cartesians (his disciples) were forced to brave the ridicule of their contemporaries by declaring that animals were mere machines. This meant denying not only that animals had thoughts but even that they felt pain. They were obliged to say that the sound of an animal apparently in pain was to be understood as a merely mechanical noise. Some of the noises produced (mechanically) by bagpipes struck some seventeenth-century philosophers as uncannily like cries of pain. And on the Cartesian theory even human cries of pain are largely produced mechanically. (Descartes was well aware of the close similarity between human physiology and that of many animals.) But whereas, in the case of humans, the cries are at least sometimes accompanied by feelings of pain, they are no more so on the Cartesian account in the case of animals than they are in the case of bagpipes.

This conclusion was generally dismissed as absurd in the seventeenth century and was seen as a serious difficulty for the Cartesian position. Most people then, as now, were as aware of continuities between ourselves and (other) animals as they were of discontinuities. Aristotle (384–322 BC), whose thought on such matters was still immensely influential, had marked humankind out as the political animal – a rather special kind of animal but an animal none the less. Cartesianism claimed the virtue, from the point of view of religion, of setting humankind well above the rest of creation, belonging more to a higher order of beings (together with angels and other spirits) which had thoughts and feelings. But it flew in the face of a perception of continuities between the species, which put humankind at the top of the league, so to speak, and not in a separate league from other animals.

Some philosophers noted that, once you start doubting whether the pain behaviour of animals is good enough evidence to ascribe pains to them, you can quickly end up doubting whether there are any pains anywhere except your own. And indeed some philosophers have claimed that it is impossible to prove that there are. At all events the basis on which we ascribe pain to other humans – similar responses to similar stimuli – is much the same as that on which we ascribe pain to animals. Both cry out, cringe, avoid sources of pain, and so on. Humans additionally can describe their pains and tell others where they feel them. But these are comparative refinements. There is no more reason to doubt that, if you accidentally tread on the cat, and it yowls, you have caused it pain, than if you similarly stand on someone's toe and they cry 'Ouch!' There are no doubt tricky cases about more elementary forms of life which raise questions about the physiological apparatus needed for pain to be experienced. But there are also (at the time of writing) just such questions about whether and, if so, when a human foetus can feel pain.

PROBLEMS OF PERSONAL IDENTITY

The Cartesian dualist faces problems about animals because of insisting on a hard distinction between creatures with any kind of feeling and mere machines. It may be possible to preserve a kind of dualism that allows souls to animals but which distinguishes between animals with lesser souls and creatures capable of immortality. To be capable of immortality a creature needs more than consciousness or feeling. The question of what more leads us into the topic of the next section. For it might be argued that it needs self-consciousness; that it needs to be aware of itself as having a past it can remember and a future it can imagine. It means it must have some kind of sense of self-identity. Moreover, immortality as commonly thought of is usually reserved for persons – though not usually only for human persons. So immortality appears to require personal identity, i.e. the conscious continuation of the same person from this life on to the next. What is involved in such a view of immortality and how far Cartesian dualism is congenial to it are questions we will be considering in the next section.

IMMORTALITY AND PERSONAL IDENTITY

When we consider what is needed for a satisfactory account of immortality there are two quite different but equally fundamental questions to be asked. First, there is the question about what kind of immortality needs to be defended. Secondly, there is the question whether a particular philosophical theory is consistent with the immortality sought and whether it makes it at all probable. Let us consider first why personal identity is important for the kind of immortality that has commonly been hoped for.

WHAT KIND OF IMMORTALITY DO WE WANT?

Not everyone wants immortality and not every religion proclaims an afterlife. There are those for whom the prospect of annihilation or, at any rate, a loss of any sense of their own continuing existence would be preferable to many kinds of continuing existence. And some religions claim that there is no survival for individuals as such. But many people do hope for individual survival in some form, and individual survival is, for many religions, a central item of belief. Even today there is a widespread belief that we will some day be reunited with those we love. And, if this were what being immortal involved, we would need to be able to identify them and they us, and all of us would need to be able to recollect our pasts and our associations with one another.

Orthodox religion, though it does not contradict this happy picture many people have, commonly offers a more austere view, in which the future life is a scene of judgement on us for the lives we have lived. But it attaches no less importance to the continuing identity of us as persons. Christian, Jewish and Muslim theologians will all insist that an individual must remain the same person in the afterlife because all individuals are liable to be rewarded or punished in the afterlife depending on how they conducted themselves in this life. And it simply makes no sense to talk about reward and punishment in the afterlife if souls lose their individuality and continuing identity. Whoever is rewarding and punishing must at least believe that they are rewarding or punishing individuals for the good or evil *these very* individuals have done. It is a miscarriage of justice if the wrong person is punished. But it is not punishment at all if the person harmed is not even supposed to have done the evil. God, as conceived in religions like Christianity, is omniscient and so makes no mistakes. But not even God can punish evil-doers unless they continue to exist. Moreover, in most religions that teach about an afterlife with rewards and punishments, the punishment would lose its point if the individuals could not be brought to remember the sins they committed. Indeed some memory of one's past seems to be an essential part of any self-identity.

This point is one made by the German philosopher G. W. Leibniz[11] (1646–1716), who criticized Descartes for not giving enough weight to this and to the problems involved:

> Such immortality without memory is altogether useless for morality, for it upsets all reward and punishment. What use, Sir, would it be to you to become King of China on condition that you forgot what you had been? Would it not come to the same thing if God, at the same time as he destroyed you, created a King of China?
>
> (Letter to an unidentified correspondent, probably dating from the late 1670s, in Leibniz (1988), p. 128)

Leibniz is a little harsh in offering this as a criticism of Descartes since Descartes did not deny, nor was he committed to denying, that memory and self-identity were necessary to an immortality worth having. It is simply that he claimed to have a view of mind and body that supported belief in immortality and failed to explain what else was needed if the immortality was to be worth having. But, harsh or not, Leibniz was making an important point.

It is one taken up in a more modern idiom by Anthony Quinton in a more recent discussion of immortality:

> if somebody says, well I am perfectly prepared for a thousand dollars to freeze you and store you for a modest rental geared to the cost of living and unfreeze you – unfortunately we have not got all of the bugs out of this yet – you will, when woken, of course continue to exist, but you will be unlikely to recover any memories of your life now ... what is the value of the assurance of continuation when it doesn't involve any recollections of your existing life?
>
> (From the transcript of a radio discussion, in Lewis (1978), p. 63)

Quinton's point is interesting in that he considers the possibility of a future life outside the context of traditional religion. Some might take the risk. But we can understand people being unwilling to pay to be resuscitated on these terms.

Not any life after death is one we would want. Some people's Heaven might well be other people's Hell. Some people want to be reunited with others who died before them. There are others for whom that is the last thing they want. A traditional picture of Heaven, which offers the prospect of an eternity of choral singing, may delight some and fill others with a sense of boredom. Clearly an eternity of choral singing would be for these others not their just reward but a punishment. It is much more difficult to describe a Heaven that everyone would want to go to than it is to describe a Hell that everyone would wish to avoid. Popular religion seems to reflect certain preferences (such as the idea that we should be reunited with our loved ones) which not everyone will have. Orthodox religion is often less specific. In religions that believe in a Heaven and a Hell, however, it is essential that those who are in Heaven should be delighted to be there and those who are in Hell should wish they were anywhere else. It is essential because otherwise Heaven would not be the ultimate reward or Hell the ultimate place of punishment.

Belief in a Heaven and a Hell is a matter of faith for those who subscribe to a particular religion. Belief in or at least the hope or fear of immortality involving personal identity is not confined, however, to people who believe in rewards and punishments in an afterlife. Even those who do not share any orthodox religious view about an afterlife might and commonly do hope for an afterlife. But, as we have seen, in these differing cases immortality still presupposes personal identity. For these reasons personal identity has become an important topic in discussions of immortality.

A DUALIST ACCOUNT OF PERSONAL IDENTITY

Assuming, then, that an account of immortality will need to accommodate personal identity, we need to consider how far Cartesian dualism is congenial to belief in immortality. We have already noted the criticism that if all that survived the death of a body was an endless stream of thoughts or a continuing consciousness this would not be enough for the kind of immortality that involved reward and punishment. The criticism seems to be that this kind of immortality involves continuing personal identity and that this in turn involves memory. The continued existence of the same person requires not just a string of thoughts but some *self-consciousness*. This will involve memory and a sense of continuity between thoughts, feelings and deeds of the past and those of the present as connected with the same person. Descartes himself did not consider these difficulties about the nature of personal identity. They were first addressed by one of the most important English philosophers, John Locke (1632–1704).[12]

Locke was in many important respects a different kind of philosopher from Descartes[13] – much less influenced by the abstract mathematical sciences and much more by those that stressed observation and experiment – but he was none the less influenced by the French philosopher in a number of ways. This is reflected in his treatment of personal identity.[14] Locke frequently writes as if, like Descartes, he accepts the view that the true person or self is a 'conscious thinking thing':

> Self is that conscious thinking thing ... which is sensible, or conscious of Pleasure and Pain, capable of Happiness or Misery, and so is concern'd for it *self*, as far as that consciousness extends.
>
> (Locke (1690), *Essay*, Book II, Ch. XXVII, sect. 17)

Consciousness can 'extend' itself backwards in time, as Locke thinks of it, by recollecting past experiences. The identity of the person, he claims, reaches as far as consciousness is extended:

> since consciousness always accompanies thinking, and 'tis this, that makes every one to be, what he calls *self*, and thereby distinguishes himself from all other thinking things, in this

alone consists personal Identity, i.e. the sameness of a rational Being: And as far as this consciousness can be extended backwards to any past Action or Thought, so far reaches the Identity of that *Person*; it is the *same* self now it was then; and 'tis by the same *self* with this present one that now reflects on it, that that Action was done.

(Locke (1690), *Essay*, Book II, Ch. XXVII, sect. 9)

That which the *consciousness* of this present thinking thing can join [sc. 'to'] it self, makes the same *Person*, and is one *self* with it, and with nothing else; and so attributes to it *self*, and owns all the Actions of that thing, as its own, as far as that consciousness reaches, and no farther; as every one who reflects will perceive.

(Locke (1690), *Essay*, Book II, Ch. XXVII, sect. 17)

Though not so intended Locke's account of personal identity provides a way of elaborating the Cartesian account of how dualism fits with a belief in immortality which accommodates personal identity. The question is whether dualists (who take the essential person to be a soul conceived as quite separate from a body) can give a satisfactory account of the conditions under which a person can be said to be the same person as one who did certain things in the past. If they cannot, then this has serious consequences for dualist accounts of immortality as immortality is commonly conceived. Locke's account points the direction for any dualist account of personal identity. Broadly, as we have seen, he puts the weight on memory: in his own terms 'as far as this consciousness can be extended backwards to any past Action or Thought, so far reaches the Identity of that *Person*'.

Before we consider whether this account is correct we need to be as clear as we can be what it means. In the first place it is clear that Locke is talking about personal memory or recollection. There are many other kinds of memory, for instance of things we have learned. Our memory of dates in history – for instance, that the Battle of Hastings was fought in 1066 – even if it is about past events, does not in Locke's terms involve extending our consciousness back to them. And, of course, many of the things we remember are not past events. (We can, for instance, remember what seven times five equals, what the inverse square law is, and so on.) None the less we have a special relationship to our own past that we do not have to any one else's. Locke expresses this by talking of extending our consciousness backwards and claiming that our selves or our personal identity extend just as far as that consciousness extends.

The next question is: what exactly does Locke claim is the connection between personal identity and personal memory?

Philosophers have often found it useful to clarify an account such as Locke's account of personal identity in terms of necessary and sufficient conditions. This kind of clarification can be explained by reference to an example. As the word 'bachelor' is used in legal contexts there are three conditions which must be met for a person X to be a bachelor: the person must be male, must be adult (i.e. old enough to marry) and must be eligible to be married (e.g. not married already). Each of these is said to be a *necessary condition* of X being a bachelor. If any one of them is not met by X, then X is not a bachelor. No one of them is a *sufficient condition* for X being a bachelor since it does not follow from the fact that X is male that X is a bachelor (some males are married), and so on. But, taken together, they constitute a sufficient condition of X being a bachelor, i.e. if they are all met then X must be a bachelor.

This is a relatively homely and unphilosophical example. But philosophers have found analysis in terms of necessary and sufficient conditions to be a useful way of clarifying difficult concepts such as knowledge. And it provides a framework within which to attempt to clarify what someone means by some problematic term. In this way we can ask ourselves whether Locke is claiming that personal memory (extending our consciousness backwards) is:

(a) a necessary condition of personal identity;
(b) a sufficient condition of personal identity;
(c) both.

More precisely, questions about necessary and sufficient conditions of personal identity can be expressed in terms of the connection between propositions. For example, propositions 1 and 2 below concern personal identity and personal memory:

1 'X is the person who did A' (where person X and action A are both unique).
2 'X remembers doing A'.

In (a), (b) and (c) below are conditions which *might* relate to the truth of the first proposition if we accept that personal identity is related to personal memory.

(a) Only if the second proposition is true does the first hold. That is, proposition 2 is necessary for proposition 1 to be true, and proposition 1 is false if X does not remember doing A.
(b) If (provided only) the second proposition is true, then the first proposition holds. That is, proposition 2 is a sufficient condition for the truth of proposition 1.
(c) If, and only if, the second proposition is true is the first true. That is, proposition 2 is necessary and sufficient for proposition 1.

EXERCISE 1.2

PERSONAL IDENTITY AND PERSONAL MEMORY

Which of (a), (b) or (c) best describes Locke's condition(s)? That is, under what conditions does Locke hold proposition 1 to be true?

It may help you to think in terms of an example Locke himself gives which is intended to exemplify his view of the connection between memory and personal identity:

> Had I the same consciousness, that I saw the Ark and *Noah's* Flood, as that I saw an overflowing of the *Thames* last winter, or as that I write now, I could no more doubt that I, that write this now, that saw the *Thames* overflow'd last Winter, and that

view'd the Flood at the general Deluge, was the same *self* … than that I that write this am the same *my self* now whilst I write … that I was Yesterday.

(Locke (1690), *Essay*, Book II, Ch. XXVII, sect. 16)

DISCUSSION

One key sentence in the Locke passage I quoted earlier is the one I have already drawn out: 'as far as this consciousness can be extended backwards to any past Action or Thought, so far reaches the Identity of that *Person*'. This implies that memory is at least a sufficient condition of personal identity. This is confirmed by Locke's example: the fact that the consciousness of the person who is writing now can be extended to seeing the overflowing of the Thames or (fancifully) even witnessing Noah's flood is sufficient to conclude that the person who is writing now is the same person as the one who saw the overflowing of the Thames (etc.). So, if for something like these reasons you put (b), you were right to do so.

It is not so clear from Locke's example that he intends that memory is a necessary condition of personal identity. The evidence that he does, however, is in his remark that personal identity reaches 'as far as that consciousness reaches, and no farther'. The addition of the phrase 'and no farther' makes it clear that if the present writer does *not* remember witnessing Noah's flood then he or she is not the same person as someone who did witness that flood. If you put (a) for something like this reason you did well.

Thus Locke holds that memory is *both* a necessary *and* a sufficient condition of personal identity. In other words 'X is the person who did A' is true *if, and only if,* 'X remembers doing A'.

Given this analysis of Locke's account of personal identity in terms of necessary and sufficient conditions, it is possible further to see how it might be criticized. For Locke's claim is that it is *always true* that 'X is the person who did A' is true *if, and only if,* 'X remembers doing A', whoever X is and whatever A is. We can show the claim to be false if we can think of *counter-examples* that show that memory is not necessary or that it is not sufficient. Let us look at these two lines of criticism in turn.

MEMORY AS A NECESSARY CONDITION OF PERSONAL IDENTITY

To test the claim that memory is a necessary condition of personal identity, what we need to look for is a persuasive counter-example, where personal identity is clearly retained even though the necessary condition of memory is not met. If we cannot think of such a counter-example this may be because the claim is such a strong one that examples that appear to go against it turn out, on examination, not to be good counter-examples at all. (It might be too that we are not very good at thinking up counter-examples, which requires a certain kind of imagination and skill.) If, however, we do succeed in finding a really good counter-example then we can then conclude that the claim is false.

The phrase 'counter-example' is a relatively modern one. But philosophers have actually been using it at least since Plato. Locke's account of personal identity provoked the Scottish common-sense philosopher Thomas Reid (1710–96) to produce this imaginary example:

> Suppose a brave officer to have been flogged when a boy at school for robbing an orchard, to have taken a standard from the enemy in his first campaign, and to have been made a general in advanced life; suppose, also, which must be admitted to be possible, that, when he took the standard, he was conscious of having been flogged at school, and that, when made a general, he was conscious of his taking the standard, but had absolutely lost the consciousness of his flogging. These things being supposed, it follows ... that he who was flogged at school is the same person who took the standard, and that he who took the standard is the same person who was made a general. Whence it follows, if there be any truth in logic, that the general is the same person with him who was flogged at school. But the general's consciousness does not reach so far back as his flogging; therefore ... he is not the person who was flogged. Therefore the general is, and at the same time is not, the same person with him who was flogged at school.
>
> (Reid (1785), Essay VI, Ch. 5)

Reid's intention in this argument is to produce a *reductio ad absurdum*, i.e. to show how a patently unacceptable conclusion (in this case a contradiction) results if we make a particular assumption or set of assumptions. But the absurdity only results if one accepts both a theory and the example that gives a conclusion which contradicts it. Both kinds of argument are *ad hominem* in character and so are based on assumptions that the person against whom they are being offered either does or is expected to accept.

EXERCISE 1.3

IDENTIFYING ASSUMPTIONS

Try to identify in the case of Reid's argument what these assumptions are. (Hint: One of them should be obvious. The other is the one he is invoking when he inserts the phrase 'if there be any truth in logic'.)

Check your answer against the one at the back of the book before reading on.

DISCUSSION

The second assumption in my answer (that if X is identical with Y and Y is identical with Z, then X is identical with Z) is a *necessary truth* about relations of identity. Reid appears to have thought of it as a *logical truth*, i.e. a truth about what you can infer about relations of identity. It is the assumption he is invoking when he says what follows 'if there be any truth in logic'. Assumption 2 is what he relies on in concluding that the general 'is the same person with' the boy who was flogged at school. Reid's example shows how the contradictory conclusion follows from assumption 1. This assumption has the consequence that the general was not the same person as the boy who was flogged if he could not recall being flogged. This is what one would suppose in this case if one held memory to be a necessary condition of personal identity. It is evidently this assumption Reid intends should be rejected.

This may look like a knock-down argument against Locke. But Locke had already considered some of the difficult cases that appear to arise for his position where people are unable to recall things they actually did. It is likely that he would have responded to Reid by referring to a distinction between the conditions under which someone can be said to be *the same man* and the conditions under which they can be said to be *the same person*. Memory is not necessary for someone to be the same man and that, Locke might have replied, is all the counter-example shows. In short, it misfires. It *is* necessary for X and Y to have the same body if he is to be counted as the same man, but the same soul, consciousness or person could, on Locke's account, inhabit different bodies.

Reid might reply that the distinction does not help since the general is not only the same man but, we would all agree, also the same person. Reid's example is not, however, given in enough detail, from Locke's point of view. Consciousness of one's past actions is necessary, according to Locke, if one is to be accountable for what one did. For Locke it is therefore crucial whether one is *capable* of recalling one's past and unimportant that one may happen to have forgotten it. Where someone is really incapable of recalling their past we may have a case, according to Locke, where there are two persons in one body. Locke discusses such a case of split personality where the 'sober' person is not held to account for what the 'mad' person did (or the other way around). But his view of the past offences that we conveniently forget – as perhaps the general in Reid's example was doing – seems to be that these are not irretrievably out of our consciousness. Locke's remarks about the Day of Judgement seem to provide the nearest to a direct answer:

> in the great Day, wherein the Secrets of all Hearts shall be laid open, it may be reasonable to think, no one shall be made to answer for what he knows nothing of; but shall receive his Doom, his Conscience accusing or excusing him.
>
> (Locke (1690), *Essay*, Book II, Ch. XXVII, sect. 22)

It is no doubt true that an omnipotent God, if there is one, could compensate for the fallibility of human memory and ensure that our consciousness does extend to all the things that we have done. But it would be a step in the wrong direction for Locke to invoke a just and omnipotent God to underwrite his account of personal identity. It is a philosophical equivalent of jumping out of the frying pan into the fire. For there are at least as many problems about defending belief in the existence of a just and omnipotent God as there are about Locke's account of personal identity. Even if there were not those problems, it can be regarded as a kind of cheating in philosophy to bring God in to sort out a problem that we ought to be able to resolve ourselves. It would, for this reason, have been wrong for Locke to bring in God at this stage. It seems, then, that there are real difficulties for his claim that memory is a necessary condition of personal identity.

MEMORY AS A SUFFICIENT CONDITION OF PERSONAL IDENTITY

In one way it seems obvious that memory must be a sufficient condition of personal identity. If I remember breaking the bank at Monte Carlo (and there was only one person who did) then I am the person who broke the bank (etc.). But this is a trivial truth, since it is true by definition that I can only remember doing the things I have actually done. The verb 'to remember' is, in this respect, like certain other verbs: for instance, I can only *know* what is true and I can only *see* what is actually there. But, of course, I can *claim* to remember something which I do not actually remember because it never happened just as I can *claim* to know something which is not in fact true. Our memories let us down not only because we cannot always recall things we actually did but because we are prone to believe that we have done things we never did. Sometimes, for example, people have vivid dreams in which they do certain things of quite an everyday sort and end up mistakenly believing (and claiming to 'remember') that they have actually done them. In this and in other ways we can *think* we 'distinctly' remember having done something though in fact we have not done it.

In the light of these considerations it seems as if there is an ambiguity in Locke's talk of extending our consciousness to the past. Does it mean correctly remembering? Or does it mean seeming to remember correctly? When I think I am remembering someone I am actually meeting for the first time – confusing them with someone who looks similar, or something like that – I am in a perfectly good sense *extending my consciousness to the past*. That phrase could, of course, be restricted to cases where someone really is remembering, where consciousness is extended to the actual past. But one reason we make mistakes with memory is that the state of backward-extended consciousness may be just the same, even if it relates to a fictional and not to the actual past. It is possible that a review of my memories and apparent memories might enable me to construct a coherent past for myself. But I would have no way of settling any doubt as to whether it was my real past or whether, like many if not most autobiographers, I was making myself into a person I would rather have been. Memory as a backward extension of consciousness to what may turn out to be an imagined past is not a sufficient condition of personal identity.

SUMMARY

To sum up this quite complex and lengthy discussion. We have seen that, for a variety of reasons, the immortality which many wish to defend is one that retains individuality and personal identity. Any philosophical account of immortality in this sense must therefore be able to give an account of how personal identity is retained after death. Dualism has come to seem the most promising basis for belief in immortality. For it to be satisfactory, however, a dualist account of personal identity is needed. Here, what has seemed the most promising direction in which to look is to memory and Locke's claim that memory is a necessary and sufficient condition of personal identity has been taken up by dualists and used to defend their cause. However, there are counter-examples and other difficulties for this account of personal identity. The conclusion is that dualism has difficulties in giving an account of the immortality it has seemed to many to help support.

There is an obvious way out of these difficulties about personal identity for someone who is not a dualist. They might say – as many have done – that bodily continuity is important for personal identity. That is an obvious way forward from Reid's example. The general is the same person as the child who was flogged at school at least partly because the creature that was a child but who grew up into the creature who became the general is the same. This is not the place, however, to consider an alternative account of personal identity. It is sufficient to note that those who have taken this view must reject dualism and the dualist basis for immortality.

In the next chapter we will consider the implications for immortality of the view, held amongst others by materialists, that persons are essentially embodied. There is, however, one form of monism which is as opposed to materialism as is Cartesian dualism and yet as opposed to dualism as any other form of monism. This is idealistic monism, or idealism for short – the view that the basic entities of the universe are minds or souls or the like and that matter either does not exist or has only a derivative reality. Idealism is an important strand of the history of Western philosophy and a dominant school of thought in present-day Indian philosophy. It has been less fashionable in the West in recent decades, though there still are distinguished advocates teaching in leading British and American universities. Moreover, it is a philosophical point of view which has been seen as particularly congenial to religion and, more specifically, to belief in an afterlife. It is worth our giving some consideration to whether idealism provides a good foundation for believing that, after we die, we will continue to exist as persons.

IDEALISM AND IMMORTALITY

One of the most serious problems faced by Cartesian dualism is that it makes the mind and the body so different that it becomes impossible to conceive how the one can have any effect on the other. The mind, not being in space, seems unable to get any leverage on physical things, so it becomes entirely mysterious how, when I make up my mind to do something in the material world, I can possibly bring it about. Equally, while it seems possible to trace the effects of the outside world upon our nervous systems and even on our brains, it seems impossible, if the mind is radically different from the brain, to complete tracing those effects to a state of mind. Thus quite ordinary phenomena like human action and sense perception become mysterious, if dualism is true.

Some of the followers of Descartes tried to solve this problem by accepting that, strictly speaking, the mind produces no effects on the body and vice versa. These 'Cartesians', as they were called, suggested that the regularity with which certain mental events are followed by certain bodily events, and vice versa, was due to laws of nature established by God. Indeed, or so they claimed, the power to produce effects in the natural world or in our minds belongs exclusively to

God. It is God, these Cartesians claimed, who makes it appear that mind and body interact. Strictly speaking, mind and body do not interact. Strictly speaking, what happens is that, on the 'occasion' of my willing my arm to move, God causes it to move. And so on. The French philosopher Nicolas Malebranche (1638–1715)[15] made this seem less miraculous by saying that God has a 'general will' that there should be certain laws of the connection between mind and body. But his form of *occasionalism*, as this view is called, still has it that it is God who is the *true cause* of my arm moving on the occasion of my willing it to do so.

EXERCISE 1.4

OCCASIONALISM

There are obvious difficulties for this view in the sense that it conflicts with commonly held beliefs. Try to think of two of them.

DISCUSSION

The most obvious difficulty, perhaps, is that occasionalism assumes that there is a God and so the solution it offers is of no interest to an atheist or indeed to anyone who has serious doubts about the existence of God. It rescues Cartesian dualism from the difficulties about how minds and bodies can interact only to plunge it into difficulties that seem no less great. Out of the frying pan into the fire, we might think.

The other obvious difficulty is that most of us assume that, whether there is a God or not, there are 'true causes' in the world we know. When a house is destroyed by fire an act of God (lightning strike) may be one possible cause but, on investigation, it may turn out that the true cause is a fault in the electric wiring, or a gas leak, or arson. There is a very important reason for not saying it is always an act of God. It is important to settle the true cause of a fire because people want to apportion blame, know how to avoid the reoccurrence of such a tragedy, and so on. It is a difficulty for Malebranche's view that it appears to put all the blame for the evils of the world on God. But (we will be discussing the problem of evil later) we can let this difficulty pass for the moment. Even if there were no religious objection to God taking all the blame, a society that really took this seriously would be lucky to survive for long. For practical purposes we need to be able to learn from the past and knowing where people did something wrong (the careless cigarette etc.) or failed to do what they should (have their wiring checked etc.) is necessary to such learning. So the belief that there are true causes in nature, specifically that we bring about changes in the world, is well entrenched and is not easily explained away.

Nowadays both these difficulties with occasionalism would commonly be thought very serious. But, in Malebranche's day, there were several arguments for the existence of God which were regarded as very impressive (one of which we will consider in Chapter 3). Indeed, for reasons we will not go into here, no one objected to this central plank of his occasionalism at the time.[16] Though Malebranche caused great controversy amongst philosophers in his own time, their objections were directed to other aspects of his philosophy. Many objected to the denial that humans were true causes and this was one point of departure for a young Irish admirer of Malebranche's philosophy, George Berkeley[17] (1685–1753).

Berkeley suggested what might be seen as an amendment to Malebranche's occasionalism, allowing that all spirits – including humans – were in their nature 'active' and that they should all be admitted as true causes, as well as God. Berkeley followed Malebranche, however, in saying that the other causes we observe in nature are not true causes but only 'occasions'. But what do we actually perceive? The usual view, which Berkeley inherited, was that perception consisted of having mental contents ('ideas') and that these were produced by external material objects. On this view, external material objects must be thought of as causes. But, for occasionalists, they are not. Moreover, Berkeley supposed, our ideas must have some cause. Sometimes, when we imagine things, we ourselves are the cause of our ideas. But not all our ideas are caused by ourselves. Some of them have an external cause. For Berkeley, this cause must be a spirit and, he suggests, the ideas we have when we see tables, sunsets and so on are all produced in us directly by God. Thus Berkeley was led (or, at any rate, sought to lead his readers) into idealism, claiming that everything was a spirit or an idea – a mental content of a spirit.

There are a number of other arguments Berkeley used in order to subvert the philosophical belief in matter and support his idealism. One of them is an application of the principle I referred to earlier as Occam's Razor. This argument may have been directed particularly against Malebranche. Matter, according to Malebranche, is not directly experienced, nor is it the cause of what we directly experience. He none the less thought that a Christian should believe in the existence of matter since it was implied by the Bible and the teaching of the Church. Berkeley, who thought the belief in matter did no good to the cause of religion, was not impressed by this last consideration, holding that the existence of matter was not a biblical doctrine. Thus, it seemed to him that those (like Malebranche) whom he referred to as 'the patrons of matter' are committed to supposing 'an innumerable multitude of created beings, which they acknowledge are not capable of producing any one effect in nature, and which therefore are made to no manner of purpose' (Berkeley (1710), Part I, sect. 53). Berkeley's point is that there is no good reason to suppose the existence of what philosophers have called 'material substances'. To the objection that he was undermining the new science of the day by his rejection of matter, Berkeley crisply replied:

> there is not any one *phenomenon* explained on that supposition [the existence of matter], which may not be as well explained without it.
>
> (Berkeley (1710), Part I, sect. 50)

In other words, the new science had no need to suppose such theoretical entities and, using Occam's Razor, we should reject them.

Berkeley's idealism was greeted with ridicule by many of his contemporaries but it enjoyed something of a revival in the late nineteenth century and he came to be acknowledged as a great philosopher. It is only in the twentieth century that some aspects of his thought, such as in the philosophy of science, have been properly appreciated.[18]

BERKELEY'S ARGUMENT FOR IMMORTALITY

Berkeley was not only himself a religious believer but a dedicated philosophical defender of the Christian religion. His idealism not only provided him with what he regarded as a philosophically more defensible position than materialism. It also enabled him to demonstrate the immortality of the soul. Here is a section from Berkeley's major work, *The Principles of Human Knowledge* (1710), in which he discusses this topic:

> 141 It must not be supposed, that they who assert the natural immortality of the soul are of opinion, that it is absolutely incapable of annihilation even by the infinite power of the Creator who first gave it being: but only that it is not liable to be broken or dissolved by the ordinary Laws of Nature or motion. They indeed, who hold the soul of man to be only a thin vital flame, or system of animal spirits, make it perishing and corruptible as the body, since there is nothing more easily dissipated than such a being, which it is naturally impossible should survive the ruin of the tabernacle, wherein it is enclosed. And this notion hath been greedily embraced and cherished by the worst part of mankind, as the most effective antidote to all impressions of virtue and religion. But it hath been made evident, that bodies of what frame so ever, are barely passive ideas in the mind, which is more distant and heterogeneous from them, than light is from darkness. We have shown that the soul is indivisible, incorporeal, unextended, and that it is consequently incorruptible. Nothing can be plainer, than that the motions, changes, decays, and dissolutions which we hourly see befall natural bodies (and which is what we mean by the *course of Nature*) cannot possibly affect an active, simple, uncompounded substance: such a being therefore is indissoluble by the force of Nature, that is to say, *the soul of man is naturally immortal*.
>
> (Berkeley (1710))

We need not trouble ourselves with what exactly were the materialistic views ('man [is] only a thin vital flame' etc.) Berkeley was opposing and who held them. It is sufficient to note here that the doctrine is an ancient one and was quite widespread in the early eighteenth century. It was then generally assumed that materialism involved a denial of the immortality of the soul. That is what Berkeley thought and our concern here is with Berkeley's own argument. Part at least of that argument should already be familiar from earlier arguments for immortality in this book.

EXERCISE 1.5

BERKELEY ON IMMORTALITY

Read the passage above again and note your answers to these questions:

1   What do you take to be Berkeley's argument for immortality? (It is condensed and needs some reconstructing.)
2   What objections can be made to Berkeley's argument? (If you cannot think of any, I suggest you look back at the section 'The Platonic argument from the simplicity of the soul'.)

Check your answer against the one at the back of the book before reading on.

DISCUSSION

1   You may have been struck by Berkeley's claim in the passage to have 'shown that the soul is indivisible' (etc.). He did not, in fact, show this in the published edition of his *Principles*. There is a brief argument in the manuscript that 'the soul is without composition, one pure simple undivided being'. But this was left out of the published editions. The condensed nature of Berkeley's argument may be due to a lapse in editing his manuscript for publication. But there is nothing original in his argument and he might have expected his readers to be familiar with it. The argument from the activity of the soul to its immortality may also have been derived from Plato.[19] But this argument, that the soul is capable of moving itself and whatever is capable of moving itself is indestructible, was not so widely used.
2   Berkeley's argument for immortality brings out how, in some respects, idealistic monism need not be different from radical dualism. The Cartesian dualist is at least drawn to the idealist view that the *essential person* is a pure (what dualists would call 'disembodied') spirit. Plato, though he often writes like a dualist, is commonly interpreted as a kind of idealist, as allowing to the material world at best a shadowy reality. It should not surprise us, therefore, if some objections to the dualist account of minds also apply to the accounts given by idealists. Idealists are just as likely to be tempted to make memory the criterion of personal identity. Berkeley, as it happens, has a quite original account of his own. But the way the problem about animals arises for him illustrates the tendency for similar problems to arise for idealist accounts of immortality as arise for dualist ones.

BERKELEY AND THE ANIMALS DILEMMA

EXERCISE 1.6

BERKELEY AND ANIMALS

Bearing in mind my earlier section 'The animals dilemma', how would you expect the animals dilemma to arise for Berkeley, given that he holds that the only substances (real entities) are *spirits*, whose nature it is to act and to perceive?

DISCUSSION

Berkeley concludes that spirits are naturally immortal. The question arises whether animals are or are not spirits. It looks as if Berkeley ought to say they are, if spirits are characterized by being able to perceive and to act. Animals have senses and perceive in ways that can be compared with human perception. Moreover, many animals are capable of some actions – for instance, a cat can catch a mouse. If they are spirits then, on his account, they are immortal. And, if they are not, there is a problem about how they fit in.

Berkeley did not discuss this topic much in his written work, but his inclination seems to have been to say that animals were an inferior sort of spirit and to reject the Cartesian view that they were mere machines. He evidently discussed it during a visit to America, where he met Samuel Johnson,[20] who had similar philosophical sympathies to his own. Johnson sought to pursue in correspondence with him the implications of combining the view that animals were some kind of spirits with Berkeley's argument for immortality:

> I think I once heard you allow a principle of perception and spontaneous motion in beasts. Now if their *esse* [a Latin word which in this context can be translated 'being'] as well as ours consists in perceiving, upon what is the natural immortality of our soul founded that will not equally conclude in favour of them?
>
> (Letter dated 5 February 1730, Berkeley (1975), p. 352)

Berkeley replied to Johnson's letter but, unfortunately for us, did not answer this particular question. It is not clear indeed how he could have replied effectively without making a significant modification to his system.

It would not involve too much change, perhaps, to allow immortality to animal spirits as well as to those of humans. But the ethical and religious implications of doing so would not have escaped his attention. If animals are naturally immortal then it is not clear why they do not have an equal status in God's eyes with human beings. It is difficult to imagine the good Bishop Berkeley being willing to think such thoughts. And yet he was familiar with the doctrines of the ancient followers of Pythagoras, who extended the natural immortality argument to animals. They believed that souls migrated from one body to another when any living thing died. Their doctrine is therefore usually referred to as the transmigration of souls. They accepted the ethical implications of this doctrine for the treatment of animals – they were vegetarians. The Pythagoreans did not, however, think of this natural immortality as a desirable state. On the contrary the incessant round of rebirth as a different animal was one from which they sought to escape. They believed that humans could hope to escape eventually by being absorbed into the universal soul of which they were a part. The Pythagorean view has affinities with Hinduism that have led some to conjecture that there were influences from the Indian subcontinent on early Greek philosophy. But, whatever its origins, it is a very different view from any which a Christian bishop could be expected to teach.

It seems, then, that there is no obvious way out of the dilemma posed by animals for Berkeley, namely: *either* animals are spirits, in which case they too need to be admitted as naturally immortal and have something like the status of humans; *or else* they are not, and Berkeley needs to explain more exactly how, in his terms, he can distinguish animals from spirits.

In discussing idealism we have been concerned with whether it is likely to fare much better than Cartesian dualism if it is used, as it was by Berkeley, to support belief in immortality. We have only discussed the animals problem in detail. But, while Berkeley's problem is not the same as that of Descartes, it is clear he has unresolved difficulties about animals. As to the other problems, it seems clear, in the first place, that an idealist might equally be tempted to rely on memory as the criterion of personal identity and face similar difficulties on this point to those that face the dualist. It seems, in the second place, that idealism, like dualism, is bound to conceive of minds or spirits as substances. (Berkeley did so quite explicitly.) The objection that there is no good reason to believe that there are such entities arises just as much for idealism as it does for dualism.

It seems, then, that neither Cartesian dualism nor idealism is likely to provide a firm philosophical basis on which to believe in an afterlife. In the next chapter we will consider whether it is possible to believe in an afterlife even though it is not assumed that minds or souls can exist independently of bodies. This will lead us to discuss the question whether accepting materialism is consistent with belief in an afterlife. But before passing on to these questions it is worth our discussing two views of human destiny which both involve what is sometimes called transmigration of souls.

THE TRANSMIGRATION OF SOULS

Belief in something like transmigration of souls has been and still is widespread as a form of belief in immortality. It is particularly associated with Hinduism and other religions of Indian origin, where it is expressed by the term 'Samsara' or 'wandering'. The soul, in these religions, is caught in a continuing process of life and death in many differing forms, ranging from deities through humans and animals to evil spirits. The form in which souls are reborn will be appropriate to their previous lives, according to a doctrine known as Karma. It is also widely believed that the soul may seek eventual liberation (Moksha in Hinduism, Nirvana in Buddhism) from the endless cycle of birth and rebirth.

These ideas were, as I mentioned earlier, taken up by the Pythagoreans and even Plato seems to have endorsed them. They have also influenced some Jewish and Christian groups, though in a modified form. For instance, the influential Kabbalistic teacher Isaac Luria (1534–72)[21] taught that each human soul goes through twelve lives (always in the human form) before eventually achieving salvation. This idea was taken up by the Christian Kabbalist philosopher Francis van Helmont (1614–98), and through him was accepted by some of the early English Quakers.[22]

The transmigration of souls clearly involves a dualist view of the relation between soul and body. The same soul pursues its career (wanderings), on this account, by being joined to a succession of different bodies. Those who subscribe to such a doctrine need to face the difficulties we saw earlier for explaining personal identity on a dualist basis. There are other distinctive difficulties, some empirical (i.e. turning on facts of experience) and others philosophical.

There is a simple empirical difficulty, namely that the number of living things (in the Pythagorean version) and the number of humans (in Luria's *Kabbala*) will need to remain constant or at least – since new souls might be created – not decline. It would be difficult to disprove this, in the case of living things in general. But there have been disasters that have temporarily reduced human populations by millions. In the fourteenth century, for instance, the Bubonic Plague devastated the human population of Europe and Central Asia. There is no evidence that this was compensated for by a growth of populations elsewhere in the world. The empirical evidence suggests that the human population of the world has sometimes declined. The Kabbalistic theory that each person has twelve lives, no more and no less, cannot accommodate this. Nor can the theory easily be modified so that some people have fewer than the standard twelve lives. For the point of the theory is that twelve lives are necessary (and sufficient) to allow everyone who has misused one or two lives to get themselves morally fit for life in Heaven. The theory cannot allow that souls are propelled into an afterlife because too many are dying and there are not enough new human bodies for them to go to.

I said it would be difficult to prove that the total population of living things was subject to reductions at particular times. But the earth has in the past been subject to bombardment by meteors and scientists believe that the material ejected by the impact has sometimes obscured the sun for long enough to change the climate and cause the extinction of large numbers of species. If this is so, then it seems likely that at times there has been a reduction in the total number of living things on the earth. There would, supposing that to have been true, be similar objections to the Pythagorean theory of the transmigration of souls.

There are other difficulties about the body-hopping which souls are supposed to be capable of in these theories of transmigration of souls. It is difficult to pin down exactly why body-hopping seems incredible. In such cases it is useful to look at the attempts by other philosophers to pinpoint the difficulty. Transmigration of souls or what is sometimes called *metempsychosis* was a discussion point in late-seventeenth-century philosophy. Leibniz considered this doctrine when writing about J. G. Wachter's book *The Kabbalah Explained* and offered this objection to the doctrine of transmigration:

> The author remarks that the doctrine of the revivification of souls into bodies, was toler-
> ated by Christ and his disciples, and by the early Christians. But it should be recognized
> that in reality there is no transition of the soul from one body to another, except insofar as
> the body itself is insensibly changed. Metempsychosis [i.e. transmigration of souls] would
> be against the rule that nothing takes place by leaps. The transition of the soul from one
> body to another, would be the same as the leap of a body from one place to another, without
> traversing the intermediate space.[23]

The 'rule' Leibniz refers to was generally accepted in scientific circles in his day. His point, as he makes clear elsewhere, is that all change in nature happens grad-ually and not all at once. However fast a change is, there is always a process, with intermediate stages. For example, if I raise my arm from my side to above my head, I can do this slowly or quickly. But, in each case, my arm gradually changes position. There are certain contexts – particularly social and political ones – where the word 'gradual' implies a process which is slow. But, at any rate in natural processes, speed does not affect whether or not something is gradual, only whether we can *see* it as gradual. A humming-bird in flight changes its wing positions so quickly that we cannot see the intermediate positions. So we cannot *see* that the changes are gradual. But, if we see the flight of a humming-bird in slow motion, then we can see the intermediate positions and the illusion of 'jumps' disappears. The rule Leibniz refers to is usually stated by saying that there are no 'jumps' or 'leaps' in nature and it is sometimes called 'the principle of continuity', since the claim is that all natural processes are continuous. It is this principle which, Leibniz holds, is violated by the theory of transmigration.

Leibniz took this to be a further reason for supposing that the process of surviving bodily death should be more one of transformation of the same bodily being, rather on analogy with the transformation of a chrysalis into a butterfly. Just as the same animal continues to live but in a new form, so the same human can be transformed by the process known in the Judaeo-Christian–Muslim tradi-tions as the *resurrection* of the body.

Belief in the resurrection originated in Judaism but was a matter of contro-versy during the life of Jesus, with the Pharisees believing it and the Sadducees denying it. The Christians believed that Jesus of Nazareth, after being crucified and buried, rose again from the dead, even appearing to his disciples. It became an article of the Christian faith to believe that everyone will be raised from the dead at some time and made to answer for their conduct in this life. The details are a matter of controversy but broadly the assumption is not only that people will live again in bodily form but that they will in some sense have the same body as they had before. Faced with the difficulties about believing in separate substan-tial souls some theologians[24] and philosophers have reflected with some relief that the Platonic commitment to the immortality of a detached soul was never the view the orthodox should have been taking.

There may be something in this. But in truth orthodoxy has tried to have it both ways. The common Christian view was, for a long time, that the resurrection of the dead will not take place until the time of the Last Judgement and that, in the meantime, the souls of the dead exist in an 'intermediate state', without a body. At the Last Judgement the souls of the dead will, according to this once common teaching, be reunited to their bodies. So, at least on this view, the resurrection of the dead is a further complication and not an alternative to the view that the souls of the dead exist in a disembodied state.

None the less it seems worth trying to dispense with this 'intermediate state' and with commitment to dualism or belief in disembodied souls and their attendant difficulties. This is the direction we will take in the next chapter.

SUMMARY

This chapter has been particularly concerned with the views about the soul and immortality associated with mind–body dualism. We considered the connection between Descartes's philosophy of mind and his view of its implications for belief in immortality. We considered the Platonic argument for the immortality of the soul based on its supposed simplicity or indivisibility. We noted that the argument was not conclusive and that there were, on the contrary, reasons for rejecting the view that souls or minds are entities or substances at all. Though Cartesian dualism has often been thought congenial to belief in immortality, there are difficulties arising from questions about the souls of animals. There are difficulties also about supposing that the conditions for personal identity can be met by disembodied souls. Similar difficulties arise for idealism, another philosophical standpoint thought to be congenial to belief in immortality. One form of belief in immortality involves acceptance of the transmigration of souls from one life form to another. This doctrine involves the difficulties of dualism as well as further difficulties of its own.

FURTHER READING

For an authoritative review of Descartes's position on immortality, see J. G. Cottingham's 'Cartesian dualism: theology, metaphysics, and science', in *The Cambridge Companion to Descartes*, ed. J. Cottingham, Cambridge University Press, 1992, pp. 236–57. Modern defences of dualism include J. Foster's *The Immaterial Self*, Routledge, 1991, and *The Case for Dualism*, ed. J. R. Smythies and J. Beloff, University of Charlottesville Press, 1989. For a modern defence of belief in immortality on dualist lines, see H. D. Lewis's *The Self and Immortality*, Macmillan, 1993. For a recent critique, see N. Everitt's 'Substance Dualism and Disembodied Existence', *Faith and Philosophy* (April, 2000). For a clear and lively account of some of the difficulties for belief in immortality, see J. Perry's *A Dialogue on Personal Identity and Immortality*, Hackett, 1978. The best available collection of readings on philosophical issues to do with immortality generally is *Immortality*, ed. P. Edwards, Prometheus Books, 1997. This collection includes both historical and recent readings on the transmigration of souls. Another excellent collection of readings on a related topic is *Personal Identity*, ed. J. Perry, University of California Press, 1975.

NOTES

1   In a letter to Huygens, reproduced in Descartes (1991), p. 208.
2   The argument is in *Phaedo* 78B–80C. Plato also used other arguments which have been taken up by later philosophers, though they are not discussed here. For a good and accessible account of Plato's thought in general and on the soul in particular, see Crowe (1984).
3   The reader for whom my account of elementary logic is too brief or unsatisfactory is recommended to read Warburton (1996).
4   I do not discuss premise 3 directly.
5   Kant's *Critique of Pure Reason* (1781) was a watershed in the history of European philosophy. It was severely critical of the rationalistic arguments for immortality and of the traditional arguments for the existence of God. Kant's writings had a major impact on subsequent work in ethics and aesthetics, as well as metaphysics and philosophy of religion. His 'moral argument' for the existence of God is discussed in Chapter 4. For a general introduction to Kant's philosophy, see the entry in Craig (1998). For a more substantial treatment of those aspects of his thought pertinent to this book, see Wood (1970).
6   Particularly in his 'Paralogisms of the Transcendental Dialectic'.
7   For an introduction to Ryle's philosophy, see the entries in Brown, Collinson and Wilkinson (1996) and Craig (1998). For a fuller account, see Lyons (1980).
8   For an account of Occam which includes discussion of his 'razor', see McCord Adams (1987).
9   For an account of this principle in a scientific context, see the entry on 'Simplicity' in Edwards (1967). For a critique, see Sober (1994).
10 See the section on 'Idealism and immortality' below.
11 For an introduction to Leibniz's philosophy, see MacDonald Ross (1984). I have dealt with Leibniz's account of the soul more fully in Brown (1998).
12 John Locke became a major influence on eighteenth-century and subsequent philosophy through the publication of *An Essay Concerning Human Understanding* (1690). He was also a major influence on English political philosophy, through works like his second *Treatise of Government* (also 1690) and his *Letter Concerning Toleration* (English translation, 1690). For a good general introduction to Locke, which positions him in relation to Descartes and devotes a chapter to his important discussion of personal identity, see Jolley (1999).
13 For instance, Locke rejected Descartes's view that many of our ideas (including the idea of God) were *innate* in all humans, i.e. that the idea was imprinted on all of us from birth. Locke claimed, on the contrary, that all our ideas derived from sense experience or a kind of inner experience he called 'reflection'. Some ideas, like our idea of red, are simple and such simple ideas are the raw materials from which we construct more complex ideas. According to Locke our idea of God is one we have, directly or indirectly, constructed from our experience.
14 *An Essay Concerning Human Understanding*, Book II, Ch. XXXVII, sect. 2. This chapter contains much of Locke's important discussion of personal identity. Locke actually claims that there are three sorts of substances that we have any idea of: namely, God, 'finite intelligences' and 'bodies'. He finally agrees with Descartes that God too is an intelligence (an infinite one) but he thinks this needs more argument than Descartes had given it. Though he is ultimately unwilling to endorse it he does not rule out Cartesian dualism.
15 Malebranche's main work was his *Search after Truth* (1674–5). For an introduction to his thought, see the entry in Craig (1998). For a fuller treatment of various aspects of his philosophy and its influence, see Nadler (2000).
16 The objection appears for the first time, so far as I know, in the writings of David Hume (1711–16) and even then only implicitly. Hume's *Treatise of Human Nature* (1739–40) might be seen as involving a kind of occasionalism without God.
17 For a good introduction to Berkeley's life and philosophy, which discusses the background to his idealism and his argument for immortality, see Berman (1994).
18 See, for instance, K. R. Popper's 'A Note on Berkeley as Precursor of Mach and Einstein' in Popper (1965).
19 *Phaedrus*, 245C–246A.
20 This Samuel Johnson, sometimes referred to as the 'father of American philosophy', is not the same as the English Samuel Johnson who thought he could refute Berkeley by kicking a stone. On Berkeley's correspondent see Berman (1994).
21 For more on Luria and on the Kabbalah generally, the still definitive work is Scholem (1941).

22   See van Helmont's *Two Hundred Queries ... concerning the Doctrine of the Revolution of Humane Souls* (1684). Van Helmont's English books were published by London Quakers and his doctrine of the revolution of human souls was defended in William Clarke's *Eight Queries*. See the entry in Craig (1998) for a brief introduction and Brown (1997) for further details of van Helmont's philosophy.

23   The Latin title of the work by Wachter was his *Elucidarius cabalisticus* (1706). Leibniz's remarks (in Latin) were published with a French translation *en face* in a work entitled *Réfutation inédit de Spinoza*, ed. A Foucher de Careil, Paris, 1854. The passage quoted is a translation from p. 76. Both these works are republished with other works under the title *Johann Georg Wachter: De primordiis Christianae religionis*, ed. Winfried Schröder (Stuttgart: Bad Cannstatt, 1995). Leibniz's critique of transmigration is discussed in Brown (1998).

24   See especially Cullmann (1958).

2 Bodily survival

OBJECTIVES

By the end of your work on this chapter you should:

■ Be able to distinguish different forms of the doctrine of the resurrection of the body and identify some of the difficulties that have been raised for belief in bodily survival.

■ Be able to state and discuss Peter Van Inwagen's materialist theory of the resurrection.

■ Have read and be able to offer a critical assessment of Linda Badham's argument against the possibility of the resurrection.

■ Be able to state and discuss the supposed implications of Darwinism and materialism for belief in an afterlife.

THE RESURRECTION OF THE BODY

To defend the view that minds or souls can exist in a separate disembodied state in some future life it is necessary to defend an appropriate view of the mind–body relation. In the previous chapter we considered two theories according to which immortality would involve a disembodied existence: Cartesian dualism and idealism. These theories face similar problems when used to support belief in immortality, conceived as involving the existence of disembodied souls. These, however, are not the only theories and immortality does not have to be conceived as involving a disembodied existence.

In this chapter we will consider approaches to the problem of life after death in which persons are thought of as essentially embodied. We will also consider whether it is possible to give a rational defence of the doctrine, common to Judaism, Christianity and Islam, that persons exist in the afterlife in a bodily form. There are, as usual, variants on what is believed to be the correct doctrine. But the central idea is that the dead are somehow brought back to life, i.e. that life is restored to them in a bodily form. Belief in what is called 'the resurrection of the body' was a development in Judaism two centuries before Jesus of Nazareth. Jesus is credited in the Christian Bible not only with having miraculously raised others from the dead but with himself 'rising' on the third day after he was crucified, dead and buried. Belief in the resurrection involves belief in the same person living again with what is in some sense the very same body.

Belief in the resurrection of the body seems to fit best with acceptance of a monistic view of human beings and indeed seems consistent with some forms of materialism. But it would be wrong to suppose that it excludes substance dualism. It was traditionally believed by Christians that the dead were all raised together on the Day of Judgement. It was commonly believed that the souls of the dead, prior to the general resurrection, existed in a state of separation from the body to which they would later be reunited. These disembodied souls were acknowledged to enjoy only a reduced ('incomplete') existence and not to flourish as Plato imagined the soul would when freed from the body. None the less this view involves a commitment to such souls as separate existences, and so involves substance dualism.

Belief in the resurrection can in this way fit with dualism. But, in view of the difficulties there are for dualism, it is noteworthy that belief in the resurrection promises to fit well with monist, even with materialist, beliefs. At a time when many philosophers of mind ask *which* form of materialism is true rather than, as previously, *whether* any form of materialism is true, philosophical interest in the possibility of the dead being resurrected has naturally increased. Those who believe in the resurrection believe that the complete person – considered as a psycho-physical unit – can be restored to life even after the body has disintegrated. Materialists, like others, may find it difficult to believe that this is possible. But, on the face of it, the resurrection of persons as bodily beings is consistent with persons being fundamentally material, whereas their survival as disembodied souls would obviously not be. Just as the survival of a disembodied or pure soul is what a dualist or idealist would expect who hoped for immortality, so the resurrection of the person as a psycho-physical unity is what a materialist might hope for, someone who believed that persons can only exist as material beings.

A MATERIALIST THEORY OF THE RESURRECTION

It is true that, historically speaking, materialists have tended to deny the existence of God and of an afterlife. For various reasons materialism has historically been a radical option and is associated with holding anti-religious and anti-establishment (especially anti-Church) views. It used to be impossible to embrace a philosophical materialism on its own without risking your reputation being ruined by people who would accuse you of trying to subvert the Church or the State.[1] But, while these associations are still important for some materialists (especially of the older generation), materialism has become much more of a mainstream view. There are still radical materialists who believe that, as science progresses, so our whole mentalistic vocabulary will come to be seen as no more than 'folk psychology',[2] as a way of speaking that, rather like talk of the sun 'rising' in the morning, will be seen to embody a false view of the world. But this programme of elimination is seen by others as no more than 'a gleam in the eyes'[3] and its implications (for religion, for instance) are, accordingly, not regarded seriously. Other kinds of materialist, though they will deny the existence of non-material things, are not thereby committed to dismissing religious experience. They are not debarred by virtue of being in some sense materialists from considering the possibility of survival after death in a bodily form.

To be sure there is a big difference between the attitude of traditional dualists and that of modern materialists towards the afterlife. Traditional dualists regarded survival of the soul after death as at least probable and some of them, as we saw, even regarded it as demonstrable. From the standpoint of materialism, by contrast, survival after death is at best improbable. A materialist might (some do) believe in God, however, and might accordingly believe that the resurrection of the dead is something that God could and will accomplish. The resurrection of the dead has always been inherently improbable from a common-sense standpoint. Belief in the resurrection, even on the part of dualists, was a matter of faith. That does not mean there was no reason to believe in it. But the reasons people thought they had were inconclusive and indirect. They tended to depend on prior belief in the existence of an omnipotent God who could, if it formed part of the divine purpose, do anything that was inherently possible. There were also arguments about whether, if there was a creator of the universe, he was particularly interested in what humans got up to or in securing a better existence for any of them in some future life. But not everything can be argued about at once.[4] Arguments about the resurrection have, accordingly, tended to grant for the sake of argument that there is an omnipotent God who might want to bring about the resurrection of the dead. They have tended to focus on whether it is inherently possible anyway.

A contemporary philosopher, Peter Van Inwagen, has argued that the only way to defend the resurrection on a materialistic basis is to suppose that, when someone dies, God preserves whatever constitutes the physical core of the person. It is not enough, he argues, that God is able to bring together all the atoms that formerly constituted that person. For the atoms that constitute a person, from a materialistic standpoint, vary at different times and thus the materialist is faced with problems that do not face the dualist. Van Inwagen explains in these terms:

> Suppose that … God proposes to bring back Socrates from the dead. How shall he accomplish this? How shall even omnipotence bring back a particular person who lived long ago and has returned to the dust? – whose former atoms have been, for millennia, spread pretty evenly throughout the biosphere? This question does not confront the dualist, who will say either that there is no need to bring back Socrates (because, so to speak, Socrates has never left), or else that Socrates can be brought back simply by providing his soul (which still exists) with a newly created human body. But what shall the materialist say? From the point of view of the materialist, it looks as if asking God to bring Socrates back is like asking him to bring back the snows of yesteryear or the light of other days. For what can even omnipotence do but reassemble? And reassembly is not enough, for Socrates was composed of different atoms at different times. If someone says, 'If God now reassembles

the atoms that composed Socrates at the moment of his death, those reassembled atoms will once more compose Socrates', there is an obvious objection to his thesis. If God can reassemble the atoms that composed Socrates at the moment of his death in 399 BC – and no doubt he can –, he can also reassemble the atoms that composed Socrates at some particular instant in 409 BC. In fact, if there is no overlap between the two sets of atoms, God could do both of these things, and set the resulting men side by side. And which would be Socrates? Neither or both, it would seem, and since not both, neither … In the end, there would seem to be no way round the following requirement: if Socrates was a material thing, a living organism, then, if a man who lives at some time after Socrates' death and physical dissolution is to be Socrates, there will have to be some material and causal continuity between the matter that composed Socrates at the moment of his death and the matter that at any time composes that man … But **physical dissolution** and **material and causal continuity** are hard to reconcile.

(Van Inwagen (n.d.), pp. 2–3)

EXERCISE 2.1

MATERIALISM AND RESURRECTION

1   What problem, according to Van Inwagen, faces a materialist account of the resurrection that does not arise for dualists?
2   What does he suggest as the solution to this problem?

DISCUSSION

1   The problem is that if there is no more to Socrates than the matter that constitutes him then, since this matter can be quite different at different times, it is logically possible for two individuals with an equal claim to being Socrates to co-exist. Dualists need not concern themselves with this problem since they hold there is more to Socrates than anything material.
2   Van Inwagen suggests that, though materialists cannot allow any extra immaterial element of Socrates, they should require that for any person at a time after Socrates' death to be the same as Socrates there will have to be material and causal continuity between the matter that constitutes each of them.

Van Inwagen does not elaborate on what he means by 'material and causal continuity'. But he seems to have in mind considerations about how material things can retain their identity through change. A living thing – a tree, for example – is constantly changing but, from one day to the next, there is a very substantial material continuity even if, over a long enough period, the matter of which the tree is composed changes completely. The tree also has a continuous history of things that have happened to it – diseases, lightning strikes, holes drilled by woodpeckers, and so on – and there is a causal continuity between the tree that is now marked in certain ways and the tree to which these things happened. Trees usually remain in the same place. But there is no problem with the thought that a tree that is transplanted is still the same tree. It may even be possible to transplant a crucial part of a dying tree and get it to grow again. The tree could then be said to have been resurrected. But then part of the tree never died. So this is not a case where the tree has been entirely destroyed. Once the tree has been destroyed, it lacks the material and causal continuity with any other tree in virtue of which we could say they were the same. Complete dissolution seems to rule out material and causal continuity. So to insist on material and causal continuity, as Van Inwagen thinks a materialist needs to do, means denying that, when people die, their bodies are completely dissolved.

Elsewhere Van Inwagen has developed this suggestion:

> It is of course true that men apparently cease to exist: those who are cremated, for example. But it contradicts nothing in the creeds to suppose that this is not what really happens, and that God preserves our corpses contrary to all appearance ... Perhaps at the moment of each man's death, God removes his corpse and replaces it with a simulacrum which is what is burned or rots. Or perhaps God is not so wholesale as this: perhaps He removes for 'safekeeping' only the 'core person' – the brain and central nervous system. These are details.
>
> (Van Inwagen (1997), p. 246)

Van Inwagen's conclusion is that the only option available to someone who favours a materialistic account of the resurrection is to deny that the core person is actually destroyed at death. He is aware of the obvious objections, that there is no evidence that the core person is preserved at death and that it is strange that God has gone to such lengths to make it look as if people not only die but 'pass into nothingness'. But he suggests that God has reasons for not making it easy for people to believe.

Once the argument is taken in this direction the positive reasons people might have for believing in immortality will depend on their reasons for believing that there is a god, a controlling intelligence whose purposes call for our survival. Whether or not there is reason to believe in such a being is a matter we will go into in the next part of this book. But, even if we suppose there is some reason to believe that our survival after death would fit the purposes of a higher being who could underwrite it, it might none the less be impossible to reconcile with *other* beliefs we hold about the world. We can, perhaps, modify our beliefs so as to make them consistent with one another. But, at the end of the day, we may find that, on balance, the basis for any belief in immortality is controversial and that there is good ground for accepting certain views that make it improbable.

Rightly or wrongly, the belief is nowadays widespread that science has undermined the basis for any reasonable expectation about a life after death. One contemporary philosopher who has argued that no kind of case can be made for bodily survival in the context of what is suggested by modern science is Linda Badham. She argues that 'the implications of modern science are far more damaging to doctrines of life after death than many Christian writers have supposed'. We will begin by considering whether the objections to bodily survival are as overwhelming as Badham and others have claimed.

OBJECTIONS TO BODILY SURVIVAL

Philosophers who consider the question of immortality tend to divide into those who see little prospect of defending disembodied existence and those who see little likelihood of defending the possibility of bodily survival. Those who write on the subject usually begin with what they take to be damning criticisms of the approach they reject before moving on to a more detailed treatment of what they regard as the more hopeful prospect. Linda Badham is no exception. She begins her chapter on the problems of life after death (in Badham and Badham (1987)) by offering some trenchant objections to what she claims is the traditional Christian notion of the resurrection of the body, and therefore to bodily survival. She thinks the best prospect of defending immortality is by maintaining the possibility of disembodied existence.

Now read the first part (entitled 'Resurrection of the Body (this Flesh)') of Linda Badham's 'Problems about the Resurrection of the Body' (Reading 1).

Reading
pp.133–5

EXERCISE 2.2

OBJECTIONS TO BODILY SURVIVAL (1)

Summarize in one or two sentences the three objections Badham offers. Check your answer against the one at the back of the book before reading on.

DISCUSSION

(a) The Cannibals Problem is one that had been much discussed by early Christian philosophers who puzzled about the resurrection. One solution was to say that not all the matter that constitutes a person is necessary to that person's identity. In addition to much matter that is replaceable there is a physical essence of each person that cannot be destroyed and which persists through death, constituting the core from which the resurrected person is recreated. The traditional thought had been that, just as some seeds are so tough they can withstand fire and then grow into living things, so there is this naturally indestructible part of humans which survives death and becomes again a living thing at the resurrection. Following the suggestion of a Jewish Rabbi, this was thought to be an indestructible bone at the base of the spine.[5] No seeds, however, are really naturally indestructible and indeed few would nowadays pin hopes of resurrection on empirical evidence that there is some indestructible physical part of us, whether a bone or anything else. A theory like Van Inwagen's, however, which makes the preservation of a core person something God undertakes, might serve instead as the basis for a modern answer to the Cannibals Problem. For the unfortunate who is devoured by cannibals is, thanks to God's intervention, salvaged in a form that is materially and causally continous with the person who has been killed and will be resurrected. There is no competition between him and any cannibal over the parts of his flesh that have been eaten since particular pieces of the flesh are not necessary to the identity of either, even on a materialist account. Even if a particulr cannibal were to eat an entire missionary alone there would, on Van Inwagen's account, be no question of the missionary becoming part of the cannibal or of their identities being confused.

(b) The second objection is about the state of the body when resurrected. It can perhaps be stated more sharply as a dilemma. Either the body will still be mortal and so its problems will only be postponed by a resuscitation; or else, if it is made immune to further deterioration, we cannot speak of it as flesh at all, still less as the same flesh. It may be replied, however, that Badham is making her case too easy by obliging the believer to subscribe to a particularly implausible version of what is involved in life after death. There are problems about translation from the biblical languages, where 'flesh' does not have its modern meaning, and the biblical belief might better be represented, it could be argued, by talking about 'the same body'.[6] Things can retain the same identity over a period of time even though there may be many changes to their parts. An individual person remains the same person and has the same body even though they have been given, thanks to modern surgery, a number of artificial parts. Perhaps something can retain its identity even when all the parts are changed. There are ancient woods which have remained the same woods for hundreds of years even though none of the individual trees that comprised them in mediaeval times are still extant.

(c) The 'too many people' objection invites the reply that it involves an unsuitable idea of God to think that the numbers of people in Heaven would pose a problem. Even if it is compounded by the thought that God might care for an infinitely large number of species in infinitely many other worlds, it seems to involve an unworthy notion of God to suggest he could not cope, as if immortality would pose a refugee problem for those administering the afterlife.

I do not think, for the reasons I have given, that Badham's objections to the idea of a literal resurrection are conclusive. This is only the first stage of her argument, however. She moves on to consider the view that our earthly bodies are not revived but rather replaced by an exactly similar body in some other world.

Now read the second part (entitled 'Resurrection of the Body (Transformed)') of Linda Badham's 'Problems about the Resurrection of the Body' (Reading 1).

Reading
pp. 135–6

EXERCISE 2.3

OBJECTIONS TO BODILY SURVIVAL (2)

1 Summarize her objection briefly in your own words.
2 Consider, briefly, whether you think it is a telling objection.

DISCUSSION

1 Badham points out that people who hope for personal survival will not be satisfied by the assurance that an exactly similar being will be brought into existence after they are dead. For what they are hoping for is that they themselves and not some replica will live after they have died.

2 Badham's objection here relates to a point made earlier in discussing what minimally must be involved in personal immortality, namely that there should be identity of person between this life and the life to come. I earlier noted there are reasons for taking bodily continuity as a necessary condition of personal identity. If there is no bodily continuity then there is the problem that Badham raises, namely that it is impossible to tell whether the new body is the same body as the one it replaces or whether it is merely a replica. It can be added that, from the point of view of the orthodox, it is an absurdity to suppose that a replica of me could be 'punished' for what I have done wrong or 'rewarded' for what I have done right. It is difficult to see on what view of immortality the existence of replicas would fulfil what was hoped for. As we saw in Chapter 1, hopes and fears of immortality are nearly always connected with the expectation that the same person will survive or live again. Thus Badham's objection seems to me telling.

But, though Badham's objection to replicas seems to me a telling one, her overall argument against the possibility of bodily survival is less convincing. It depends upon supposing that, in the resurrection, either all of the matter of the deceased's body is restored to life or else new matter is created which is exactly the same. But this is a false dichotomy. It is possible that the unique physical core (bits of the brain and genetic material) of a person is somehow retained and provides the basis in the afterlife for that person not only to be, but to be recognized as, the same person. At the same time it has to be admitted that there is no evidence that this happens and so, unless one believes in an omnipotent God who could underwrite such transformations, the doctrine of the resurrection appears to be incredible.

DARWINISM AND IMMORTAL SOULS

On the face of it, Darwinism is hard to reconcile with the kind of belief in the soul that religious people have. Since human life has arisen, according to Darwin's theory, from lower forms of life, it seems to have the implication that there is nothing special about us compared with other species; at any rate, we are not so special that we should flatter ourselves we are destined for eternity. This implication was immediately seized upon by Darwin's critics.

Darwin himself was careful, in the *Origin of Species*, to avoid discussing the implications of his theory of natural selection for understanding the human situation. But a reviewer in the periodical *Athenaeum* alleged that Darwin's 'creed' was that man 'was born yesterday – he will perish tomorrow' (18 November 1859, p. 660). The reviewer seems to have gleaned that the human race was a late product of a long evolutionary process which, like other species, is going to disappear. And this, as it seems to me, is a reasonable inference. It is natural to assume a symmetry between human origins and human destiny and to infer that if humans have such lowly origins then they are not destined for eternity and have no special place in the mind of the Creator.

Darwinism was and still is vehemently opposed by many religious groups as inconsistent with their fundamental beliefs. But over the years it has become more, rather than less, entrenched in the life sciences[7] and many of the major groups have looked for and believed they have found ways of making acceptance of Darwinism possible for their adherents. The basic strategy has been to interpret Darwinism as less far reaching in its implications than had previously been supposed. For instance, it might be claimed that the evolution of animal species was just as Darwin supposed and that indeed the human species evolved from the higher primates just as Darwin supposed. But this, it might be claimed, only affects our material nature. It is consistent with this that our spiritual nature should have a quite different origin and should have been specially conferred on us in accordance with God's original purposes for the creation. A religious believer can thus accept Darwinism as a scientific hypothesis without accepting the interpretation put upon it by certain philosophers, such as Daniel Dennett.[8] This is the strategy now adopted by the Catholic Church in relation to Darwinism, since the Church has allowed Darwinian doctrines to be accepted for animals and the bodily aspects of humans but insists that this does not affect the Church's teaching about the soul. The pronouncement of Pope Pius XII in 1953 used these words:

> The teaching of the Church leaves the doctrine of evolution an open question, as long as it confines its speculations to the development, from other living matter already in existence, of the human body ... That souls are immediately created by God is a view which the Catholic faith imposes on us.

The Catholic teaching is that God specially creates and adds each soul to the human embryo at some point before birth. This teaching is consistent with the principle that there should be a symmetry between what we believe about human origins and what we believe about human destiny. Darwinism makes human origins seem much more humble than is suggested by the Bible or conventional religious belief. There seems no more reason to suppose that humans are naturally immortal than other species or that humans enjoy any divine preferment. It seems as if those who hold that humans are immortal or are specially favoured by God can give only a qualified endorsement of Darwinism and must reject its more radical forms. They can only be, as Catholics are now allowed to be, what are sometimes called 'conservative Darwinists'.

Conservative Darwinism is a point of view which seeks to combine two sets of ideas that have seemed to others to be irreconcilable.[9] The question arises whether the strategy works. There are many options available to the religious believer who wishes to combine traditional belief in an afterlife with a broad acceptance of the scientific basis of contemporary biological science. But the broad strategy has to be to show that the well-confirmed ('Darwinian') results of contemporary biological science do not have the implications some have drawn from them. It may be possible to deny the principle that there is a symmetry between human origins and human destiny. But here we will confine ourselves to those who accept this principle and who accept the Darwinian story about the evolution of the human species. Unlike fundamentalists, they will accept, in the light of the theory of natural selection, that the biblical account of the special divine creation of the human species is not literally true. It is, they might say, a myth designed to encapsulate the truth that humans (they do not have to say, 'only humans') are made by God in his image. That truth needs to be expressed in some other way. Some philosophers and theologians – especially Catholics – have followed the traditional thought that humans are not mere animals but that, in the case of humans, a rational soul is added to each individual embryo.

This way of reconciling Darwinism with traditional religious beliefs about the soul involves a dichotomy between the spiritual and the animal aspects of human beings. It may be consistent with the theory of natural selection, but we might ask how it stands up as a theory about the mind–body relationship. At first it may seem as if it involves a commitment to substance dualism and therefore is exposed to all the difficulties that faced Descartes's version of that theory. That might seem the most obvious interpretation of Pope Pius XII's distinction between 'the human body', which may have evolved as Darwinists claim, and 'souls', which are 'immediately created by God'. But this remark need not involve the implication that the soul is a separate substance from the body. On the contrary, Catholic writers commonly stress the unity of persons as psycho-physical beings. For instance, the author of the entry on 'Evolution, Human' in the *New Catholic Encyclopedia*, R. J. Nogar, is equally dismissive of both Cartesian dualism and of the view that people are mere animals:

> A perennial and serious dispute relating to human nature is the mind–body problem. Although man is one in nature and person, the laws of his mind are not simply reducible to the laws of organic bodies. Even when distinguishing between biological man and psychosocial man, one must preserve the indivisibility of human nature in its spatio-temporal context and see the laws of man's free and intelligent spirit and the laws of organic bodies as co-ordinate rather than as opposing principles of human life. It is not easy to conserve the delicate balance that this insight requires. At one extreme is the tendency to separate the human spirit and the body by a type of Platonic idealization. An example of this is the dualism of R. Descartes (1596–1650), in which the overspiritual soul becomes a detached governor of an overmechanized organic body. At the other extreme is the tendency to reduce the mind–body relationship to animal psychology and behavior, giving no recognition to man's mind as a truly spiritual entity. Neither pure spirit nor brute animal,

man is an organic spirit and a spiritual organism.

(Nogar in Catholic University of America (1967), Vol. V, p. 683)

Father Nogar declares himself against Cartesian dualism because it involves an overspiritualizing and idealizing of the soul and we may assume he would reject idealism on the same ground. At the same time it seems clear that he would have to reject some forms of materialism, certainly eliminative materialism, which in his phrase give 'no recognition to man's mind as a truly spiritual entity'. He favours what he refers to as the 'traditional Greek doctrine of hylomorphism' as the account 'most capable of providing the delicate balance ... demanded by this dual nature of the human person' (op. cit., p. 683). The word 'hylomorphism' was concocted from the Greek words for matter (*hulé*) and form (*morphé*) and refers to a doctrine owing to Aristotle in particular, that every sensible thing is a composite of matter and form. This doctrine was commonly glossed by saying that everything has both a material and a spiritual component, which together make it a substance. It is, however, implausible, to say the least, to suppose that a rock has a soul and, for this reason, hylomorphism was commonly limited to living things. But, in this form, the doctrine requires a fundamental dichotomy between the living and the non-living, which has been called into question by scientific developments that suggest that living things have evolved from inanimate things. If this suggestion is correct then there is a fundamental continuity between living and non-living things and hence any theory that requires a fundamental dichotomy between living and non-living things is no longer tenable. Hylomorphism has been accepted by a number of great philosophers in the past (notably, from the point of view of Catholic theologians, by Thomas Aquinas) but it is not usually mentioned in modern surveys of the options in the philosophy of mind.[10]

The nub of the difficulty seems to be that the conservative Darwinist, by making the spiritual and mental a special divine addition to human nature, is opposed to even those moderate forms of materialism that are consistent with belief in an afterlife. For even those moderate forms of materialism insist that our mental (and spiritual) life depends on our material nature. This strategy for supporting conservative Darwinism thus leads to far greater philosophical difficulties than are at first apparent. The dichotomy between an animal and a spiritual nature sounds at first an easy and familiar one (especially to religious people) but it turns out to be less easy to support in terms of contemporary philosophy of mind. It is also liable to erosion by the results of animal psychologists, who have made the contrast between the distinctively human and the merely animal much less sharp and easy to draw than had previously been supposed.

Those who wish to defend belief in an afterlife as at least consistent with contemporary tendencies in science and philosophy have to square their belief with a broad acceptance of Darwinism and with some kind of materialism. But, it seems, they cannot have it both ways. Considerations drawn from the philosophy of mind have made some of the views traditionally associated with belief in an afterlife – including dualism, idealism and hylomorphism – appear difficult to hold and made some kind of materialism comparatively plausible. But conservative Darwinists, because of the position it seems they are obliged to take on the origins of human mental nature, cannot accept materialism and must instead defend one of the less plausible options in the philosophy of mind. It could be that difficulties with any form of materialism will once again turn the tide. But, on the evidence and the arguments currently available, conservative Darwinism, as a view about the soul, seems to be a difficult position to sustain. These difficulties are cumulative, since even though it may be possible separately to reconcile belief in an afterlife with contemporary philosophy of mind (and therefore with materialism) or with contemporary biological science (and therefore with Darwinism), it does not seem at all easy to defend belief in an afterlife on both fronts at once.

SUMMARY

In this chapter we have seen that while materialism is inconsistent with belief in the survival of disembodied minds it appears consistent with belief in bodily resurrection. We considered a possible materialistic theory of bodily resurrection (that of Van Inwagen) which proves to be resistant to some objections that have been made to believing in the resurrection. The theory is, however, inherently improbable and depends for its credibility on belief in an omnipotent God who is willing to underwrite survival in a bodily state. We also considered an argument against immortality based on Darwinist reflections on our humble origins. We looked at a strategy religious believers might adopt in order to counter this argument by suggesting that God implants mental/spiritual natures in the human embryo at some point before birth. We saw, however, that this was an anti-materialist strategy. The overall strategy of reconciling materialism as well as Darwinism with belief in an afterlife is one which seems unlikely to succeed.

FURTHER READING

An excellent general reader is P. Edwards (ed.), *Immortality*, Prometheus Books, 1997. This work includes a reprint of P. Van Inwagen's paper 'The Possibility of Resurrection'. Another good collection is S. T. Davis (ed.), *Death and Afterlife*, Macmillan, 1989. The best attempt by a recent philosopher to come to terms with Darwinian thinking in ways consistent with religious beliefs is R. Swinburne's *The Evolution of the Soul*, Clarendon Press, revised edition, 1997. Swinburne defends a form of dualism but does not claim that souls can function apart from bodies. For a good debate between a materialist and a dualist about personal identity, see S. Shoemaker and R. Swinburne, *Personal Identity*, Blackwell, 1984.

NOTES

1 A good example is the philosopher John Locke, a pious Anglican and loyal supporter of William and Mary, who speculated in a few obscure passages of his *Essay Concerning Human Understanding* (1690) that God, being omnipotent, had the power to add thought to matter. These speculations, which run contrary to Locke's considered position, were seized on by ultra-conservatives, who made Locke into a demonic figure, and also by genuine radicals, who exaggerated the affinity of Locke's thought with their own. See Brown (1996) for an example of an ultra-conservative reaction.

2 I have in mind eliminative materialists such as Paul Churchland. See, for instance, Churchland (1984).

3 This is how Hilary Putnam summarizes his own pessimism about the prospects for the programme of eliminative materialism (Putnam (1988), pp. 70f.).

4 Arguments for and against belief in a designer of the universe who has purposes of which we might be a part form the topic of the next part of this book.

5   The Rabbi was Joshua ben Hananiah. See the entry on 'Luz of the Spine' in *Encyclopaedia Judaica* (Jerusalem: Keter, 1972).

6 The Bible sometimes implies, for instance, that the resurrected body will be 'incorruptible'. How it could none the less be the same body is a 'mystery'.

7 As is argued by Janet Radcliffe Richards, for instance (Radcliffe Richards (2000), Ch. 1).

8 See his *Darwin's Dangerous Idea* (Dennett, 1995).

9 Radical Darwinists, by contrast, are those who regard Darwinism as inconsistent with some traditional ideas and who hold therefore that those ideas should be rejected.

10 It is not, for instance, mentioned in Wilkinson (2000) or in Warner and Szubka (1994).

II Purpose in the universe

In this part we will be concerned with arguments for and against believing that the universe was designed and more particularly with arguments for and against believing that it was designed for appropriate purposes by a wholly good and omnipotent being. In Chapter 3 we will consider the 'argument from design' and the implications of Darwinism for continuing to believe in a designed universe. We will also consider an argument for design from modern science which purports to show that life on earth could not have come about wholly by chance. In Chapter 4 we will look at several arguments based on common moral notions and moral experience in favour of believing in a moral 'governor' of the universe. In Chapter 5 we will consider problems that arise out of both natural and moral evil for believing in a wholly benevolent and omnipotent deity.

3 Arguments for a designer

Philosophers have argued for millennia about whether or not there is a God. But their arguments have often established at best the existence of a perfect being or a first cause who might, for all the arguments showed to the contrary, have no interest whatever in humans and whose existence or otherwise has no obvious implications for our situation. Two of the classical arguments, however, are intended to show that there is a higher intelligence who designed the universe and whose purposes were served by creating it. One group of arguments is concerned to establish that there is a moral purpose in the universe. These arguments, which we will consider in the next chapter, are known simply as 'moral arguments' for the existence of God. The second argument, which is generally referred to as the 'argument from design', aims to establish that there is purpose in the natural order. We will consider this argument in this chapter. We will also consider an argument, based on modern scientific ideas, that it is too much of a coincidence that just the right conditions obtained in the universe to produce life as we know it.

THE ARGUMENT FROM DESIGN

The first argument we will be considering is an old one — more than 2000 years old, since it is found at least as far back as Cicero. It is generally known as the argument from design and also, more grandly, as the teleological argument, *telos* being the Greek word for purpose. One of the most famous exponents of the argument was an Anglican clergyman, William Paley (1743–1805),[1] whose *Natural Theology* was an influential book in the nineteenth century and was prescribed for students at Cambridge. Paley was an important influence on the young Charles Darwin, whose later ideas have been taken by some, as we will see, to undermine belief in a designed universe.

ARGUMENTS FROM ANALOGY

Paley's argument is an *argument from analogy*. It is important to distinguish such arguments from *deductive* arguments of the kind we discussed in Chapter 1, where it would be inconsistent to accept the premises and deny the conclusion. The distinction can be brought out by giving examples of each that differ only in one crucial (italicized) feature:

A DEDUCTIVE ARGUMENT

| Premise 1 | Apples have cores with pips. |
| Premise 2 | Pears *are* apples. |

Therefore

| Conclusion | Pears have cores with pips. |

AN ARGUMENT FROM ANALOGY

| Premise 1 | Apples have cores with pips. |
| Premise 2a | Pears *are like* apples. |

Therefore

| Conclusion | Pears have cores with pips. |

I have deliberately minimized the difference between these arguments. The obvious difference lies in the second premise. In the deductive argument this might also be expressed by saying:

| Premise 2 | Pears *are a kind* of apple. |

Or

| Premise 2 | Pears *are a sub-class* of apple. |

This premise is, of course, untrue. And so this deductive argument is *unsound*. It is none the less *valid*. Moreover the conclusion is true. But it is unsound because a similar argument using premise 2 would readily lead to a false conclusion. For example:

Premise 1a   Apples are round.

Premise 2   Pears are apples.

Therefore

Conclusion   Pears are round.

Going back to our first deductive argument, what is wrong with it is that premise 2 is false. It is too strong. What is true is that pears are like apples. (They are part of the same large family of trees.) That is a weaker claim and the argument from analogy is a weaker argument than a deductive argument. But the argument from analogy may still be a good one.

Put more generally, arguments from analogy rely on the principle that if two things are similar in some known respect they are likely to be similar in other respects. The point of such arguments is that they enable us to draw conclusions as to likely similarities where these are not already known. The awkward thing with such arguments, however, is that they presuppose a sense of where the analogy holds and will help us to new truths and where it does not and would let us down. Pears (usually) look and taste quite different from apples, so the analogy is obviously limited. But, just because the limitations of the analogy are mostly obvious, it can be helpful to draw it. Gardening books often tell their readers how to look after apples and then, in the section on pears, largely refer back to what was said about apples.

PALEY'S ANALOGY

Paley's version of the argument from design may be stated very crudely as a simple argument from analogy:

Premise 1   Watches invariably have a designer.

Premise 2   The universe is like a watch.

Therefore

Conclusion   The universe has a designer.

This is a crude statement of the argument because, so stated, it is not remotely convincing. But Paley's argument is quite a subtle one. In his *Natural Theology* (1802) he argues that we would still think that something was a watch, so long as it had the observable properties of a watch, even if we did not know about its origins. Whatever we supposed about its origins, the fact that the various parts of a watch work together so as to tell the time would be evidence that it had a designer. Paley invites us to suppose, as a thought experiment, that watches are capable of producing other watches. None the less, he insists:

> The machine we are inspecting demonstrates, by its construction, contrivance and design. Contrivance must have had a contriver; design, a designer; whether the machine immediately proceeded from another machine or not.
>
> (Paley (1838), p. 71)

In other words it is not the simple fact that all the watches we happen to know about had a designer that is Paley's starting-point. His point is that anything that exhibits, as a watch does, such intricate adaptation of means to end, whose parts work together to serve a particular function, is a contrivance and so must have had a contriver. His argument is, then, that the universe is analogous to a watch in this respect:

> every indication of contrivance, every manifestation of design, which existed in the watch, exists in the works of nature; with the difference, on the side of nature, of being greater and more, and that in a degree which exceeds all computation. I mean that the contrivances of nature surpass the contrivances of art, in the complexity, subtility and curiosity of the mechanism.
>
> (op. cit., p. 9)

Paley develops his argument by comparing an eye with a telescope:

> As far as the examination of the instrument goes, there is precisely the same proof that the eye was made for vision, as there is that the telescope was made for assisting it. They are made on the same principles; both being adjusted to the laws by which the transmission and refraction of rays of light are regulated. I speak not of the laws themselves; but such laws being fixed, the construction, in both cases, is adapted to them. For instance; these laws require, in order to produce the same effect, that the rays of light, in passing from water into the eye, should be refracted by a more convex surface, than when it passes out of air into the eye. Accordingly we find that the eye of a fish, in that part of it called the crystalline lens, is much rounder than the eye of terrestrial animals. What plainer manifestation of design can there be than this difference? What could a mathematical instrument-maker have done more to shew his knowledge of his principle, his application of that knowledge, his suiting of his means to his end ... ?
>
> (op. cit., pp. 9–10)

EXERCISE 3.1

ARGUMENT FROM ANALOGY

What do you think of this analogy? Do you think there is precisely the same proof that the eye was made for vision as there is that the telescope was made to make distant objects appear larger to us?

DISCUSSION

There is one important point at which the analogy breaks down. Even if we have not personally seen someone design a telescope, we have enough familiarity with design processes to know how artefacts are commonly made to serve human purposes. We have no experience whatever, on the other hand, of any design processes relating to the works of nature. We do not know whether the order in nature came about by anything like the processes which result in human artefacts having the order they have. This makes it uncertain whether there is much of an analogy between the eye and the telescope.

This objection is given further force by noting that there are cases of order in nature which have been misattributed to design. There are many geological features of this kind. For instance, there are the misnamed 'parallel roads' in Glen Roy. What you see do indeed look just like three old unmade roads that run parallel to one another up the glen. But, as Charles Darwin realized when he had visited Glen Roy in 1838, they are not roads at all but actually old beaches. Darwin thought, mistakenly, that they were sea beaches, remembering that he had discovered the remains of such beaches high up in the Andes. But it is now thought that they marked the shores of glacial lochs that have since disappeared. They were not, then, put there on purpose. Another striking example is the so-called Giant's Causeway in County Antrim, which consists of highly regular stones appearing to be a pavement sloping into the sea and which was assumed, at least in legend, to have been put there on purpose by a giant. These stones are actually thousands of basalt columns formed during a process of post-volcanic cooling. I expect you will have seen other examples.

The general point to be taken from this is that Paley was wrong in supposing that there was not a problem about what objects 'demonstrate ... contrivance and design'. There are plenty of objects whose apparent construction (shape etc.) has led people mistakenly to attribute design. The growth of scientific knowledge since Paley's day has made the existence of such objects familiar even to lay people like myself. Particularly important has been the theory of natural selection.

DARWINISM AND DESIGN

Darwin went to Cambridge in 1827 to study theology, no doubt seeing the life of a parson in a quiet country parish as leaving plenty of room for the pursuit of his already passionate interest in the natural world. It was indeed commonplace at the time to see in the natural world abundant evidence of a wise and good designer. Paley's arguments were given particular prominence and in Cambridge his books were set texts for students of theology. At the time Darwin was entirely persuaded by such arguments. But once he had hit on the idea of natural selection he came to think that there was no need to postulate an intelligent being in order to explain the marvellous adaptations in nature and hence that the argument from design was no longer acceptable. As he put it in his *Autobiography*:[2]

The old argument from design in nature, as given by Paley, which formerly seemed to me so conclusive, fails, now that the law of natural selection has been discovered. We can no longer argue that, for instance, the beautiful hinge of a bivalve shell must have been made by an intelligent being, like the hinge of a door by man. There seems to be no more design in the variability of organic beings and in the action of natural selection, than in the course which the wind blows.

(Charles Darwin in de Beer (1974), pp. 50f.)

Darwin's point was that the variability in nature is quite random and that the reason why we find so many good adaptations is not because of design but because of the processes of natural selection. The species we see around us are mostly survivors of a long and ruthless process which has weeded out those species that are less well adapted. Given that process, we should expect to find an abundance of good adaptive features in nature.

When he wrote the *Origin of Species*, Darwin still believed in some kind of intelligent 'First Cause' of the universe, though the tendency of his subsequent thought was, he confessed, in the direction of agnosticism.[3] There were, for him, many mysteries about the world, like the origin of life or the emergence of the human mind, which science had not explained. Perhaps because these gaps now look like they have been or could be filled, modern Darwinians are more confident in asserting that there is no need to suppose an intelligent creator of the natural world. Thus Richard Dawkins,[4] in a book entitled (with Paley in mind) *The Blind Watchmaker*, gives this account of the implications of Darwin for Paley's design argument:

Paley's argument is made with passionate sincerity and it is informed by the best biological scholarship of his day, but it is wrong, gloriously and utterly wrong. The analogy between telescope and eye, between watch and living organism, is false. All appearances to the contrary, the only watchmaker in nature is the blind forces of physics, albeit deployed in a very special way. A true watchmaker has foresight: he designs his cogs and springs, and plans their interconnections, with a future purpose in his mind's eyes. Natural selection, the blind, unconscious, automatic process which Darwin discovered, and which we now know is the explanation for the existence and apparently purposeful form of all life, has no purpose in mind. It has no plan for the future. It has no vision, no foresight, no sight at all. If it can be said to play the role of watchmaker in nature, it is the blind watchmaker.

(Dawkins (1988), p. 5)

If Dawkins is right, then Paley's argument from design is simply out of date, and the hypothesis of a purpose behind the workings of nature has been proved 'gloriously wrong' by subsequent scientific developments.

The view that science has simply shown that the argument from design is wrong has, however, been disputed by some philosophers. Anthony Kenny, for instance, has written:

if the argument from design ever had any value, it has not been substantially affected by the scientific investigation of living organisms from Descartes through Darwin to the present day. If Descartes is correct in regarding the activities of animals as mechanistically explicable, then a system may operate teleologically [i.e. 'purposefully'] while being mechanistic in structure. If Darwin is correct in ascribing the origin of species to natural selection, then the production of a teleological structure may be due in the first instance to factors which are purely mechanistic. But both may be right and yet the ultimate explanation of the phenomena be finalistic [i.e. in terms of purposes]. The only argument refuted by Darwin would be one which said wherever there is adaptation to environment we must see the immediate activity of an intelligent being ... The argument was only that the ultimate explanation of such adaptation must be found in intelligence; and if the argument was correct, then any Darwinian success merely inserts an extra step between the phenomena and their ultimate explanation.

(Kenny (1969), p. 118)

Kenny is not writing with Paley's argument in view but on behalf of the much earlier argument of Thomas Aquinas (1224–74). None the less it can be urged on behalf of Paley that he is not concerned to maintain that *the immediate cause* of all order in the universe is an intelligent being. Paley expressly imagined that watches might bring other watches into existence. This process would be a mechanistic one. But Paley's point is that we do need a designer at the beginning in order to explain the existence of clocks at all. So Paley's view might be taken to be consistent with accepting a mechanistic view of science and holding only that the universe must ultimately be explained in terms of purpose.

We looked earlier at a short extract from Dawkins's *The Blind Watchmaker*, in which he comments directly on Paley's argument. Later, in a chapter entitled 'Doomed Rivals', he turns his attention to the kind of position Kenny had in mind when he suggested that those who believe in a designer of the universe need only believe that this is the ultimate explanation of order, not that it is the immediate explanation.

Now read the Dawkins extract (Reading 2) and attempt Exercise 3.2.

Reading
pp. 137–8

EXERCISE 3.2

DARWINISM AND CREATIONISM

Make a note (two or three sentences) of your answers to the following questions:

1   What does Dawkins mean by talking of creationism as one of the 'alleged alternatives' to the theory of natural selection?
2   Does he claim to have disproved creationism or the view that evolution is guided by a Providence?
3   What do you think he means by saying that creationism and 'guided evolution' are doomed rivals?

Check your answer against the one at the back of the book before reading on.

DISCUSSION

As often in philosophy, the debate continues. I will offer some points by way of conclusion. First, as to the logic of the situation, it would be quite wrong to interpret Darwinism as *disproving* the existence of a designer of the universe. Darwinism is quite compatible with the existence of purpose in the universe. That much need not be in dispute. What is not clear is whether the particular argument for a designer known as the argument from design has been rendered totally unconvincing. On this question it seems to me that science has identified an increasing number of objects that many people have just assumed to have been designed but, as it turns out, wrongly. Natural selection does not do more than further increase that number and so has further weakened the analogy between nature and human artefacts like the watch without which Paley's argument does not get off the ground. If the argument can still be presented, it will have to be presented in a very different way from the way it was presented by Paley.

A MODERN ARGUMENT FOR DESIGN

Darwinian explanations of order in the natural world may not have undermined the arguments of William Paley entirely. But they have put paid to the suggestion that design is manifest in nature: that we only have to examine the eye of a fish or any of a huge variety of phenomena to see it as something designed. To that extent Darwinism has put paid to the argument *from* design, i.e. from observed design in nature to a hypothesized designer. But, in recent decades, some scientists have become more and more impressed with a new line of argument for believing that the universe had a designer.

The arguments begin from a puzzle surrounding certain physical constants governing the emergence of our universe – for instance, the rate at which it expands. If these constants were only very slightly different from what they are, the universe as we know it would never have come about. Either by chance or by what looks like fine tuning, the conditions were just right for the sequence of developments that has resulted, for instance, in a universe that contains life as we know it, including scientists observing and theorizing about it. Writers on the puzzle commonly refer, because of this human dimension, to what they call 'the anthropic principle' – *anthropos* being the Greek word for 'human' – though the literature yields varied conceptions of what exactly this means. An early statement of the principle emphasized that the 'possibility of life as we know it in the Universe depends on the values of a few basic physical constants – and is in some respects remarkably sensitive to their numerical values'.[5] However it is named, there appears to be a principle at work in virtue of which the conditions were just those that are needed if life as we know it is to be possible.

A number of scientists and philosophers believe that such considerations provide the basis for a revival of the traditional teleological argument. The argument is summarized and reviewed in a non-technical way by Russell Stannard in the extract in Reading 3 from his *Grounds for Reasonable Belief*.

 Reading
pp. 139–41

Now read the Stannard extract (Reading 3) and attempt Exercise 3.3.

EXERCISE 3.3

MODERN ARGUMENT FOR DESIGN

Make a note (in a sentence or two) of what you take to be the fundamental features of the 'modern argument for design' and of the two reservations that Stannard expresses about concluding (on the basis of the argument) that the fundamental fabric of the universe has been designed and hence that there is a God.

Check your answer against the one at the back of the book before reading on.

DISCUSSION

Here I will take the scientific position to be as stated and focus on the argument. There are many arguments that infer design or intention from something's being too much of a coincidence. These can be countered either by producing a satisfactory alternative explanation or by arguing that the coincidence is not too great. In the first of his two reservations Stannard envisages the possibility of an alternative explanation and, in the second, his argument seems to be that, while the coincidence that the conditions are right for life to emerge is too great if there is only this one universe, it would not be too great if there were an infinite number of them.

In fact, although he mentions this second reservation, he does not make it in his own name. Rather he presents the suggestion that this is only one of an infinite number of universes as a 'counter-proposal'. Against it he points out that we have no way of knowing about other universes since they do not interact with our own. The proposal is a mere 'metaphysical speculation' and is not a testable scientific hypothesis. The second objection refers to Occam's Razor – the principle that enjoins us not to multiply theoretical entities beyond necessity and always to prefer the simplest hypothesis that is consistent with the facts. This principle, he claims, is on the side of those who believe there is a designer God and only one universe rather than those who believe that there is no God and an infinite number of universes.

There are several criticisms that might be offered of the modern argument for design. I will focus on two here. They are:

1 That the argument assumes that it makes sense to speak of how probable it is that the universe we know should have come into being, but that this is highly problematic.
2 That the appeal to Occam's Razor cannot decide the issue since it could equally be used on the other side.

I elaborate on these criticisms below, under the headings 'Probability and the argument for design' and 'Occam's Razor and the argument for design'.

PROBABILITY AND THE ARGUMENT FOR DESIGN

Unbelievers are invited by Russell Stannard's argument to accept that, if the universe was not designed so as to be suitable for life as we know it to evolve in it, then it was by the sheerest chance that it turned out to be so. But it may be objected that it only makes sense to talk of the 'chances' of a particular outcome where there is at least one alternative outcome. We are familiar with coins with different sides ('heads' and 'tails') and this is part of the background against which it makes sense to say that there is a 50/50 chance of making the correct call in a coin-tossing game. The universe is, however, the only one we know about and, for all we know, the only one there is. Because of its uniqueness there is not the contrast with other universes that is needed to make sense of the suggestion that it is or is not a coincidence (improbable matter of chance) that this universe is the way it is.

This problem is acknowledged by the physicist P. C. W. Davies in his book on the anthropic principle entitled *The Accidental Universe*. Davies suggests this way of making sense of saying that it is highly improbable that there should be a universe containing life as we know it:

> One could envisage a huge collection of possible universes – a world-ensemble – each varying slightly from the others so that somewhere among the ensemble would be a universe in which every conceivable value for each fundamental constant, and every conceivable initial arrangement of matter and motion, were realized to within a certain accuracy. The famous coincidences then acquire a rather more concrete status. Imagine the Creator equipped with a pin, blindly choosing one of the universes at random from among the vast collection of contenders, the chance of His picking a universe compatible with life as we know it is then exceedingly small.
>
> (Davies (1982), p. 123)

Davies concedes that we do not know how to measure probabilities between possible universes and so we cannot say how improbable it is that our universe is suitable for our habitation: 'Nevertheless, accepting the world-ensemble concept enables one to assert the general fact that our world is indeed extremely unlikely on *a priori* grounds, and that we are immensely fortunate to exist, even if we cannot assert precisely *how* fortunate.'

OCCAM'S RAZOR AND THE ARGUMENT FOR DESIGN

Although Occam's Razor is most commonly expressed in the dictum 'Entities are not to be multiplied without necessity', it has, historically, been fused with associated principles of simplicity such as that, other things being equal, the theory to be preferred is the one that makes the fewest or the least elaborate assumptions. Occam's Razor has been applied in metaphysics as well as in science, as we saw in Chapters 1 and 2. But its statement has varied somewhat and, partly for this reason, its use often remains controversial. This has a bearing on the use of it by Russell Stannard and others. For if it is a question of not assuming more entities than is strictly necessary then we should reject the hypothesis of an infinite

EXERCISE 3.4

PROBABILITY AND THE ARGUMENT FOR DESIGN

Consider whether Davies's way of making sense of the suggestion that our universe is extremely unlikely would help someone like Russell Stannard who infers from this suggestion that the universe had a designer.

DISCUSSION

The suggestion that our universe is extremely unlikely is made sense of by Davies in terms of a model which presupposes a Creator who chooses between different possible worlds. Stannard rejects the view that there is a plurality of actual universes. But, even though Davies's talk of a 'world-ensemble' is not entirely clear, there is no reason why he or others who argue in a similar fashion should not accept the picture of a God who chooses to create this particular universe rather than any of a huge number of alternative possibilities. But if we need to bring in a Creator to make sense of the suggestion that this universe is extremely unlikely then that suggestion cannot be admitted as a premise of an argument intended to convince atheists that the universe had a designer. At the most it might persuade someone who already believed in some kind of Creator that the peculiar character of the universe offers hints as to the nature of that Creator. It will only do even this if there are no other objections to the argument. To use it in argument with atheists would be largely to *beg the question*, i.e. to assume too much of what is at issue. Davies's way of making sense of the suggestion that the universe is extremely unlikely is not helpful for Stannard's project. On the contrary it underlines a difficulty for that project, namely that it needs premises that the unbeliever may complain do not make sense as they stand and perhaps only make sense on the assumption that the universe has a Creator.

number of universes and prefer the hypothesis of a designer God and a single universe. But it could be argued that the point of Occam's Razor is not to reduce the sheer number of entities assumed but the number of new theoretical concepts. Thus it might be said that the real simplification in the Copernican theory (as developed by the time of Newton) is that it enabled scientists to drop the previously fundamental distinction between celestial bodies and terrestrial ones and between the celestial sciences like mathematical astronomy and the terrestrial ones like physics. Likewise the simplification involved in Berkeley's idealism (discussed in Chapter 1) is a conceptual one. His objection is just as much to assuming any corporeal or material substances as it is to an infinite number of them.

So interpreted, Occam's Razor could be invoked on the other side, against those like Stannard who prefer the hypothesis of a designer God and only one universe. For they are the ones who, within the context of scientific theory, are offering the conceptually more elaborate hypothesis. The other hypothesis, of an infinite number of universes, can be seen as conceptually simpler. These other universes, on the hypothesis, are understood in terms of our physics, only their constants (rate of expansion, gravitation, etc.) are different from those scientists have determined for our universe. There does not seem to be the kind of conceptual add-on which is involved in an explanation in terms of a designer God.

Thus it is not clear that Occam's Razor will settle this dispute for us. That is not to say that it is useless, since there are cases where it gives the same result whichever way it is interpreted. It is always good sense to avoid unnecessary complexity. But in this particular case it is controversial which hypotheses are simper (less complex) and so the application of the principle is controversial. It is not available, therefore, as a decisive weapon on the side of Stannard or others who offer a similar modern argument for design.

NATURAL AND REVEALED THEOLOGY

If there were a successful version of the argument from design this would make it reasonable to believe that there is an intelligence behind the creation of the universe. But it would not establish that there is only one being responsible, nor would it establish that this being or beings had any interest in us. The fact that humans have evolved on this planet might, from the point of view of such beings, be a very minor, temporary and local matter. They might have been interested in seeing how much variety could be got over time in a universe that is fundamentally the same. We just do not know enough about the rest of the universe to conclude, even assuming that it was created by these intelligences, that our existence was any part of their purpose in creating it. The creation of the universe might be thought of as a leisure pursuit of these intelligences. The emergence of the human species might have been part of a cosmic game that was being played out. It might be within the purpose of the game that we have emerged as a species, even that we have a point of view, ask questions about the purpose of the universe, worship deities, and so on. But it need not be part of the purpose of the game that our point of view matters or indeed that it matters whether we worship the right deities or not, what we do with our lives, or whatever. If there are purposes behind the origin of the universe – and, of course, that remains a big *if* – they will not necessarily give our existence any particular significance.

It is possible, then, that the universe was created with a purpose but not with a moral purpose. Religions (Judaism, Islam and Christianity, for instance) do none the less teach that God did have a moral purpose in creating the universe, that God does mind a great deal how we conduct our lives and indeed that the good will eventually be rewarded and the wicked punished. As we saw before, belief in that purpose is an integral part of many orthodox views of life after death. The question is whether it is possible to support belief in such a purpose without appealing to revelation, for instance to what is written in the Bible or the Koran. The problem about appealing to revelation is that the argument only works with those who are already believers. For instance, it can be argued:

Premise 1   Whatever is taught in the Koran is inspired by God.
Premise 2   Teachings that are inspired by God are true.

Premise 3	The Koran teaches that the good will be rewarded and the wicked punished.
Conclusion	Therefore (it is true that) the good will be rewarded and the wicked punished.

EXERCISE 3.5

VALIDITY

Assess whether this argument is valid or invalid, explaining your decision. Check your answer against the one at the back of the book before reading on.

DISCUSSION

Appeals to revelation are characteristically made within the context of a particular religion, by one believer in arguing with another. They share premises like premise 1 above. But sometimes a non-believer can also appeal to revelation, at least for the sake of argument. Thus a non-believer could seek to discredit a Church-goer who committed adultery by such an argument as this:

Premise 1	What the Bible teaches is true (assumed for the sake of argument).
Premise 2	The Bible teaches that adultery is wrong.
Premise 3	She has committed adultery.
Conclusion	Therefore, she has done wrong.

The non-believer does not believe premise 1 and so, if she believes the conclusion, it will be for other reasons.

But arguments that depend on appeals to revelation are often not helpful for the simple reason that any non-believers to whom they are addressed are not in the least tempted to accept the key premise. This is why the arguments of *natural theology* (which forms part of *philosophy of religion*) are of more general interest. For they purport to be based on premises which it is hoped any reasonable person would accept. The arguments of natural theology are those that are based on reason alone, which has traditionally been assumed to be natural and common to all human beings, in contrast with revelations, which are imparted only to a chosen few. An argument, based on the Koran or the Bible, which concluded that there was a moral order in the universe – certain behaviour that is good, other behaviour that is bad, reward for the good, punishment for the bad, etc. – would probably be unnecessary for those inside those religious traditions and carry no conviction for those outside. What is needed is an argument whose premises would be accepted by any reasonable person. And many reasonable people are outside any religious tradition. What is needed is an argument in natural theology, such as the moral arguments for the existence of God, which we will consider in the next chapter.

SUMMARY

We have seen that the argument from design, as presented by Paley, depended on drawing an analogy between the purpose-serving order to be observed in a human artefact such as a watch or a telescope and the purpose-serving order taken as apparent in the natural world. Just as the existence of a designer may be inferred from the existence of such order in artefacts so the existence of a designer God can be inferred from the existence of such order in nature. The analogy is seen not to hold, however, where an alternative (non-purposive) explanation for the existence of purpose-serving order in the natural world can be provided which does not involve design. Darwin's theory of natural selection provides the basis for such alternative (mechanistic) explanations of the purpose-serving features of the living world.

In recent decades consideration of the conditions necessary for life to evolve has led scientists to puzzle at the fact that it seems improbable that just the right conditions were present by chance. This has led some to infer that the universe was designed and fine tuned so that life would evolve. We noted two lines of objection. First, it is not easy to attach sense to talk of it being 'improbable' that the world is as it is. Secondly, if it were supposed that there is an infinite number of universes, it is not surprising that one of them accidentally had just the right conditions for life to evolve on it somewhere at some time. To this supposition, however, it was objected that it is a simpler and so preferable hypothesis that there is a designer God and only one universe than that there is an infinite number of them. This objection, however, seems to be based on a controversial application of the principle of Occam's Razor. Thus there is insufficient reason to accept the conclusion of the new argument for a designer of the universe.

Arguments that claim to establish that the universe had a designer do not, in any case, purport to indicate the purposes for which the universe may have been created. This could be claimed, however, on behalf of the so-called 'moral' arguments for the existence of God, which purport to establish the existence of a moral order in the universe of which we are an integral part. We will consider these arguments in the next chapter.

FURTHER READING

Hume's *Dialogues Concerning Natural Religion* remains one of the best critical discussions of the traditional argument from design. Many of those who argue, partly on the basis of arguments for design, in favour of believing in the existence of God claim that the case is a cumulative one and does not turn on a single argument. Two good examples of such a cumulative defence are F. R. Tennant's *Philosophical Theology*, Cambridge University Press, 1930, and R. Swinburne's *The Existence of God*, Clarendon Press, 1979. For the modern argument, *The Anthropic Cosmological Principle*, ed. J. Barrow and F. Tiplers, Clarendon Press, 1986, and M. A. Corey's *God and the New Cosmology: The Anthropic Design Argument*, Rowman and Littlefield, 1993, are recommended.

NOTES

1 William Paley was an Anglican theologian who taught at Cambridge and subsequently became Archdeacon of Carlisle. His major works, *The Principles of Moral and Political Philosophy* (1785), *A View of the Evidence for Christianity* (1794) and *Natural Theology* (1802), became required reading for undergraduates at Cambridge and as late as 1831 Charles Darwin had to swot them up for an examination. Clark (1974) is a good critical introduction to Paley's thought.

2 Mostly written in 1876, though with later additions. Darwin's family insisted that some parts, critical of orthodox theology, were omitted in early published versions and it was not until 1958 that a complete, critical and unexpurgated edition was published.

3 De Beer, 1974, p. 54. Darwin had long given up belief in anything like the Christian God, for reasons discussed in Chapter 5.

4 Born in 1941, Richard Dawkins is a zoologist and a leading advocate of radical Darwinism, i.e. someone who holds that Darwinian ideas are inconsistent with and therefore should lead us to reject some received opinions. He is the author of *The Selfish Gene* (1976, 2nd edition 1989), *The Extended Phenotype* (1982) and *River out of Eden* (1995).

5 Carr and Rees (1979), p. 612.

NOTES

4 Arguments for a moral order

There are a number of arguments for the existence of God that take their starting-point from commonly held views about morality and moral experience. Not every view of morality and moral experience needs to be completed by supposing that there is a moral order underwritten by a god who is concerned with how people conduct their lives. But some do need, or have been thought to require, such a completion. And these views of morality and moral experience provide the basis for one or other of the moral arguments. We will consider four such arguments in this chapter.

THE ARGUMENT FROM MORAL DUTIES AS IMPERATIVES

There are those who think of ethics in terms of the fulfilment of *duties*: to keep our promises, to tell the truth, to respect other people's property, and so on. But what is a duty? A duty, it is tempting to reply, is something we ought (morally) to do: we ought to keep our promises, and so on. But this answer takes us round in a circle. For we need to know what this moral 'ought' is. None the less the answer suggests we need to distinguish between what we *morally* ought to do and *other* things we ought to do.

Suppose, for example, someone said to you: 'You ought to take care on this surface when it is wet.' You would not understand this as a reminder of your duty. You would, I think, take it as a piece of advice. As a piece of advice it assumes something about your situation, for instance that you do not want to fall. If that assumption is wrong, then the advice is wrongly directed. So this prudential – as it is sometimes called – 'ought' has got a qualification attached to it. It is not a qualification that is normally made. But sometimes it is: 'If you don't want to fall in the water, don't skate on the ice today!' An insight of Immanuel Kant's was that a statement of moral duty lacks this kind of qualification. Whereas a piece of advice is a hypothetical (qualified) imperative, a reminder of moral duty is, according to Kant, a categorical (unqualified) imperative.[1]

One way of testing Kant's claim is to think of a statement of what we morally ought to do and see what happens to it when we add a qualification about the person it is addressed to. For example, by itself, 'You ought to pay your taxes' sounds like a statement of moral duty. But, with the qualification 'If you don't want to risk a heavy fine' added in front of it, it becomes a piece of advice.

Kant's moral philosophy is one, though not the only one, in which a moral duty is thought of as absolute, in terms of unqualified imperatives. We ought always to tell the truth, according to those who think in this way. Our particular circumstances do not make any difference. Such ways of thinking about duty are easily distinguishable, for instance, from those moral theories according to which whether or not we ought to tell the truth would depend on what would be the likely *consequences* all round in any particular situation.

Suppose, then, that statements of moral duty are categorical imperatives. The question then arises as to how they differ from ordinary imperatives. When a sergeant major orders soldiers to come to attention, he or she issues the order 'Attention!' In this case, and usually with orders (which are imperatives), the person issuing them has an authority in virtue of which those to whom it is addressed have a duty to obey the order given. If a civilian makes the order or (in usual circumstances) the order is addressed to civilians, it has no authority. By contrast, statements of moral duty can be addressed by anyone to anyone.

What, then, is the source of the authority absolute moral imperatives have? Some people, though not Kant, have found the following argument persuasive:

Premise 1	All imperatives derive from some authority.
Premise 2	Moral imperatives do not derive from any human authority.
Premise 3	Moral imperatives must, however, derive from some appropriate authority.
Premise 4	The only appropriate authority for moral imperatives is God.
Conclusion	Therefore moral imperatives derive their authority from God.

We are assuming premise 1 on the basis of the previous discussion. The case for premise 2 is based on the reflection that anyone can remind anyone else of their moral duty, even if the person being reminded is a king or a priest or someone who otherwise enjoys a position of authority. Premise 3 derives from premise 1. Premise 4 is arrived at by eliminating a myriad of inappropriate sources, like Mount Everest or the planet Jupiter. The conclusion is inferred from premises 3 and 4.

EXERCISE 4.1

VALIDITY AND SOUNDNESS

Do you find this a compelling argument? If not, why not?

DISCUSSION

The argument is a valid one. But I do not find it compelling because it seems to me unsound. In particular premise 1 seems to me questionable. It involves an invalid argument from what was said before. Though all orders derive from some authority and all orders are imperatives, not all imperatives are orders and so 1 does not follow. The fallacy involved is sometimes called *affirming the consequent*. The invalid form of argument involved is:

If p, then q
q
Therefore p.

Put in that form the argument was:

If something is an order, then it is an imperative.
Statements of moral duty are imperatives.
Therefore statements of moral duty are orders.

It is only orders that depend on some personal authority. Some religious people have construed moral duties as divine commands. The Ten Commandments which Jews and Christians believe Moses brought down from Mount Sinai ('You shall not steal', 'Honour your father and your mother', and so on) are such divine commands. Someone who already believed they were might be tempted by the argument we have been discussing. But to think of the Ten Commandments as an unproblematic example of moral duties would already be to import God into morality.

There is a further difficulty. Even if there is a god who commands humans to fulfil a range of moral duties (not to steal etc.), a difficult question arises whether they are duties just because God commands them. If so, then morality seems to be a matter of God's whim. Morality becomes arbitrary, a matter of pleasing the deity. If, on the other hand, they are duties independently of the will of God and God commands us to do them because it is right to do them, the authority for doing them rests not in a command structure but in whatever makes them duties independently of the will of God. This problem, which philosophers have discussed at least since Plato, does not have an easy resolution. Those philosophers who have followed Plato dislike the notion of a deity who is like a human monarch at the head of an ultimately arbitrary command structure. They have said rather that moral duties are grounded in objective truths which are grasped by reason and do not depend on God's will. God commands humans to fulfil their duties because it is good that they should do so. It is not because of God's commands that they are good. The source of morality does not lie in orders. The existence of a God issuing commands is not required, therefore, to explain the authority that moral imperatives have.

THE ARGUMENT FROM CONSCIENCE

Statements of moral duties are like orders in some respects. But to suppose that they need a personal authority is to stretch the comparison too far. None the less people have often thought of their moral obligations as like obligations to a person even when no other human was involved. Indeed morality is often conceived as a matter of following the dictates of conscience and conscience itself is often thought of as some kind of other 'voice' inside us which tells us what to do, reminds us we have to do it and reprimands us if we do not. Our moral experience, in particular our awareness of conscience, has been taken by some as an argument for believing in a moral governor of the universe. This is argued by John Henry Newman (1801–90)[2] in his *Essay in Aid of a Grammar of Assent*.

Reading
pp. 143–5

Now read the extract from Newman's *Grammar of Assent* (Reading 4, 'The argument from conscience'). It is quite dense and you may need to read it more than once. Then attempt Exercises 4.2 and 4.3.

EXERCISE 4.2

ARGUMENT FROM CONSCIENCE (1)

Summarize what you take to be Newman's argument as concisely as you can in a short paragraph. Check your answer against the one at the back of the book before reading on.

EXERCISE 4.3

ARGUMENT FROM CONSCIENCE (2)

Make notes of any points that strike you as relevant to a critical evaluation of the argument.

DISCUSSION

Newman does not explain what he means by claiming that conscience is 'legitimate' but it seems to be that, at least some of the time, certain objects arouse in us *appropriate* responses of blame and approval, regret and satisfaction, and so on. That seems to be part of the point of comparing conscience with taste. Newman makes it clear that the promptings of conscience are 'not in all cases correct' (paragraph 2) and does not stress conscience as a 'moral sense' enabling us to tell what is right and wrong. Its 'legitimacy' does not turn on accepting the contentious view that our moral feelings are a guide to what is right and wrong. He is willing to allow that the elements of morals might more reliably be discovered by the 'intellect'. His emphasis is on the role of conscience as an internal force which demands that we do what is right and avoid what is wrong, what he calls its 'primary and most authoritative aspect' (paragraph 3).

How plausible Newman's argument appears to us will turn in part on how far his account of conscience squares with our own moral experience. It seems to me, however, that he is describing the moral experience of someone who already believes in God. Thus, for instance, he says that conscience is a 'voice' that 'is ever forcing on us by threats and by promises that we must follow the right and avoid the wrong' (paragraph 3). Conscience is, moreover, intimately connected with certain emotions – 'especially fear' and a 'bad conscience' with 'self-reproach, poignant shame, haunting remorse, chill dismay at the prospect of the future'. These references to threats and promises, to fear of the future, are evidently not references to *worldly* punishments (threats) and rewards (promises). For if they were it would be the voice of prudence and self-interest that would be speaking to us. Moreover people who act out of fear *for themselves* are not obviously acting morally at all but out of self-interest. In making so much of fear Newman seems to be describing a distinctively religious conscience. Only someone who believed in an afterlife with punishment for the wicked would associate conscience with threats and promises, with fear or with 'chill dismay at the prospect of the future'. If that is true then it would be tantamount to *begging the question* to bring in these emotions as part of an argument for the existence of a 'Supreme Governor' of the world. For only such a 'Supreme Governor' could ensure that the virtuous were rewarded and the wicked punished in some future life. Thus to assume the threats and promises that Newman thinks conscience can make is already to assume what the argument was setting out to prove. It begs the question.

Another related objection is to the list of emotions Newman associates with conscience, as ones on which, as he puts it, 'conscience has an intimate bearing' (paragraph 4). Of those he includes, only self-reproach and remorse seem to me to be always and essentially connected with conscience. I am not sure self-reproach is strictly an emotion at all but, since it is closely connected with remorse it will be sufficient to consider remorse. Remorse is, in a strong sense, a moral emotion. It is a special kind of regret which people only feel when they have done something wrong or at least think they have. Having a conscience and being able to feel remorse are closely tied together. Remorseless foes are ones who can do harm to one another without having a bad conscience about it. A philosophical study of conscience would need to say a good deal about remorse and vice versa.

Not all the emotions Newman lists, however, are as closely associated with conscience as remorse is. Fear and shame, for instance, may be felt when the issues are not moral ones at all. This can be seen by producing suitable *counter-examples*. Let us start with the case of fear. If someone puts a few small items from the supermarket shelves into their pocket and not into the trolley, they may approach the check-out in a state of fear. But their worry need not be at all prompted by conscience but only by the risk of being caught. If so, once they are out of the store and past the point where their pilfering might be challenged, they will feel a sense of relief. Where conscience is involved, however, there will be some remorse even when the risk of being caught is past. Similarly, to take a case of shame: someone may feel ashamed at being seen scruffily dressed by a neighbour or feel ashamed by the press coverage of their court appearance. Moral issues need not be involved at all. What makes someone afraid, in the first case, has to do with their sense of how likely it is that they will get caught. What makes someone feel ashamed has to do with how they think other people will see them and with the adverse view of themselves this gives. There seems, however, to be a further difference between fear and shame. Fear seems only incidentally to have anything to do with morality and to have primarily to do with self-protection and therefore self-interest. An utterly fearless person could be a paragon of morality – even a saint. But it is different in the case of shame. It is difficult to think of a better phrase to give someone the lowest possible ranking as a moral being than to refer to them as 'utterly shameless'. The word 'utterly' is important here, since people can rebel against social norms in a limited way and make a kind of boast of their shamelessness in some particular regard. Thus, in a society where elitism is disapproved of, people may rebel and say, for example, that they are 'shameless elitists' (about musical education, perhaps) or 'shameless cowards' (if they reject the military virtues). The rebellion might even take the form of systematically shameless behaviour. But usually this is carefully defined, as in stag nights and hen parties, where the principals are allowed to act in an utterly shameless way without putting their fundamental decency in doubt. Shame is thus a significant emotion for morality. I will make a suggestion shortly about what that significance is. None the less the feeling of shame, like that of fear, is compounded rather than caused by a bad conscience.

Returning to Newman's argument, we have seen that, in its final and crucial stages, it involves these premises:

Premise 1	The emotions associated with the promptings of conscience are always elicited by something outside us.
Premise 2	This 'something outside us' must be an 'intelligent being'.
Premise 3	It is not an 'earthly object'.
Conclusion	The emotions associated with the promptings of conscience are always elicited by something 'Supernatural and Divine'.

I hope this looks to you to be well on the way to being a valid argument, if we grant those extra assumptions that would entitle Newman to infer that, if there is nothing in the world around us that causes these emotions, then it must be an intelligent supernatural being. Obviously it could be a guardian angel but, once the argument has got off the ground, it would be quibbling to make a fuss about such later stages of the argument. The question is whether it can get off the ground. For that, premises 1–3 are necessary. Let us suppose that the argument is valid or, at any rate, that it can readily be made into a valid argument. The important question then becomes whether it is sound, i.e. whether these premises are true.

EXERCISE 4.4

NEWMAN AND CONSCIENCE

Do you think Newman's arguments for accepting these premises are satisfactory? Consider whether you are willing to accept premises 1–3 and, if not, why not.

DISCUSSION

I am not convinced by premise 1, i.e. that the emotions associated with the prompt-ings of conscience are always elicited by something outside us. It seems plausible only for those emotions, like fear, which are loosely associated with morality and conscience, to say that they are elicited by something outside us. In the case of the emotions that are always and uncontroversially associated with conscience – self-reproach and remorse – this is not plausible. In the case of self-reproach, it is the offender alone who is the cause of the discontentment he or she feels. No one else need be involved. Equally, someone's feelings of remorse can be caused entirely by their own reflection on what they have done.

I am inclined to accept premise 2 for at least those cases where moral emotions have an external cause. It seems that another 'intelligent being' needs to be involved, either actually or in prospect, where someone feels shame. People who are ashamed will characteristically hide their faces (in shame) from others. Shame can, of course, be secret (hidden from others). But the shame that is felt seems then to be caused by the prospect, however remote, that others might find out.

Newman's line of thought has failed at earlier stages in the case of emotions like remorse, which does not need an external cause. If we follow it through for the more favourable case of shame, however, it seems to fail at premise 3. Other people ('earthly' objects, in his quaint phrase) seem to serve as the usual causes of feelings of shame, including moral shame. There is no *need* to invoke a 'Moral Governor'. Of course those who already believe will feel shame before God. But that is not to say that we need to postulate a god in order to explain our having a conscience.

Newman is only one of many who have thought that a satisfactory explanation of conscience and its workings needed to bring in a deity. But those who are content with a naturalistic explanation – one that does not invoke a supernatural being – will not accept such an argument. In a later section (see p. 117) we will refer briefly to a naturalistic account of conscience offered by Darwin. But, what-ever the merits of Darwin's account, it seems reasonable to expect that some naturalistic account of conscience will prove satisfactory. As J. L. Mackie puts it:

If we stand back from the experience of conscience and try to understand it, it is over-whelmingly plausible to see it as an introjection into each individual of demands that come from other people; in the first place, perhaps, from his parents and immediate associates, but ultimately from the traditions and institutions of the society in which he has grown up, or of some special part of that society which has had the greatest influence upon him. In thus understanding conscience we do, admittedly, look beyond conscience itself and beyond the agent himself, but we look to natural, human, sources, not to a god.

(Mackie (1982), p. 105)

An explanation of conscience belongs more to a branch of psychology than it does to philosophy. But I think philosophy can contribute to a better understanding of conscience by showing its connection with the moral emotions, like remorse and shame. Shame is perhaps particularly interesting since it can only be felt by social beings and is connected with the need for social approval and the fear of social rejection. It fits well as a main ingredient in the kind of naturalistic account of conscience that Mackie sketches.

Those who agree with Mackie's sketch will not expect a project like Newman's to succeed. There are, however, other arguments for the existence of God that are based on other aspects of morality and which have impressed some philosophers, including one of the greatest in the Western tradition, Immanuel Kant.

KANT'S MORAL ARGUMENT FOR THE EXISTENCE OF GOD

Kant's argument for the existence of God turns in part on the principle that we do not have a duty (moral obligation) to do something unless we can do it. This is sometimes known as the *ought implies can* principle. It is easy to think of examples where it holds. Whenever we make an undertaking for the future (make an appointment, promise to do something, etc.) there is something that we *ought* to do (keep the appointment, fulfil the promise, etc.). Or at least we *ought* to do it if we *can*. If it turns out that we cannot carry out our undertaking – we catch the flu, for example – then we are relieved of the obligation to carry it out.

The 'ought implies can' principle has an intuitive plausibility about it. It seems to be embedded in our way of thinking about moral matters. For instance, if someone fails to do something they had a duty to do, others may *blame* them. But, if it turns out that this someone was not able to do it, that blame would be inappropriate. If John makes an appointment to meet George at a particular time but John's train is derailed and he is late for this reason, George (supposing him to be a reasonable person) will excuse John, i.e. will not hold him to blame for being late. What makes the failure to fulfil a duty excusable in our eyes is whatever we accept as showing that the duty could not be fulfilled in the circumstances.

There is a second principle Kant assumes in developing his argument. It is that we have a moral obligation to perfect ourselves and to attain the 'highest good' (in Latin, *summum bonum*). The highest good is a perfect state of human society in which happiness is proportioned to moral worth. But, he argues, it is impossible for us to attain this 'highest good' under the conditions of the lives we live here and now. So, he argues, not only must there be a purposive God whose will it is that we can and do attain this 'highest good' but there must be another (better) life ahead of us in which we do. As Kant himself put it:

The idea of the highest good ... cannot be realized by man himself ... yet he discovers within himself the duty to work for this end. Hence he finds himself impelled to believe in the co-operation or management of a moral Ruler of the world, by means of which alone this goal can be reached.

(Kant (1960), p. 130)

EXERCISE 4.5

KANT'S MORAL ARGUMENT (1)

Re-read Kant's argument as quoted above and set it out as a valid argument, as far as you can, adding the 'ought implies can' principle and any other implied premises you find necessary.

Check your answer against the one at the back of the book before reading on.

DISCUSSION

Strictly this superhuman agency does not have to be 'a moral Ruler of the world'. But perhaps we can, for the sake of argument, allow Kant that supplementary arguments would support saying that this highest good can only be achieved in another (better) world if, and only if, there was moral order underwritten by a supremely wise, good and powerful being.

EXERCISE 4.6

KANT'S MORAL ARGUMENT (2)

Supposing that Kant's argument can (charitably) be set out so that it is a *valid* argument, are you inclined to accept its conclusion? If not, why not? Which premise would you question?

DISCUSSION

A premise which many people would be inclined to query is number 1. One way of interpreting the 'ought implies can' principle would be to rule out as duties whatever is not humanly achievable. We may have a duty to perfect ourselves as far as we can. But we cannot have a duty to achieve what is (humanly) impossible. Kant's argument depends on an interpretation of the 'ought implies can' principle which is implausible.

There is much more that can be said in support of Kant's argument, in particular in defence of premise 1. This takes us to some fundamental aspects of his moral philosophy. Kant insisted that the only reason for doing one's duty is that it *is* one's duty. People are not acting morally if they behave well to others on the basis that, if they do, there is some chance the others will behave well to them.

Nor are they acting morally if they do the honest thing because they dare not risk being found out. Morality, for Kant, cannot be a matter of self-interest, not even of long-term enlightened self-interest.

But why should rational people act morally at all, if there is nothing in it for them? Kant refused to address that question in such a form. At the same time he had a deep sense that something would be fundamentally wrong with the moral order if virtue was not ultimately to be rewarded and wrongdoing punished:

> to be in need of happiness and also worthy of it and yet not to partake of it could not be in accordance with the complete volition of an omnipotent rational being, if we assume such only for the sake of the argument. Inasmuch as virtue and happiness together constitute the possession of the highest good for one person, and happiness in exact proportion to morality (the worth of a person and his worthiness to be happy) constitutes that of a possible world.
>
> (Kant (1956), pp. 114f.)

If there is a harmonious moral order then, according to Kant, the highest good (happiness in proportion to virtue) is realized. But such a harmonious moral order needs to be underwritten by a 'moral Ruler of the world' and requires, for humans, another world in which it is realized. Thus for Kant, both the immortality of the soul and the existence of God are what he calls 'postulates' of pure practical reason.

I have been helping Kant's argument by using such phrases as 'moral order'. But someone who was deeply unimpressed by Kant's way of thinking might protest that there is no moral order, that it is just a fact of the human situation that virtue and happiness do not necessarily go together at all. Kant is simply wrong to insist that they must do. At all events we do not need to go down the road he takes. We could settle for a more humdrum view of morality, such as *utilitarianism*, which takes for its criterion of what makes an action right or wrong considerations to do with human happiness.[3]

Kant, more than any other philosopher, has been the inspiration of moral arguments for the existence of God. But one philosopher who advocated a form of moral argument, Hastings Rashdall (1858–1924), is normally classed as a utilitarian philosopher and so as very different from Kant.[4] His argument is not open to the difficulties noted in relation to the two moral arguments we have already considered.

THE ARGUMENT FROM THE OBJECTIVITY OF MORALITY

Of the three versions of the moral argument we have already considered, the first assumes that statements of moral duties are quite strictly orders and the third assumes that as moral beings we are committed to a project we cannot complete in this life. Neither of these assumptions were made by Rashdall, whose argument turns in part on the problematic but none the less widely shared thought that there is an absolute standard of right and wrong. This standard, he argues, is as objective and therefore as independent of the wishes and desires of individuals as the facts of the external material world. But the standard does not exist in the material world. If we suppose that physics could give us a complete description of the material world, then we should not expect it to mention this standard. But, if it is objective, Rashdall supposes it must exist somewhere. Assuming a dualist dichotomy between the material and mental world, he concludes that, if it does not exist in the material world it must exist in the mental world. And this means it must exist in some mind. But, if it does not exist in our minds, there must be another Mind in which it exists. This Mind, he goes on to conclude, is God.

This is a partial summary of the argument Rashdall put forward in his *Theory of Good and Evil* (1907). Here is an extract from that book:

> An absolute Moral Law or moral ideal cannot exist *in* material things. And it does not exist in the mind of this or that individual. Only if we believe in the existence of a Mind which is the source of whatever is true in our own moral judgements, can we rationally think of the moral ideal as no less real than the world itself. Only so can we believe in an absolute standard of right and wrong, which is as independent of this or that man's actual ideas and actual desires as the facts of material nature. The belief in God … is the logical presupposition of an 'objective' or absolute Morality. A moral ideal can exist nowhere and nohow but in a mind; an absolute moral ideal can exist only in a Mind from which all Reality is derived *or at least a mind by which all Reality is controlled*. Our moral ideal can claim objective validity in so far as it can rationally be regarded as the revelation of a moral ideal eternally existing in the mind of God.
>
> (Rashdall (1907), Vol. II, p. 212, phrase in italics added by author in footnote)

EXERCISE 4.7

OBJECTIVITY OF MORALITY (1)

Why does Rashdall think that an absolute standard of right and wrong cannot exist in human minds?

DISCUSSION

The reason is that the standard is 'as independent of this or that man's actual ideas and actual desires as the facts of material nature'.

EXERCISE 4.8

OBJECTIVITY OF MORALITY (2)

Do you think his reason is a good one?

DISCUSSION

It does not seem to me a good reason. The fact that something is independent of

> my ideas and desires does not mean that it cannot be *in* my mind. There are many
> things that may be in an individual's mind which are in no way determined by that
> individual's ideas or desires. A woman selecting from her crop of potatoes which
> to put in for the local gardening show will, if she knows what the judges are
> supposed to be looking for, have in mind a standard of the 'show' potato. She
> might have ideas about how she would like to alter that standard but the standard
> that is in her mind is set independently of her ideas and desires.

Part of what is wrong with Rashdall's thinking lies in his dualist assumption
that there are two *places* where objective things may exist: in the material world,
on the one hand, or in minds, on the other. But minds are not an alternative loca-
tion for things. If someone says to you 'I have been thinking of you today' or
(which would come to the same thing) 'You have been in my mind', they are not
denying that you have been in the various places you thought you had been.
Minds are not really locations for things at all.

Yet, Rashdall appears to have thought: if ideals and standards do not exist in
the material world, where do they exist? His train of thought appears to be something like this:

Premise 1   Something is 'objective' if it exists outside individual minds and
                 'subjective' if it depends only on someone's ideas or desires.
Premise 2   Moral ideals and standards are objective.
Conclusion   There must be somewhere that moral ideals and standards exist
                 outside individual (human) minds.

But this line of thought involves an over-simple view of objectivity. It is
commonly said that the quality of being red or smelling fishy does not strictly
exist in the objects we say are red or smell fishy. On the contrary these are
subjective qualities. They are subjective in that things only look red to creatures
with colour vision or smell fishy to creatures with a sense of smell (and with
experience of the smell of fish). They are not wholly subjective, it might be said,
because there is something in the object in virtue of which it looks red to people
with normal colour vision and something in the object in virtue of which it
smells the way it does to people with a normal sense of smell and a correct
memory of how fish smell. Physics can tell us about the objective qualities of the
surface of objects in virtue of which they will look red in normal light conditions.
These are different objective qualities from those of an object we say is blue.

These reflections are intended to illustrate how the word 'objective' can quite
rightly be construed as meaning 'existing in the object'. But this construction
cannot without confusion be extended to the discussion of the objectivity or
otherwise of ideals or standards. Objectivity seems to mean something different
here. Those who have denied the objectivity of ideals and standards have not been
making claims about where they did or did not 'exist'. They have been affirming
rather that those ideals and standards are totally dependent on the ideas or desires

of individual subjects. For a subjectivist a good potato means no more than one he or she likes and a good action no more than one of which he or she approves.

Someone who wishes to defend the objectivity of moral or other ideals and standards does not need to make any claims about where such ideals and standards exist. What they need to do is to defeat the claims of the subjectivist and the relativist. Against the subjectivist, they will need to argue that such ideals and standards are not dependent on individual ideas and desires. Against the relativist, they will also need to argue that these ideals and standards are not dependent either on the ideas and preferences of particular groups of people. That is what the project of defending the objectivity of morality involves. It does not mean that those standards or ideals have to exist somewhere. The project of defending the objectivity of morality does not lead, as Rashdall supposed, to postulating God as the Mind in which those standards or ideals would have their existence.

We cannot go further here into the project of defending the objectivity of morality. We have only considered one argument, based on what I have claimed is a misconception of objectivity. There may be other arguments from the objectivity of morality which will fare better. At the same time, if what is sought is a transcultural basis for moral judgements, the most likely basis is a common human nature. To the extent that humans are the same whatever society they belong to; to the extent that they have the same needs, for instance: to that extent their duties to one another will be the same whatever society they belong to. If that suffices as a way of underpinning the objectivity of morality then there is no reason to expect that it is necessary to presuppose a god.

We have considered only a few of the arguments in favour of the existence of a purpose behind the universe. There are also arguments *against* belief in a purposive God. We have already noted one that is implicit in Darwin's thinking: that the place of chance in the evolution of species makes it improbable that there is a designer of nature. Darwin also thought there was so much cruelty in nature as to make it improbable that there is a good God who cares about what happens in the universe. This line of argument is one we will pursue in the next chapter.

SUMMARY

In this chapter we have considered four of the so-called 'moral' arguments for the existence of God. The first, based on construing duties as imperatives, made the mistake of supposing that, in all imperatives, there had to be a person who authorized them. A second argument, owing to Newman, was that it was necessary to suppose a moral governor of the universe in order to explain our experience of conscience. But not only was the argument found implausible but in any case there was a good prospect of a satisfactory psychological explanation of conscience. The third argument, which is Kant's, is that we have a duty to realize the highest good, namely happiness proportioned to virtue, but that we cannot realize this unless there is a better life and a 'moral ruler of the world' to underwrite it. We noted, however, that many would deny that we have a duty to realize the highest good, as Kant understood it. The fourth argument, that of Rashdall, is that the existence of God is presupposed by an objective or absolute standard of morality. It was suggested, however, that Rashdall has a conception of objectivity which is inappropriate for morality.

FURTHER READING

There is a good recent review of the 'Moral Arguments' by C. S. Evans in *The Blackwell Companion to the Philosophy of Religion*, ed. P. L. Quinn and C. Taliaferro, Blackwell, 1997, pp. 345–51. Recent defences of forms of moral argument for the existence of God include: H. P. Owen's *The Moral Argument for Christian Theism*, Allen & Unwin, 1965, J. Hare's *The Moral Gap: Kantian Ethics, Human Limits and God's Assistance*, Oxford University Press, 1996, and G. Mavrodes's 'Religion and the Queerness of Morality', in R. Audi and W. Wainwright (eds), *Rationality, Religious Belief and Moral Commitment*, Cornell University Press, 1986. Discussion of the relation of morality and religion is also reflected in a collection edited by P. Helm, *Divine Commands and Morality*, Oxford University Press, 1981. A good critical review is in J. L. Mackie's *The Miracle of Theism*, Clarendon Press, 1982.

NOTES

1 Kant explained this distinction in his *Groundwork of the Metaphysics of Morals* (1785).
2 Newman was for a number of years an Anglican clergyman, associated with the Oxford Movement, but in 1845 he was received into the Roman Catholic Church, of which he was eventually made a cardinal. His *Grammar of Assent* was first published in 1870. For an account of Newman's philosophy, see Ker (1990).
3 The term was introduced as the title of John Stuart Mill's *Utilitarianism* (1863), though it was already quite a well-established way of thinking about morality. See the entries in Edwards (1967) and Craig (1998) for a fuller account and bibliography.
4 For brief introductions to Rashdall see the entries in Brown, Collinson and Wilkinson (1996) and Craig (1998). There is no definitive book on his thought but a fuller account can be found in Elliot-Binns (1956).

5 | God and evil

EVIL AS A LOGICAL PROBLEM FOR RELIGIOUS BELIEF

The existence of evil is almost universally accepted as an inescapable fact of the human situation. Earthquakes, floods and epidemics; the cruelty and suffering of humans and other animals; these and other evils have made it difficult for people to see human or animal existence as meaningful. Religions have sought in different ways to make sense of evil. Some religions (ancient Zoroastrianism, for instance) think of the world as a battleground between the forces of good and the forces of evil. In some religions individuals are invited to think of themselves as having a role to play in determining the outcome of this cosmic war.

But in other religions, God is conceived as omnipotent as well as wholly good and so the victory of good over evil is assured. Indeed, according to these religions, this victory has been assured since the beginning of time. This is the position of mainstream Christianity – Catholic, Eastern Orthodox, Anglican, Methodist and many denominations. In focusing on it I am not suggesting at all that it is to be preferred to other positions or that I think it is more likely to be right. On the contrary I am focusing on it because, although widely received, it is faced with a particular difficulty.

The difficulty is that it insists on a set of beliefs which are inconsistent, i.e. which (logically) cannot all be true. These are:

Premise 1   God (a wholly good and omnipotent being) exists.

Premise 2   God (being wholly good) abhors all evil.

Premise 3   God (being omnipotent) can prevent the existence of anything he abhors.

Premise 4   Evil exists.

EXERCISE 5.1

CONSTRUCTING AN ARGUMENT (1)

To demonstrate an inconsistency we need to show how, from the agreed premises, a self-contradictory conclusion can be reached. Continue the argument so as to show how the self-contradictory conclusion (Evil both exists and does not exist) can be derived from premises 1–4 together with a further premise:

Premise 5   If anyone abhors something they will prevent it if they can.

Check your answer against the one at the back of the book before reading on.

DISCUSSION

This kind of argument is sometimes referred to as a *reductio ad absurdum*. It takes a set of premises (here 1–5) and deduces an absurdity from it, something that cannot be true, in this case a self-contradiction. Strictly speaking, however, it does not demonstrate the absurdity of the orthodox theological position. It does not, since the absurd conclusion only follows if we accept premise 5. And, although premise 5 has seemed obvious enough to some people, orthodox theologians have sought to retain premises 1–4 and avoid the inconsistency by claiming that God has purposes which justify allowing evil even though he abhors it. But there are no easy solutions to this problem, for those who accept premises 1–4.

There is a further suppressed premise that those who have discussed the logical problem of evil have usually taken for granted. It is that God is omniscient, i.e. knows everything that there is to know. No one has, to my knowledge, ever suggested that God is able to prevent evil and does prevent all the evil he knows about, only there is some evil that exists of which God does not know. That has never been suggested within the religious traditions for which the logical problem of evil arises because within those traditions it would be regarded as an impious suggestion, embodying an unworthy notion of God.

Evil is not a logical problem for all religious systems. According to the Vedanta teachings of Hinduism evil is an illusion. This has also been the view of certain Christian sects, most recently in Christian Science, whose founder, Mary Baker Eddy, wrote that 'evil is but an illusion, and it has no real basis' (Eddy (1875), p. 480). It is possible in this way to adopt the radical solution of denying premise 4. Other ways out are also controversial from the point of view of orthodox Christianity: for instance, it is sometimes the omnipotence of God that is denied.

Orthodoxy constrains the solution to this problem and, as I have already indicated, the most promising strategy for the orthodox is to try to find a way of denying premise 5. We will consider one way of pursuing this strategy in the next section. But first it is worth noting that this is not merely a logical puzzle for the orthodox. The same logical argument that poses the problem for theology about how evil can be admitted can be turned around so that it becomes an atheistical argument or at any rate a demonstration from the fact of evil that there cannot be a god as understood by the orthodox, i.e. a being who is wholly in control of what happens in the universe and whose purposes are wholly good. The logical problem is that the five premises listed above are inconsistent. That means that there is always at least one that must be rejected. It is possible to argue that, if evil exists, then either premise 2 or 3 must be rejected and that if either premise 2 or 3 is rejected then premise 1 must be rejected.

EXERCISE 5.2

CONSTRUCTING AN ARGUMENT (2)

Try to construct an argument, starting from premise 4 and using premise 5, for denying premise 1.

DISCUSSION

Here is my argument:

A Evil exists (premise 4).

B The evil that exists has not been prevented (from A, on the principle that otherwise it would not have existed).

C God has not prevented the evil that exists (if it has not been prevented, then no one, including God, has prevented it).

D If God did not prevent the evil then either he could not prevent it or he did not want to.

E If he could not prevent it then he is not omnipotent.

F   If he did not want to prevent it he is not wholly good.
G   God is either not omnipotent or is not wholly good.
H   There is no God, understood as a being who is *both* omnipotent *and* wholly good.

The argument from D to H takes the form of a *dilemma*. (We encountered a dilemma before, in Chapter 2.) The orthodox believer, who admits the fact of evil in the world, is apparently confronted by an unpalatable choice between denying that God is wholly good and denying that he is omnipotent.

There is a way out of the dilemma, however, and of resolving the logical problem of evil. I mentioned earlier that theologians have commonly denied premise 5 – by saying that while God abhors evil he allows it. He might allow it, for instance, because evil is necessary if he is to achieve the good purposes he has for the universe as a whole. We will consider this line of escape in the next section.

THE FREE-WILL DEFENCE

The logical problem of evil has most commonly been addressed in the Christian tradition by focusing on human free will. Broadly, it has been argued that God's purposes for humankind could not be achieved without allowing humans free will. God could not allow humans free will without allowing for the possibility that they would choose to do evil. God does not will the evil that they choose to do. His will is that they should freely choose the good. Thus, although God does allow evil, he is in no way responsible for the evil that there is. This is the line of argument taken up by John Hick.[1]

Reading
pp. 147–9

Reading 5, John Hick's 'The problem of evil: the free-will defence', is a summary of the traditional free-will defence, the objections to it of some contemporary philosophical critics and part of Hick's reply to those objections. Read the extract now, and attempt the following exercise.

EXERCISE 5.3

FREE-WILL DEFENCE

1   You will find that Hick identifies three phases of the 'free-will defence'. Summarize in two or three sentences of your own words what the first two phases are.
2   Hick takes the first two phases to be uncontroversial. He replies to the objection to the third phase of the 'free-will defence' in his own way. Summarize the objection and Hick's reply to it.

Check your answer against the one at the back of the book before reading on.

EXERCISE 5.4

FREE-WILL DEFENCE AND EVIL

Make a note of any thoughts you have as to whether the free-will defence is satisfactory as a way of getting out of the logical problem of evil.

DISCUSSION

Articulating and defending your own point of view in philosophy is one of the
hardest but most rewarding parts of the subject. You might have tried to tackle this
question narrowly by focusing exclusively on the debate to which Hick is
contributing. Or you might have tried to take a wider view and begun by asking
what exactly the free-will defence was supposed to show.

Beginning with the narrower question of who is right in the debate between
those who have advocated and those who have criticized the free-will defence, it
might be argued, against Hick, that he is veering in the direction of making God
take risks in creating persons and of saying that there are outcomes which God
cannot foresee and which are outside his control. If Hick is committed to doing
this he is involved in denying two of God's attributes: omniscience (which we have
not met before) and omnipotence. The denial of omnipotence would lead him in the
direction of a radical dissolution of the logical problem by denying one of the
premises (namely premise 1) on which it arises and whose acceptance is one of
the constraints on an 'orthodox' solution. If we were to speak on behalf of the
critics to whom Hick is replying we might say that they are arguing (*ad hominem*)
within those constraints and for him to avoid their criticism by stepping outside
them is a kind of cheating. Unfortunately, however, we are touching here on a deep
problem as to whether, if God not only knows what I will do but has in some sense
(because he is omnipotent) fore-ordained that I will do it, I will do it freely. Hick
seems to be inclined to answer 'No' (I will not in those circumstances do it freely)
whereas his critics are assuming that there is no inconsistency in talking about
God fore-ordaining my free actions.

We cannot go much into this problem here. Some philosophers, myself
included, do not see why it follows, if someone's actions are wholly predictable,
that they are for that reason alone not 'free' in doing them. People may be wholly
predictable, for example, when they are acting entirely rationally and in character. The fact that their human nature is not something chosen by them does not
mean in that situation that they do not act freely. It does not seem to matter how
they came by those natures. If that is so, it makes no difference whether those
natures are a chance result of evolutionary processes or whether they are
specially selected by a supervising deity. Free action is still possible, at least for
some people some of the time. Thus it seems to me that Hick is wrong in
thinking that he can avoid the criticism of those who claim that God could have
arranged a world in which everyone freely chose to act rightly and well. There is

no obvious inconsistency in the suggestion that God could have made us so that we would all freely act in the ways he wanted all of the time.

There is, however, another line of defence open to those who seek to resolve the logical problem of evil by arguing that some evil is inevitable to achieve the ends willed by God. It may still be the case that the critics of the free-will defence are demanding the logically impossible. That this is so becomes apparent if we recap the debate so far in slightly different language.

The critics of the free-will defence point out, quite correctly, that if God is really wholly good and omnipotent then the world we live in, as we find it, must be the best possible world. The actual world must, in short, be Utopia. Their argument is that since this is not Utopia (because, for a start, humans do evil things) there is either no god at all or, at any rate, there is not one who is both wholly good and omnipotent. The free-will defence urges that you cannot have Utopia without free will and free will means some evil. But the critics reply that the true Utopia would be one in which everybody freely chooses to do good and there is no evil. There is no contradiction, say the critics, in supposing that God might have created this true Utopia. Since he evidently did not, if there is a god he is either not wholly good or else he is not omnipotent.

EXERCISE 5.5

UTOPIA AND FREE WILL

Can you spot what the defender of the free-will argument needs to do in order to counter this criticism?

DISCUSSION

What is needed is an argument to show that the Utopia demanded by the critics is a logical impossibility. To see whether it is we need to consider what exactly such a Utopia would involve. It is a world in which everyone always freely chooses to do the good, where everybody perfectly exercises the virtues. Those who claim that such a Utopia can actually exist are committed to the general claim that the virtues can be exercised in a world in which there are no evils. This kind of general claim is in principle open to refutation by counter-example. All that is needed to refute it is an example (which the person making the claim cannot reasonably refuse to accept) of a virtue that cannot be exercised except in a world in which there are evils.

EXERCISE 5.6

VIRTUE AND THE NEED FOR EVIL

Can you think of such virtues, that can only be exercised where there are evils?

DISCUSSION

In Utopia everyone would be nice to everyone else. But many of our virtues could not be exercised. In a world in which no one suffered evils, it would not be possible to exercise virtues like compassion. In a world in which no one was threatened by evils, it would not be possible to exercise virtues like courage. If no one did any evil, it would not be possible to exercise virtues like forgiveness or magnanimity. For many of our virtues to be exercised there would have to be not only a good deal of natural evil – for which humans are not to blame – but also a good deal of moral evil, for which they are. It seems possible then to counter the claim that the best of all possible worlds would include no evil.

The free-will defence does not by itself explain why there are natural evils for which humans are not responsible. But if the purpose of the universe were to produce virtuous people, then there is reason to think there would need to be quite a lot of evil in it, both natural and moral evil, so that they could develop the desired virtues. This has led some to a further line of defence of belief in a good God in the face of evil. It is to say that the purpose of our existence in this life is to make us morally fit for a better one. This is sometimes referred to as *the vale of soul-making* defence. The suggestion is that the whole of the natural world, including its blessings and its evils, is there as a kind of moral training ground for human souls.

However, there is a further objection that while some evil may be necessary there is a disproportionate amount of it in our world. Not only is there too much of it but a great deal of it serves no purpose in the moral training of anyone. There are a number of aspects to this problem of pointless suffering. Many young children, for example, suffer terribly without being given the chance to develop their characters. Much suffering of adults is simply overwhelming and provides no chance of character building. Then there is the suffering of animals which seems to be entirely pointless and unjustifiable. These are all complicated topics on which a good deal has been written. We cannot go into them all here. But the issue of animal suffering as a problem for belief in a good God deserves particular attention.

ANIMAL SUFFERING

The problem posed for belief in a benevolent creator by animal suffering was one that particularly struck Charles Darwin, who wrote in his *Autobiography* of 1876:

> That there is much suffering in the world no one disputes. Some have attempted to explain this in reference to man by imagining that it serves for his moral improvement. But the number of men in the world is as nothing compared with that of all other sentient beings, and these often suffer greatly without any moral improvement. A being so powerful and so full of knowledge as God who could create the universe, is to our finite minds omnipotent and omniscient, and it revolts our understanding to suppose that his benevolence is not unbounded, for what advantage can there be in the sufferings of millions of the lower animals throughout almost endless time?
>
> (Darwin in de Beer (1974), p. 52)

Darwin continued to believe in the existence of a creator of the universe. But he ceased to believe in the God of Christian orthodoxy. The reason for his disbelief was the sufferings of millions of the 'lower animals'. This is a theme he took up just after the publication of his *Origin of Species*, when he wrote to a friend:

> I had no intention to write atheistically. But I own that I cannot see as plainly as others do, and as I should wish to do, evidence of design and beneficence on all sides of us. There seems to me too much misery in the world. I cannot persuade myself that a beneficent and omnipotent God would have designedly created the Ichneumonidae [a species of parasitic wasp] with the express intention of their feeding within the living bodies of Caterpillars, or that a cat should play with mice.
>
> (Darwin (1887), Vol. II, p. 262)

Darwin went on to say that while he believed that the universe was subject to 'designed laws', it seemed to him that the details, 'whether for good or ill', were 'left to chance'. He still apparently believed in a designer of the universe, so far as concerned its origin and general laws. But he could no longer believe in the God of William Paley and orthodox Christianity, who cared about the details. He ceased to believe that God was wholly benevolent in his purposes towards his creation.

Darwin was secretive about his unbelief and his route to it is therefore difficult, if not impossible to trace. In his *Notebooks* (Summer, 1842) he recorded what seems to have then been a way of reconciling animal suffering with God having a good purpose for the world:

> From the concealed war of nature we can see the highest good, which we can conceive, the creation of the higher animals has directly come.

The thought here seems to be that the end justifies the means and that animal suffering can be justified because it leads through evolution to the emergence of the human species. But, if Darwin was at one time satisfied with that view, he seems to have come to think that animal suffering was disproportionate and so not justified in relation to the evolution of the human species. There was, to his mind, too much animal suffering in nature to square with belief in a good purpose controlling the world.

Reading pp.151–4

Reading 6, John Hick's 'The problem of animal suffering', is the second extract from his *Evil and the God of Love*. It addresses the specific problem of animal suffering. Read the extract now, and attempt the following exercise.

EXERCISE 5.7

ANIMAL SUFFERING

1 What exactly is the author's problem and what, in brief, is his solution to it?
2 Does his solution work? Can you give an objection to it?
3 To what extent, if at all, do you find his treatment convincing?

DISCUSSION

1 Hick's problem is, 'Why ... does an all-powerful and infinitely loving Creator permit the pain and carnage of animal life?' This is both a problem about the pain animals suffer and about the violence of nature. The author's answer to the question about pain is that pain, in those creatures who suffer it, is 'part of their equipment for survival'. Animals benefit, as humans do, by possessing the equipment for survival and so it can be thought of as part of the plan of a benevolent God. As to the violence of nature, Hick argues that animals experience the world quite differently from humans, that death is not a problem for them as it is for us since they live their lives from moment to moment oblivious as to what may lie ahead for them. This aspect of the problem evaporates, he argues, once we see that it is a mistake to project the fears and anxieties we have about ourselves onto creatures who are incapable of feeling them.

2 The answer only works, so far as pain is concerned, to the extent that pain serves the purpose of enabling animals to avoid danger. There remains the problem of pain which does not serve its purpose, exceeds what is necessary to serve its purpose or continues long afterwards. Even granting that Hick's account is broadly correct, the existence of unnecessary pain (which is not needed to alert an animal to danger) has still got to be explained. Given that God is all-loving and omnipotent, there should not be such unnecessary pain at all.

Hick's answer to the problem about the mental suffering of animals is to deny its reality. But, while he is right to say, for instance, that animals do not have the kind of fear of death humans can have, that is not because they do not feel fear at all. Humans can fear events that are not imminent, as animals cannot. But we can be as confident in saying that some animals suffer terror as that they suffer physical pain. That is what presumably offended Darwin about cats playing with mice. If the mouse was not in a state of terror this would not be a case of cruelty.

On both points, it seems to me, Hick goes some way towards reconciling the existence of animal suffering with belief in a wholly good omnipotent

Creator. But he fails to come to grips satisfactorily with some persistent difficulties.

3   I have already indicated some points at which I find Hick's treatment unconvincing. I was struck by the blandness of his claim, towards the end of the extract, that 'in general' an animal 'lives from instant to instant, either in healthy and presumably pleasurable activity, or in a pleasant state of torpor'. This may be true of well-cared-for farm animals or pets. But the picture Darwin offers of animals in the state of nature is much less attractive. What Hick says is not true presumably of those caterpillars who are being devoured by the parasites inside them. And surely many animals struggle through their short lives in constant pain through illness or injury. Even if animal life is not 'a dark ocean of agonizing fear and pain', it is beset by much more agonizing fear and pain than Hick acknowledges.

Hick's book, it is only fair to note, was written more than thirty years ago and, in the intervening period, there have been major changes in our attitude towards animals. Someone writing a similar book now would probably find this topic a much more challenging one in relation to traditional religious belief.

This discussion might go on much longer. It may be possible to preserve consistency, as Hick tries to do, by being sceptical about the extent to which animals suffer. It may be possible, in that way, to escape the dilemma posed by the fact of animal suffering against the existence of an all-good omnipotent Creator. But this would be a hollow victory for a religious apologist if it involved adopting a view of evil which others were unable to share. For, if people's religious beliefs affect their view of evil, it is also true that the view they take of evil affects the kind of religious belief that is possible for them. Thus, even if it is not possible to demonstrate that belief in a wholly good and powerful God is inconsistent with the evil that there is in the world, someone's experience of the world can make it incredible for them, as it did for Darwin, that the world has a wholly good and powerful Creator. Even if the logical problem of evil can be resolved at least with some degree of satisfaction, there remains what we can call the empirical problem, to which we will now turn.

THE EMPIRICAL PROBLEM OF EVIL

As we have already seen, Darwin's experiences as a biologist led him away from religious orthodoxy to the view that God is not benevolent. Whereas he continued, at least for a while, to accept the hypothesis of design, he ceased to believe that the designer of the laws of the universe cared about the details. He ceased to believe in the existence of a benevolent designer as a hypothesis that could be fitted with the facts of animal suffering. Darwin seems to have been aware of the logical problem and to have argued for rejecting belief in God's benevolence rather than in his omnipotence. As he put it: 'A being so powerful and so full of knowledge as God who could create the universe, is to our finite minds omnipotent and omniscient.' But he was much more overwhelmed by what he took to be evidence for a lack of benevolence:

> I cannot see as plainly as others do, and as I should wish to do, evidence of design and beneficence on all sides of us. There seems to me too much misery in the world.
>
> (Darwin (1887), Vol. II, p. 262)

This problem about what is probable on the basis of the evidence of what is known about suffering in the world is the empirical problem of evil. It was posed by David Hume in his *Dialogues Concerning Natural Religion*. The sceptic Philo concedes that there may be no inconsistency in believing in a wholly good and omnipotent God in the face of evil. He considers the hypothetical example of a creature who, before being brought into this world, is *already* assured — perhaps by a 'very solid argument', though Hume did not think there was such an argument — that the world was the workmanship of a perfectly benevolent being. Such a creature would be very disappointed with what he found in the world, but he would not need to retract his belief that it was the workmanship of a perfectly benevolent being. For he may reflect on the limitations of his own understanding and the possibility that the evils of the world might be seen in a better light through the eyes of a less limited being than himself. But this is not the actual position, as the sceptical character in the *Dialogues* (Philo) goes on to claim:

> But supposing, which is the real case with regard to man, that this creature is not antecedently convinced of a supreme intelligence, benevolent, and powerful, but is left to gather such a belief from the appearances of things – this entirely alters the case, nor will he ever find any reason for such a conclusion. He may be fully convinced of the narrow limits of his understanding, but this will not help him in forming an inference concerning the goodness of superior powers, since he must form that inference from what he knows, not from what he is ignorant of. The more you exaggerate his weakness and ignorance, the more diffident you render him, and give him the greater suspicion that such subjects are beyond the reach of his faculties.
>
> (Part XI, para. 2)

There has been some controversy amongst scholars as to how far Philo speaks for Hume himself in the *Dialogues*. This controversy relates, however, to whether or not Hume himself thought that anything could be concluded from the argument from design. It seems clear that, on the problem of evil, Philo does speak for Hume and that character and author both held that, even if belief in a good God could be sustained in the face of the logical problem of evil, the empirical problem of evil was insuperable. Even if belief in a good God cannot be shown to be inconsistent with the recognition of evil in the world, it is not a belief that anyone could reasonably arrive at on the basis of their experience of the world alone.

Philo also, I am sure, spoke for Hume when he uttered these words specifically in relation to the human situation:

> there is no view of human life or of the condition of mankind from which, without the

greatest violence, we can infer the moral attributes or learn that infinite benevolence, conjoined with infinite power and infinite wisdom, which we must discover by the eyes of faith alone.

(Part X, last para.)

As we will see in the next part, this apparent reliance on faith in face of the failure of the arguments of natural theology is characteristic of Hume. Faith, on his account, involves a miracle as a result of which people are able to hold beliefs that go entirely contrary to the normal principles according to which their beliefs are formed. However, it becomes clear, once we know what Hume's views about miracles are, that his apparent defence of faith is back-handed and that 'the eyes of faith' only appear to reveal anything to people who are credulous. Yet the point would hold good, on a more positive account of faith, that belief in a good God is something to be believed as a matter of faith and not as a generalization based on detached observation of the world.

SUMMARY

In this chapter we have considered evil both as a logical problem and as an empirical problem. The logical problem concerns the consistency of certain quite widely held religious beliefs: specifically, whether it is possible to believe in a wholly good and omnipotent being who governs the world and at the same time admit the existence of evil. The empirical problem is that, if people did not have a prior commitment to believe the contrary, their experience of the world and its evils would lead them to atheism. They would be led, at any rate, to believe that, if there is an intelligence governing what happens in the world, it is either less than wholly good or less than omnipotent. The empirical problem can be solved if belief in a wholly good and omnipotent being can be defended in some other way. But the logical problem is more difficult. We considered one line of solution which rests on the argument that God cannot achieve his ends unless humans have free will and, if they do, there is bound to be some evil. Even if this contentious solution were allowed, however, there remains a great deal of evil in the world which cannot all be laid at the door of human free will. We considered animal suffering as a case in point. It is difficult for believers to offer a rational explanation of the existence of so much natural evil in a world that is supposed to have been created by a wholly good and omnipotent being. If they do so this may be because they see the world through the 'eyes of faith'.

FURTHER READING

J. Hick's *Evil and the God of Love*, Macmillan, 1966, can be recommended to anyone who wishes to have a fuller introduction to this topic. Hick develops what is referred to as 'the vale of soul-making' view. The logical problem of evil has been posed well by J. L. Mackie in his 'Evil and Omnipotence', *Mind* LXIV

(1955). See also E. Madden and P. Hare, *Evil and the Concept of God*, Charles C. Thomas, 1966. For a good selection of contemporary writings on the topic, I recommend *The Problem of Evil*, ed. M. McCord and R. M. Adams, Oxford University Press, 1990. See also *The Problem of Evil: Selected Readings*, ed. M. L. Peterson, University of Notre Dame Press, 1992.

NOTE

1   John Hick (born 1922) is one of the major British philosophers of religion of recent years. His books include *Faith and Knowledge* (1957), *Evil and the God of Love* (1966), *Death and Eternal Life* (1976), *Problems of Religious Pluralism* (1985). For a brief account of Hick see the entry in Brown, Collinson and Wilkinson (1996).

III Faith and revelation

In the previous two parts we have considered how far it is reasonable to believe in life after death or in a moral purpose behind the universe. Religious belief or faith is, however, commonly held to be based, not on reason, but on the acceptance of the truths of revelation. This invites the question whether it is reasonable to accept claims as revealed truths. One historical answer to this question is that it is reasonable so long as there is good reason to associate those claims with genuine divine interventions such as miracles. In Chapter 6 we will study Hume's celebrated essay 'Of Miracles' in which he subjects this argument to critical scrutiny. Hume's essay becomes a general critique of faith considered as the acceptance of truths based on revelation and contrary to the evidence of one's own experience. 'A wise man', he insists on the contrary, 'proportions his belief to the evidence.' Hume's discussion raises questions about 'the ethics of belief', i.e. whether it is right to hold beliefs except where they are fully supported by the evidence. In Chapter 7 we will consider the controversy between those who regard faith as unreasonable and those who defend going beyond the evidence in what we believe, particularly in matters of religion.

6   Miracles and revelation

OBJECTIVES

By the end of your work on this chapter you should:

■ Be able to explain why miracles have been thought to provide the basis for accepting revelation.
■ Have read a substantial part of Hume's essay 'Of Miracles' and be able to explain what Hume meant by a miracle, why he thought miracles almost never happen and why he thought a miracle could never be established so as to be the foundation of any system of religion.
■ Be able to explain Hume's views on religious faith.
■ Have practised your skills of reading critically.

MIRACLES AS EVIDENCE FOR REVEALED RELIGION

The arguments we have been considering so far in favour of religious belief, such as those for immortality or for a purpose in the universe, have mostly been independent of any particular religion. They belong to what was referred to previously (Chapter 3) as natural theology – they are, that is to say, based on human experience or derived by reason alone. Natural theology is contrasted with theology which is based on an appeal to religious authority, whether it be a set of writings considered as sacred (such as the Bible or the Koran) or an institution or its leaders (such as the Church or the Pope). In the Mediterranean and Western religious traditions natural religion is contrasted with revealed religion, i.e. religion based on *revelation*, which involves the idea that God has revealed certain key truths humans need to know but which they could not work out for themselves. Christian, Jewish and Muslim philosophers and theologians have historically found common ground in discussing the arguments of natural religion. But they largely disagree when it comes to revelation since their most characteristic beliefs are founded upon different sets of writings.

Since these beliefs conflict, the claim of these texts to speak from God poses this fundamental problem: they cannot all be right. Christians believe on the basis of revelation that Jesus Christ is the Messiah, the Son of God, someone whose life and death has incalculable implications for the human situation. This absolutely fundamental point of Christian belief is entirely rejected by Jews and Muslims. Both might say that Jesus was a great religious teacher and endorse many of the things he said, for instance about moral issues. But if, they may be expected to say, Jesus did indeed believe he was the Son of God in the sense Christians claim he did, then he was at best deluded and at worst an impostor. Christians in turn have said similar things about Muhammad. If, of course, the basis on which these criticisms are made is itself revealed religion, then the arguments are question-begging, since each appeals to a revelation the other party rejects. It remains to be seen whether natural religion could provide a basis for accepting a particular religious authority as reliable and for rejecting others.

Historically it has been supposed by defenders of Christianity that natural theology could do this; that the mark of the true religion was that its teachers, being divinely inspired in what they said, were also divinely supported in what they did. Those who genuinely spoke from God showed their credentials, it was claimed, by performing genuine miracles.

Miracles have, for these reasons, a particularly prominent place in the Judaeo-Christian tradition. There are many miracles associated with the exodus of the Jews from ancient Egypt, for instance, which are taken by Jews (and Christians) to confirm the special status of Moses and the teachings (such as the Ten Commandments) revealed to him. For instance, when the Jews were trapped on the shores of the Red Sea by the pursuing Egyptian army, it is related in the Bible that the waters parted to allow them to cross safely and closed again to destroy their pursuers. Maybe, as has been suggested, it is possible to find a scientific explanation of how freak weather and tidal conditions in that part of the world might make it possible to cross safely for a short period. But no one imagines that there could be a scientific explanation of why those freak – and, if they occur at all, extremely rare – conditions should have prevailed at just such a moment of crisis as faced the Jewish people as they sought to escape from captivity to their homeland. At all events there is no doubt that the Bible presents the parting of the Red Sea to allow the Israelites to escape as a miracle. It was taken as evidence of the favour shown by God to his chosen people. Stories such as this also confirmed the view of Moses as a divinely inspired leader and in turn the divine authority of the books of the Bible attributed to him. The miracles attributed to Moses thus served to give credence to the view that the Ten Commandments were divinely authorized, indeed revealed by God to Moses.

Miracles have also traditionally been important as support for Christian claims about revelation. According to the Anglican theologian Alan Richardson,

traditional Christian theology has always regarded the miracles as the rational grounds by means of which reasonable men may believe truths which go beyond the power of reason to establish.

(Richardson (1947), p. 156)

In support of this he quotes one of the most influential of mediaeval Christian theologians, Thomas Aquinas, as arguing for the Christian revelation on the basis of the miracles which support it. Aquinas thought that, in this respect, Christianity was better founded than, for instance, Islam and criticized Muhammad for failing to offer

> any signs of supernatural agency, which alone are a fitting witness to divine inspiration, since a visible work that can be from God alone proves the teacher of truth to be invisibly inspired.
>
> (*Contra Gentiles* I, vi)

Jesus' status, according to biblical accounts, was confirmed by his ability to perform miracles and this is claimed to have been their purpose. Thus the author of the entry on Miracles in the *New Catholic Encyclopedia* writes:

> The chief purpose of Christ's miracles was to confirm His divine mission. As works of God in an eminent sense, they are a divine seal on the message of revelation Christ claimed to bring from God to man.

The assumption that miracles provide evidence of revelation and so can support the claims of a particular religion was widespread amongst Christian thinkers in the eighteenth century. But that assumption was put in question by the sceptical philosopher David Hume[1] in his classic essay 'Of Miracles'. This essay was written by Hume as a young man but it was not published until 1748. It starts from the assumption that claims to revelations are based upon miracles and these in turn on the evidence of people's senses. Hume attempts to show why it is difficult, though not impossible, to prove that a miracle has ever occurred and claims to establish conclusively that miracles can never serve as the basis for any system of religion. Partly because it is such an important text we will be looking at most of Hume's essay in some detail.

HUME'S CRITICAL APPROACH TO TESTIMONY

Many of our strongest beliefs are either based on or confirmed by our own experience. This is true of many general beliefs we hold, such as that fire is hot. But many other beliefs we hold are based on what others tell us. The reports of others, based on their experience, are referred to by Hume as 'testimony'. Testimony, as we know, is not always reliable. If you are a member of a jury in a criminal trial, you will listen to a great deal of testimony. What one witness says will commonly contradict what is said by another. We expect, in such cases, that some witnesses will have a motive for giving a false account. A jury usually has to decide, in the end, whom to believe and whom not to believe. They need to take a critical approach to testimony. The same is true, Hume takes it for granted, with reports of miracles. Here too there are reasons for being careful about what we accept on the testimony of others. In matters of probability we must always weigh the evidence on either side. This is the principle Hume applies to the 'particular instance' of testimony. He observes that 'there is no species of reasoning more common, more useful and even necessary to human life, than that which is derived from the testimony of men, and the reports of eye witnesses and spectators'. However, testimony varies in its reliability and so needs to be used critically.

We will omit Hume's introductory paragraphs – which may have been topical at the time but which are unnecessarily obscure for the modern reader – and pick up Hume's discussion a little later.

Reading
pp. 155–7

Reading 7 is an extract from David Hume's essay 'Of Miracles'. Read paragraphs 3–10 of the extract and the endnote to paragraph 10 and then attempt Exercises 6.1 and 6.2 below.

EXERCISE 6.1

HUME ON TESTIMONY AND EXPERIENCE (1)

1   What considerations does Hume think should be taken into account in evaluating testimony?
2   Does Hume think the Indian prince who refused to believe the stories about frost when he first heard them was reasonable?

Check your answer against the one at the back of the book before reading on.

EXERCISE 6.2

HUME ON TESTIMONY AND EXPERIENCE (2)

What do you think was Hume's point in mentioning the case of the Indian prince?

DISCUSSION

The point of mentioning the case of the Indian prince is that he was obviously and uncontroversially wrong and yet was (Hume thought) quite justified in his reasoning. People could be wrong in rejecting an extraordinary story even though they reasoned entirely justly. Hume's point is that, although we can only rely on our experience in such matters, our experience is limited and so our own past experience can lead us to false conclusions.

HUME'S CASE AGAINST MIRACLES

Reading
pp. 157–8, 161

We are now approaching the heart of Hume's argument. Please read paragraphs 11 and 12, including the endnote for paragraph 12, of Reading 7 (the extract from David Hume's essay 'Of Miracles'). Then attempt Exercise 6.3.

EXERCISE 6.3

HUME ON MIRACLES AND LAWS OF NATURE

1 What does Hume mean by a 'law of nature'?
2 What definitions does he give of a 'miracle'? Which is the more important in the context of his argument?
3 Why does he think that 'the proof against a miracle, from the very nature of the fact, is as entire as any argument from experience can possibly be imagined'?

Check your answer against the one at the back of the book before reading on.

DISCUSSION

I have used the word 'exception' where Hume talks about a 'violation' or a 'transgression'. Hume uses the metaphorical language appropriate to the idea that the *laws of nature* are *ordained* by somebody and so are *obeyed* by nature or *transgressed (broken, violated)* by miracles. This metaphorical language is not strictly appropriate for Hume, given that he does not believe that God ordains the laws of nature. But he is not setting out to offer a contentious definition of miracles.

What Hume offers is indeed a *strict* definition of miracles. There are those who would admit as miracles what in his terminology (see paragraphs 10 and 11) should be called *marvels*. But that broader definition includes miracles in the strict sense. The problem about marvels is that, though remarkable, it is not clear that they need be understood in supernatural terms. From the point of view of the Indian prince, ice is a marvel. Hume's contrast between a person in good health suddenly dropping dead (a mere marvel) and a dead person coming back to life (a miracle) exemplifies the distinction he has in mind.

Hume moves on to offer a 'general maxim' which summarizes his argument to date.

Now read paragraph 13 of Reading 7 (the extract from David Hume's essay 'Of Miracles'). Then attempt Exercise 6.4.

Reading
p. 158

EXERCISE 6.4

HUME ON MIRACLES

1 What is the 'general maxim' that Hume gives?
2 Does Hume consider that miracles are absolutely impossible?

Check your answer against the one at the back of the book before reading on.

THE POSSIBILITY OF MIRACLES

At the beginning of Part II of his essay, Hume writes that he has been too liberal in conceding that 'the testimony, upon which a miracle is founded, may possibly amount to a full proof'. He goes on to claim that 'there never was a miraculous event established on so full an evidence' (paragraph 14, not reproduced in Reading 7). He gives four reasons for thinking that, in practice, it would never be reasonable to conclude that it would be more miraculous were the testimony false than it would be if the event itself had occurred. These reasons are, in sum:

1 History does not provide us with cases of miracles that are attested to by a sufficient number of credible witnesses. Neither have they occurred in circumstances where all doubt as to fraud can be ruled out.
2 Human beings are naturally credulous because they find it agreeable to hear and relate remarkable stories.
3 Reports of miracles are found chiefly among 'ignorant and barbarous nations' and become less and less frequent as we approach 'the enlightened ages'.
4 The testimony for miracles that favour one system of religion is contradicted by the testimony for miracles favouring others.

Hume concludes that no human testimony can have such force as to prove a miracle as a foundation for a particular system of religion. We will come back to this conclusion. It is worth observing, however, that there could be miracles that are proved from human testimony. Hume even constructs an example to show the kind of case where he thinks the testimony should be accepted even though it could only be true if a miracle had occurred. This is in paragraph 36.

 Reading p.159

Now read paragraph 36 of Reading 7, the extract from David Hume's essay 'Of Miracles'. (We will look at paragraphs 24 and 35 later.) Then attempt Exercise 6.5.

EXERCISE 6.5

HUME'S EXAMPLE OF A POSSIBLE MIRACLE

Do you think Hume was right on his own terms to accept this as an example of a miracle?

DISCUSSION

One way to answer this question is to consider whether it is free of the four characteristic flaws of miracle stories given earlier. Hume seems to have constructed an example where there are a large number of witnesses who have no particular motive for believing that the earth was covered with darkness, where the story is not particular to a single culture and not connected with any particular religion. The example seems to have been constructed to be free of these flaws and so to serve Hume's purpose well enough.

Incidentally, it is likely that Hume's choice of example was made partly as a thinly veiled attack on the Christian story about a darkness that covered 'the land' at the time when Jesus was crucified (Matthew 27: 45). This miracle story was flawed at just the points where Hume's concocted miracle story would have been strong: that is, it lacked the cross-cultural testimony and the testimony of people who had no religious motive for believing it.

EXERCISE 6.6

HUME'S DEFINITIONS OF MIRACLES

Compare the way Hume speaks of miracles in paragraph 36 with the two defini-tions of miracle he gave earlier in the essay (paragraph 12 and endnote). Is Hume's use of the term in paragraph 36 consistent with his earlier definitions?

DISCUSSION

In paragraph 36 Hume seems to introduce a weaker definition of 'miracle' than either of the ones he introduced in paragraph 12. Miracles, in the apparently weaker sense, are 'violations of the usual course of nature', which seems to be something in between a marvel and a miracle in the strict sense. The example he gives of a total darkness over the whole earth for a period of eight days is, however, of a miracle in the strict sense for it has been the *uniform* experience of humankind (to date) that such an event does not occur. Here we come back to the point that, though laws of nature are established by a uniform experience, human experience is limited. That means that, like the Indian prince, we can quite reason-ably generalize from our experience to what later evidence shows was a false conclusion. In retrospect we can still say that it was a violation of the usual course of nature as experienced by Indians (living in low altitudes) for water to turn solid and in the same sense it is a violation of the usual course of nature as we have experienced it for there to be darkness over the earth for a period of eight days. Hume's error here looks like an inconsistency but it may be that he has simply slipped into speaking with the benefit of hindsight. For we can be mistaken about what the laws of nature are. And, when we are, we mistake the usual course of nature for a law of nature.

This interpretation is confirmed by Hume's own reaction to the hypothetical miracle being proved: 'our present philosophers, instead of doubting the fact, ought to receive it as certain, and ought to search for the causes whence it might be derived'. What Hume seems to be saying here is that the admission of a viola-tion of the accepted laws of nature makes it necessary for scientists to revise their view of how certain events come about. He even seems to think that the estab-lished order of nature might itself be subject to decay and dissolution. But, whatever the story, it is significant that he does not consider introducing a deity or an invisible agent. In conceding that this hypothetical case would be a miracle he is using the term consistently with his use in paragraph 12 but not consistently with the more 'accurate' definition he gives in his note. For, in accordance with that more 'accurate' definition, conceding that something is a miracle would be conceding that some god or invisible agent brought it about. Hume makes no such concession.

ALLEGED MIRACLES AS THE FOUNDATION OF RELIGIONS

Hume's strongest conclusion in the essay 'Of Miracles' is that no miracle can be proved so as to be the foundation of any system of religion. He argues for this most directly in paragraphs 24, 35 and 37–8.

 Reading pp. 158–60

Now read paragraphs 24, 35 and 37–8 of Reading 7 (the extract from David Hume's essay 'Of Miracles'). Then attempt Exercises 6.7 and 6.8 below.

EXERCISE 6.7

MIRACLES AS FOUNDATION FOR RELIGION (1)

Why is Hume unwilling to admit even an imaginary case where the testimony in favour of a miracle might be established so as to be the foundation of a system of religion?

Check your answer against the one at the back of the book before reading on.

EXERCISE 6.8

MIRACLES AS FOUNDATION FOR RELIGION (2)

Is Hume justified in not admitting a case where the evidence for a miracle might be such as to provide the foundation of a system of religion?

DISCUSSION

In the imaginary example of the darkness over the earth for eight days there was neither the mutual destruction of testimony which Hume thought there was where a miracle favours one religion to the exclusion of others, nor was there an evident motive for witnesses to lie. In these ways Hume is not being arbitrary in accepting the possibility of miracles which are mere violations of the usual course of nature but denying that miracles could be so proved as to be the foundation of a system of religion.

HUME ON FAITH AND REASON

Hume concludes his essay with two paragraphs (40 and 41) in which he reiterates some of its main themes and draws his conclusions.

Now read paragraphs 40 and 41 of Reading 7 (the extract from David Hume's essay 'Of Miracles'). Then attempt Exercise 6.9.

EXERCISE 6.9

FAITH AND REASON

1   Is what Hume writes in paragraph 40 consistent with his accepting the truth of the stories told in the Pentateuch? (The Pentateuch is that part of the Hebrew Bible and the Christian Old Testament – the first five books – traditionally supposed to have been written by Moses.)
2   What do you think Hume means when he concludes that 'the *Christian Religion* not only was at first attended with miracles, but even at this day cannot be believed by any reasonable person without one'?

DISCUSSION

1   Hume has engaged in an exercise of supposing that the Pentateuch was 'the production of a mere human writer and historian' rather than 'the word or testimony of God himself'. If we look at these writings as an historical document, then, on the principle of rejecting the greater miracle, we would conclude that the stories they tell are untrue. I do not think there is any reason to doubt that Hume himself thought the Pentateuch should be considered critically in the light of the historian's 'measures of probability'. There is no reason either to doubt that he considered the stories surrounding the Exodus from Egypt (such as the miraculous parting of the Red Sea to allow the Israelites, but not their enemies, to escape in safety) to be mere fabrications. But the question was whether what he wrote is *consistent* with accepting the truth of those stories. The answer is 'Yes'. Hume allows a loophole for those who want to believe the stories are true. They can refuse to subject the Bible 'to such a trial as it is, by no means, fitted to endure' and assert that it is not the production of a mere human writer at all but the word of God. This Hume links with the main thesis of the final paragraphs: 'Our most holy religion is founded on *Faith*, not on reason.' There is no contradiction therefore in believing both that there is no basis for accepting the stories of the Pentateuch as a work of history and yet at the same time accepting them as true (on faith).
2   Throughout these last two paragraphs Hume seems to be writing with the deliberate intention that he could be read in more than one way. Superficially he is advocating the position known as *fideism* – a position which many Scottish clergymen of his time would have endorsed and which was developed philosophically by such figures as Michel de Montaigne and Pierre Bayle. This position is characterized by an extreme scepticism about the power of human reason, which reduces people to a hopeless state of

uncertainty from which they can only be rescued by divine revelation. Scepticism about reason is thus combined with a profession of intense religious faith. (The Latin word for 'faith' is *fides* and the word 'fideism' is constructed from it.) Montaigne and Bayle were apparently quite sincere in their religious fideism. Hume, moreover, was a great admirer of Bayle. But, surrounded as he perceived himself to be by religious bigotry (of which he was to some extent a victim), he did not think he owed it to the public to be sincere with them. In these paragraphs he is being ironic, deliberately setting out to confuse his less discerning readers. His true beliefs are expressed earlier in his remark that 'a wise man ... proportions his belief to the evidence' (paragraph 4). The miracle of faith is a subversion of the basis on which we normally form our beliefs. Faith is therefore, on Hume's account, the characteristic not of wise people but of fools.

HUME'S CRITIQUE OF RELIGIOUS FAITH

These final paragraphs are quite a dense piece of writing and you may have rightly been struck by details on which I have made no comment. It becomes clear that Hume is attacking not only miracles but also prophecies, which he claims are a kind of miracle. His apparent fideism is a thinly disguised attack on revealed religion as a whole. Indeed, if his final remarks are ironic, he is rejecting even the possibility of sincere religious belief. Miracles are violations of the uniformly experienced order of nature. Nature, for Hume, includes not only the world studied by the natural sciences but also the human world. Thus the way our beliefs are formed, for Hume, is just as regular as any process in the natural world. Hume no more believes that there are internal miracles that subvert the principles of our understanding than he believes that there are external miracles that violate the established laws of nature. In linking faith with miracles he is doubting whether people really believe those things in which they profess to have faith.

This point needs a little explanation. Hume's essay 'Of Miracles' was placed in his *Enquiry Concerning Human Understanding* after a section entitled 'Of the Reason of Animals'. In this earlier section Hume had tried to show that animals form their beliefs in much the same way as previously he had claimed that humans do. In doing this he was not so much placing animals in the human world as making humans part of the natural world. One of Hume's main contentions in the *Enquiry* was that there are natural processes by which beliefs are formed, that there are — so to speak — laws of nature governing belief. One of the key elements in his account is what he calls 'custom', which for Hume is the great guide through life. Our beliefs about the world are formed above all by repetitions in our experience to which we become accustomed and which establish connections and eventually beliefs in our minds. It would require a miracle to believe 'contrary to custom and experience' as Hume pretends to claim actually happens with faith. But the discerning reader who has read the whole of the book in which the essay is included would be able to apply Hume's critique of miracles to the supposed miracle of faith itself. Fideists, according to this analysis, do not really believe what they profess to believe.

Hume does not hold that no one is sincere in religious belief. Only he really thinks that its true basis is in natural religion and not at all in revelation. He does not doubt the sincerity of those who believe that the existence of a providence who designed the universe can be inferred from the order we detect in it. He rejects the argument for design, which he argues against in the next section of his *Enquiry* and in his posthumously published *Dialogues Concerning Natural Religion*. But he takes it very seriously.

One outcome of Hume's treatment of faith is to suggest that fideism and scepticism about religion, so far from being as diametrically opposed as they might at first seem to be, are surprisingly close to one another. So far as trying to be rational about religious beliefs is concerned, the fideist and the sceptic are entirely agreed. There is no rational basis for Christianity or for any other religion. Curiously, though fideists may sincerely be trying to free religious belief from the demands of philosophers, the effect of their protestations may be to encourage scepticism.

Certainly the view of faith taken by Hume and his fideist predecessors as contrary to reason has seemed to others unsatisfactory. That controversy about the nature of religious faith and its relation to reason is one we will explore further in the next, concluding, chapter.

SUMMARY

In this chapter we have considered an argument for accepting revealed religion that depends on the idea that someone's words are likely to be divinely inspired if at least some of their deeds are miraculous. We have also considered Hume's objections to such an argument. Hume argues, in the first place, that there is no evidence sufficient to establish that any of the claimed historical miracles actually occurred. Indeed, by the very nature of the case – a miracle being contrary to the uniform experience of humankind – it is unlikely that the initial evidence against a miracle will ever be outweighed by the evidence in favour of it. But, in the second place, even though it is possible to imagine a case where this does happen, the miracle story would be quite different from one that supported one particular system of religion.

Christianity, for Hume, is only founded on miracles in the sense that it requires a miracle of faith for anyone to believe it. And, while Hume's conclusion was deliberately ambiguous, the interpretation favoured was that such faith was, for him, irrational – a subversion of reason. The question that remains to be considered, however, is whether Hume's account of belief is one that can be as readily applied to religious beliefs as to beliefs about the natural order.

FURTHER READING

Hume's essay is the starting-point for most recent discussions of miracles. Some, like J. L. Mackie's *The Miracle of Theism* (Clarendon Press, 1982), offer an updated version of Hume's argument. An alternative conception of what a miracle is from Hume's was offered by R. F. Holland in 'The Miraculous', *American Philosophical Quarterly* 2 (1965), 43–51. A good modern treatment of Hume's arguments is J. Houston's *Reported Miracles: A Critique of Hume* (Cambridge University Press, 1994). Two good selections of writings on this topic are *Miracles*, ed. R. Swinburne (Macmillan, 1989) and *Questions of Miracle*, ed. R. A. H. Larmer (McGill-Queen's University, 1996).

NOTE

1   David Hume (1711–76) spent most of his life in Edinburgh, where he was born. His first book, *A Treatise of Human Nature* (1739–40), is one of the greatest philosophical works in the English language. He decided not to include his essay 'Of Miracles' and published it only later in his *Philosophical Essays* (1748), later and better known as his *Enquiries*. His *Dialogues Concerning Natural Religion* were published, posthumously, in 1779. The best book on Hume's philosophy of religion is Gaskin (1978).

7 | Faith and reason

OBJECTIVES

By the end of your work on this chapter you should:

- Be able to expound and evaluate Clifford's argument that it is always wrong to go beyond the evidence in our belief.
- Be able to explain and critically comment on Pascal's wager.
- Be able to explain William James's position in relation to Clifford's argument and Pascal's wager and evaluate his defence of religious faith.
- Have extended your familiarity with philosophy by studying two classical texts on the subject of religious faith and one of the classical arguments for it.
- Have further developed your skills in reading and analysing philosophical texts.
- Have further developed your skills in philosophical argument, particularly in relation to the use of counter-examples.

Many different accounts have been given, by philosophers and religious thinkers generally, of the nature of faith. It is usually taken to be a kind of belief. On Hume's account it is a belief which is miraculously held *contrary to* reason. But faith is more commonly supposed to be *above or beyond* reason than contrary to it. Faith does, therefore, involve belief which goes beyond the evidence. To that extent it is like a conjecture, a guess or a speculation rather than a well-judged belief. Hume, as we saw in the previous chapter, held that wise people *proportion* their beliefs to the evidence. There are many instances where this seems right: our opinions about what the weather is going to be like, whether there is life on Mars, whether sweeteners are harmful for our health, and so on, are based, directly or indirectly, on the evidence that is available to us. The stronger the evidence, the more we are convinced. Most of us only have opinions worth listening to on a few matters and rely most of the time on the evidence of experts – weather forecasters, scientists, doctors, and so on. But in these cases we have opinions about the reliability of the experts. These opinions are in turn based on evidence. They can be more or less reasonable. If, for instance, I never believed the weather forecast because they sometimes got it wrong, that would seem to most people to be unreasonable. On the other hand, it may be that there are outlying parts of a region for which the general forecast is too often wrong to be worth relying on though the forecast is generally reliable for most of the region.

In everyday matters the more we proportion our beliefs to the evidence the less likely we are to be wrong. With beliefs there is always some risk of being wrong. But, by proportioning our beliefs to the evidence, we only believe strongly that something will turn out in a particular way when the chances are relatively small that it will not. We will not expect rain firmly if the forecast informs us that there is only a 10 per cent chance that rain will fall. But we might take an umbrella.

Those who do not proportion their beliefs to the evidence may not only run the risk of being wrong but run other risks as well, e.g. the risk of getting wet. But those whose beliefs are out of proportion to the evidence do not always run risks for themselves. Those who engage in casual generalizations about other people may be disadvantaging those others and not at all themselves. In these cases the belief they arrive at is called a *bias* or a *prejudice*. When it comes to forming our beliefs about other people we are expected to be fair. This is important to the extent that unfavourable beliefs can do them harm or excessively favourable beliefs can do them an undeserved good. These points apply with particular force to people such as magistrates, referees and examiners. Such persons, in their professional roles, are expected to be *objective* in their beliefs.

Though we might agree, however, that objectivity (freeing oneself from personal bias etc.) was something to aspire to in certain contexts, it may not be appropriate to aspire to it in every situation. No one usually criticizes sporting fans for holding stronger beliefs about the likely success of their teams than commentators would think warranted by the evidence. For not only is such a belief in itself harmless but it is even associated in many cases with the exercise of a virtue, namely loyalty, for instance to the fan's home town. Loyalty, where it is owed, may prevent people from being objective and even, in certain cases, make it right to hold a belief that is not proportioned to the evidence. Parents who refuse to believe that their sons are guilty of the crimes with which they are charged are not criticized for being not objective. On the contrary, they would be criticized if they merely said 'we will have to see what evidence is produced in court'. People are, unfortunately, sometimes wrongfully convicted and parents may continue to give their children the benefit of the doubt and continue to believe them to be innocent even when the evidence has seemed pretty conclusive to others. Their continuing to believe in their innocence may never be publicly vindicated. But, if it is, the media do not bill it as a case of biased relatives turning out to be right in spite of being unreasonable. The parents in such cases are cast as heroes and heroines, who stood by their convicted children in spite of the evidence and the public acrimony against them. Whether or not they are publicly vindicated, their continuing belief may also be called *faith*.

FAITH AND 'THE ETHICS OF BELIEF'

The example of the loyal parent is not, of course, an example of *religious* faith. None the less it may help to make sense of the idea that faith, even though it involves a stronger belief than the evidence supports, might be a virtue. The word *faith* carries with it particular connotations, as used by religious people, and implies that we should look favourably on the situation of anyone who shows it. But that implies a particular reading of the situation. A less favourable interpretation might be made, for instance, where it is thought that the parents are blinding themselves to the facts. In that case it might be better if the family learned to accept what had happened and showed its loyalty by helping the convicted son to come to terms with his crime and build for the future. What looks to one person like faith might look to another like escapism. It can look like faith to those who think they *could* be right or that they are actually right. It is only those for whom there is no question of their being right that it will seem like escapism.

In these remarks I have tried to suggest some links between faith and certain other ideas or concepts. I have suggested that the word faith is only used where it is regarded as a good thing to believe something and where to do so is to go beyond the evidence. There is nothing particularly profound about this. Those who think it is never good to believe in this way – who think we should only believe in proportion to the evidence – will not use the word 'faith' at all, except perhaps (as Hume did) ironically. What some call faith others may call superstition.

The claim that the wise proportion their beliefs to the evidence became a scientific orthodoxy for some in the nineteenth century. It was defended by the mathematician and philosopher of science W. K. Clifford[1] in an article entitled 'The Ethics of Belief' (Clifford, 1877a). Clifford sought to uphold the view that 'it is wrong always, everywhere, and for anyone, to believe anything upon insufficient evidence'. His article provoked a reply from the important American philosopher William James, in a lecture published in *The Will to Believe and Other Essays* (1897) which defended going beyond the evidence in belief as a practical necessity in a range of matters, including matters of religious faith. We will be looking at this controversy in some detail. But first let us look at what Clifford has to say.

CLIFFORD ON 'THE ETHICS OF BELIEF'

As I have just indicated, Clifford holds that 'it is wrong always, everywhere, and for anyone, to believe anything upon insufficient evidence'. These are the last words of the Clifford extract and sum up the position for which he has been arguing in the preceding paragraphs. We are here interested to know what argument is to be found in the preceding paragraphs for that conclusion. And this is a case where it is useful, at least to begin with, to skim-read in order get a broad grasp of the argument.

Read the Clifford extract from 'The Ethics of Belief' (Reading 8) through quickly and attempt Exercise 7.1.

Reading
pp. 163–8

EXERCISE 7.1

SKIM-READING

Make a note in a sentence or two of what you take to be the drift of Clifford's argument in Reading 8.

Check your answer against the one at the back of the book before reading on.

DISCUSSION

Clifford's conclusion would, of course, involve a very rash generalization if it were simply based on two examples. If a man tells us he has been to Skye twice in June and it rained both times, we would not think much of his conclusion if he went on without any more ado to claim that it rains all the time in Skye in June. For there is an obvious difference between something being true some of the time and it being true all of the time. Likewise it does not follow *without any more ado* from the fact that it is sometimes wrong to believe on insufficient evidence that it is always wrong.

There is, however, more to Clifford's argument. His examples are intended to be more than persuasive examples of where someone believes without sufficient evidence. But what more? We need to look at the extract again, to find what other purpose the examples serve.

EXERCISE 7.2

ETHICS OF BELIEF

Read the extract again and try to find what makes Clifford's argument stronger than that of someone who is merely arguing that because something is true in two cases it is true in all.

DISCUSSION

The examples are taken by Clifford to be illustrative of what he goes on to claim is a quite general feature of belief. The reason why, in the examples, it was thought wrong to believe on insufficient evidence is that belief is never a purely private matter (paragraph 10). It is because believing on insufficient evidence has some bad effect on others that it is wrong. But, Clifford goes on to claim, it is a quite general feature of belief that it always has some effect ('no belief held by one man, however seemingly trivial the belief, and however obscure the believer, is ever actually insignificant or without its effect on the fate of mankind'). Moreover, as Clifford goes on to argue in paragraph 11, this effect, in the case of what is believed on insufficient evidence, is always harmful.

Clifford's ethics are quite close in some respects to *utilitarianism*. The consequences of what we believe for society is, for him a crucial consideration: 'no belief ... is ever ... without its effect on the destiny of mankind'. He claims that 'fatal superstitions' can 'clog' a whole race and that what mothers inculcate in their children may either 'knit society together, or rend it in pieces'. Credulity, he insists, is a 'danger to society'; 'The credulous man is father to the liar and the cheat'. And there are other remarks that suggest that the effect on the welfare of society is what makes something right or wrong. But Clifford makes no mention of happiness or similar notions, still less of the sum of human happiness. He writes as if the very survival of human society were at risk and his language ('destiny', 'danger', 'rend it [society] in pieces') is quite dramatic. But his concern with the very survival of society and indeed the 'destiny' of the human race and the danger of superstition begins to fall in place when we learn that Clifford, although brought up as a Christian, was converted by some of Darwin's more militant followers to a strongly anti-religious form of Darwinism. His ethics are based upon Darwin, whose *Descent of Man* provided 'the simplest and clearest and most profound philosophy that was ever written' on the conscience. Clifford believed, on Darwin's authority, that humans have evolved a conscience because it was useful for the community or tribe in its struggle against other tribes or in its struggle for survival generally. As Clifford puts it elsewhere:

> The function of conscience is the preservation of the tribe as a tribe. And we rightly train our consciences if we learn to approve those actions which tend to the advantage of the community in its struggle for existence.
>
> (Clifford (1875))

Clifford took it that not only conscience but also ethics had a biological and therefore scientific basis. He insisted that conscience was 'the voice of Man within us, commanding us to work for Man' (Clifford (1877a)), deliberately choosing the phrase *the voice of Man* in opposition to the common view that conscience is *the voice of God* within us. Clifford held that his humanism, if we can call it that, promoted the good order of society whereas religion undermined conscience and morality by making duties primarily to God:

> When men respect human life for the sake of Man, tranquillity, order and progress go hand in hand; but those who only respected human life because God had forbidden murder have set their mark upon Europe in fifteen centuries of blood and fire.
>
> (Clifford (1877b))

Clifford, as we have seen, subscribes to an ethical theory according to which right and wrong are determined by what is necessary for the survival of the community. Of the mainstream theories, it is most like utilitarianism. But whereas it is quite natural for a utilitarian to extend concern to all creatures capable of feeling pleasure and pain, Clifford's ethics are confined to human beings, in so far as they depend on the idea that we have a biological urge to ensure the survival of our own species.

EXERCISE 7.3

VALIDITY

Assume that Clifford's argument can be represented as follows:

1 People have a biological urge to ensure the survival of their own species.
2 Therefore, people ought to act in a way that is likely to ensure the survival of their own species.

Is this a *valid* argument? If not, how could it be made into one?
Check your answer against the one at the back of the book before reading on.

DISCUSSION

That additional premise is, of course, controversial. But, in any case, the 'Darwinian' premise that Clifford bases his argument upon is no longer assumed by modern Darwinists. The actions of the individual, according to neo-Darwinism, are not designed to perpetuate the species as such but only their gene pool. Thus, even if the argument were made valid, it is *unsound*.

Despite the differences, Clifford's ethics have much in common with the utilitarianism of Jeremy Bentham. They largely agree, for instance, in putting the interest of the community above that of the individual and in making the consequences for the wider community crucial to whether something is right or wrong. Yet even here there is a significant difference in that, for the utilitarian, the individual always counts for one (if no more) whereas in Clifford's ethics the fate of individuals is unimportant in itself, so long as the position of society is not affected.

One reason why it is useful to identify Clifford's general ethical position is that it becomes apparent how it might be possible to argue against him on his own terms. For he is arguing that, *as a matter of fact*, believing on insufficient evidence *always* has a bad effect.

EXERCISE 7.4

CONSTRUCTING AN ARGUMENT

How might it be possible to argue against Clifford's conclusion that it is always wrong to believe on insufficient evidence?

DISCUSSION

I was hoping you would say: by producing a *counter-example*, where it is right to believe on insufficient evidence, even better if it is socially beneficial. You may have gone on to produce your own counter-example. I mentioned earlier that we might think that someone can believe something on insufficient evidence out of loyalty (of a parent to a child who is accused of wrongdoing, for example). We can add that loyalty might be represented as a virtue in evolutionary terms, as conducive to the survival of society. This might be put forward as a counter-example to Clifford's conclusion.

As this counter-example is illustrative, I will not discuss it in detail, partly because we will be looking at others when we come to the criticisms made by William James. Logically, a single counter-example would be enough to refute Clifford's conclusion. But it needs to be a counter-example he cannot reasonably refuse. In practice there are often difficulties that can be raised against a counter-example in defence of the claim it is intended to refute. Someone who shared Clifford's commitment to the 'purity of belief' might argue that loyalty requires parents to hope their child is innocent, to be willing to stand by the child anyway, but not to be willing to believe the child's story beyond what is supported by evidence. Quite often it is necessary to try out a variety of counter-examples before one is found that is widely accepted in the philosophical community as pointing to a serious difficulty with a general claim such as Clifford's.

EXERCISE 7.5

CLIFFORD AND FAITH

What view of faith do you think is implied in Clifford's article?

DISCUSSION

Clifford does not use the word 'faith' but, if faith is belief that goes beyond the evidence, then it involves what he calls 'credulity'. Clifford thinks credulity is harmful to society. He does not specify any of 'the fatal superstitions which clog [the human] race' or how mothers can transmit to their children beliefs that 'rend ... society in pieces' or how credulous societies can slip back into 'savagery'.

Clifford is not opposed to all religious belief as such but only to the way in which it is commonly held. In this respect he is not unlike Hume, for instance, when he writes that 'religious beliefs must be founded on evidence; if they are not so founded, it is wrong to hold them'. But, like Hume, he was aware that, in Christianity, people were recommended to believe without evidence. He goes on:

The rule of right conduct in this matter is exactly the opposite of that implied in the two famous texts: 'He that believeth shall not be damned', and 'Blessed are they that have not seen but have believed'. For a man who clearly felt and recognized the duty of intellectual honesty, of carefully testing every belief before he received it, and especially before he recommended it to others, it would be impossible to ascribe the profoundly immoral teaching of these texts to a true prophet or worthy leader of humanity.

(Clifford (1877b))

The texts Clifford attacks are ascribed to Jesus of Nazareth in the Gospels and so Clifford's remarks seem to be completely anti-Christian. Clifford seems, however, to have retained a great respect for Jesus of Nazareth as a moral teacher and goes on to suggest that these passages have been added by the Church. The first, he says, is from 'the well-known forged passage at the end of the second gospel' and the second 'occurs only in the late and legendary fourth gospel'. He concludes by abusing the rascal who perpetrated the fraud by misattributing these words to Jesus, referring to the former as 'a man void of intellectual honesty … who would accept and spread about any kind of baseless fiction for fear of believing too little'. But, whether these two texts were ever spoken by Jesus or not and whatever Clifford's view of Jesus may have been, it seems clear that he, like Hume, must be opposed to faith as commonly understood, which involves belief that goes beyond the evidence. On this cardinal point he was vigorously opposed by William James.[2]

WILLIAM JAMES ON THE WILL TO BELIEVE

William James wrote many defences of religious belief. But his lecture 'The Will to Believe' is probably the most famous. It is divided into ten sections. We will be looking at them in more detail and bit by bit.

Skim-read James's lecture (Reading 9), and attempt Exercise 7.6.

Reading
pp. 169–80

EXERCISE 7.6

JAMES'S 'THE WILL TO BELIEVE'

Note down your impression in one sentence of what each section of Reading 9 is about, including the unnumbered introductory section.

Check your answer against the one at the back of the book before reading on.

Having looked through the extract as a whole you should have an idea of what James is claiming, at least in outline. It is now time to consider some parts of his argument in greater detail. As you will see, if you have not already noticed, there are a number of references to Clifford and it turns out that James's criticisms of Clifford are an important part of his argument. But there is also, in sections II and III, discussion of what is called 'Pascal's wager' – an argument for belief with which James had considerable sympathy.

PASCAL'S WAGER[3]

Blaise Pascal (1623–62) was a brilliant mathematician and philosopher, as well as being a devout Catholic. He compares the choice between believing in God and not believing with the choice of betting one way or another in a game of chance. Pascal has in mind a simple game of tossing a coin where 'either heads or tails may turn up' (Pascal (1973), pp. 93–6). He points out that what it is reasonable to do depends not only on the probabilities but also on the stakes. In the decision whether to believe in God or not, the position, according to Pascal, is this: you stand to gain eternal bliss if you believe in God and you are right and, on the other hand, will lose little or nothing if you believe in God and are wrong. Even if the chances of your being right are not high it is reasonable, Pascal concludes, to stake your all on God.

Read what James has to say about Pascal in sections II and III of his lecture (Reading 9), and attempt Exercise 7.7.

Reading
pp. 171–3

EXERCISE 7.7

JAMES AND PASCAL'S WAGER

Why does James think the argument is less successful with the unbeliever than Pascal hoped? (See section II.) Under what conditions, according to James, would Pascal's argument succeed? (See also section III.) You will need to check back to section I to see what a 'living option' is.

Check your answer against the one at the back of the book before reading on.

James does not accept what he takes to be Pascal's view, that true belief can result from a mere act of will where there was no prior inclination to believe. Talk of believing 'by our volition' is 'simply silly', because belief in such a case is a 'dead option'. The idea that our opinions might be modifiable at will is, from another point of view, highly objectionable ('vile' is James's word) because it is subversive of the discipline of being objective and impartial in our beliefs which is – here he agrees with Huxley and Clifford – at the foundation of science.

There has been much debate in philosophy about whether or not the will can influence belief. It is often linked with discussion of Pascal's wager. But not always. One of Locke's arguments against religious intolerance turns on the claim that while it might be possible to coerce someone into *pretending* to believe something, it is impossible to coerce someone into sincerely *believing* something. Locke wrote: 'To believe this or that is not within the scope of the will.'[4] James's position is not dissimilar, as regards 'dead options', since what is 'irrational' from a Lockean point of view would be 'silly' in his terms. Both would think it irrational for the Inquisition to suppose that those whom they sought to convert by force could simply decide to believe what Catholics believe. But Pascal's position is more subtle than the one Locke rejects. On his account the will could have an indirect effect on belief since it is possible to get into certain habits (for instance, of going to Church, saying prayers and reading the Bible) as a result of an act of will and for these habits in turn gradually to modify belief. James's point seems to extend to the act of will: a Muslim or a Protestant would typically regard the whole project as a 'dead option'. On his account it is a project that might be embarked on by someone with the right religious education and inclination but who professed themselves unable to believe. Pascal's wager might thus work for lapsed Catholics.

JAMES'S CRITICISM OF CLIFFORD

Clifford was not the only, nor the most famous, advocate of the view that it is immoral to go beyond the evidence in our beliefs. Darwin's champion, Huxley, was a bigger name. But Clifford attempted to defend in greater detail and rigour the very views that James was particularly anxious to oppose. That seems to be why James chose to attack him.

EXERCISE 7.8

JAMES ON CLIFFORD

Look back at sections II, III, V and VII of James's lecture and make a note of your answers to these questions:

1   What was it about Clifford's views that James was particularly concerned to oppose?
2   What objections does James make to Clifford?

Check your answers against the ones at the back of the book before reading on.

EXERCISE 7.9

ASSESSING AN ARGUMENT

Do you consider these objections to be reasonable ones?

DISCUSSION

Your answer may well go on rather different lines from mine. But perhaps you spotted that James is guilty of using the word 'empiricist' as what is sometimes called a *persuader word*. He uses it to refer to the kind of person he could expect most of his audience would aspire to be: tolerant – tolerance, we are told towards the end of the lecture, is 'empiricism's glory' – open-minded and willing to accept that they might be wrong. He insinuates that Clifford is not like this. But he actually gives very little evidence. We should, therefore, treat this part of his argument with great caution. In any strict sense of the term 'empiricist' Clifford sounds very much like one – especially in his stress on proportioning our beliefs to the evidence.

The charge of being dogmatically 'anti Christian', which James levels against Clifford, seems to be based on a confusion. For, while Clifford was strongly opposed to Church Christianity and perhaps dogmatic in his rejection of the priesthood, he was more agnostic and open-minded about religion in general.

Although the general criticism of Clifford seems to me more than slightly unfair there is a much more specific criticism made in section VII. This seems to me much closer to the mark. Clifford is concerned only with the harm that he claims is invariably done if people go beyond the evidence in their beliefs. He does not consider that someone who was willing to pursue a hunch might be more likely to arrive at the truth. He is unimpressed by the fact that people who believe on insufficient evidence are sometimes right. It does not occur to him, as it does to James, that the benefits of being right might make the risk of error well worth taking.

Though we are concerned with who is nearer to being right it has to be said that there is much that is unsatisfactory about the arguments on both sides. Clifford is not very convincing when he claims that in every single case when someone goes beyond the evidence in believing something they are doing some harm to 'Man'. It seems easy for James to suggest that mistakes often do not matter very much and to point up the benefits of believing in certain cases where the evidence is not supportive. It is not so clear, however, that Clifford is bound to accept James's examples. A good counter-example to Clifford's claims would be an advance in science that was achieved by going beyond the evidence in believing something. James, however, was in no position to provide such a counter-example. For he conceded that Clifford's view of science was the correct one. He says that there is no 'forced option' in science and here the 'dispassionately judicial intellect … ought to be our ideal' (section VIII). His case is that the same ideal is not appropriate in other areas, like morality and religion, where the options are, in his terms, 'forced'.

We will consider this positive thesis of James's shortly. But it is worth dwelling briefly on the opportunity he missed to make more conclusive objections to Clifford's argument. He accuses Clifford of being excessively nervous in his scientific methodology – so anxious to avoid error that he is like the general who fails to win on the battlefield because he will not risk his troops. But though he shows signs of being dubious about it, he seems to accept Clifford's approach as basically the right one, since this very nervousness is built into scientific method:

Science has organized this nervousness into a regular *technique*, her so-called method of verification; and she has fallen so deeply in love with the method that one may even say she has ceased to care for truth by itself at all.

(Reading 9, section VIII)

Despite the hint of criticism, which he does not follow up, James accepts that it is the correct methodology in science only to conclude what is verified by experiment and observation and to hold back from conclusions where they are not empirically verified. The ideal scientist is portrayed as a 'dispassionately judicial intellect' who is not going to be swayed in his or her judgements except on the basis of a critical examination of the evidence. The scientist, in short, is someone who says 'wait and see'.

This view of science was very much the dominant one in the nineteenth century and remained a commonplace long after it became untenable. Science since Newton had appeared to grow step by step and, by the use of the correct method, was thought to be constantly building. It was assumed that Newton's theories had been verified and were a permanent part of the theoretical edifice which was constantly being extended. But, to give a very sketchy summary, scientists came to find difficulty in squaring their results with Newton. Einstein eventually came up with a quite different theory. Most relevantly, Einstein was guilty of a flagrant breach of the accepted methodology since what he produced was rich in speculation and not verified. None the less it proved possible to make precise predictions on the basis of Einstein's theory which, when there was an opportunity to test them, turned out to be astonishingly accurate. Partly for this kind of reason it came to be accepted by the scientific community. The result of this was a revolution in the philosophy of science. Out went the view that science progressed by steady and sure steps on the principle of not believing things until they had been verified. Philosophers of science began to accept that science could progress in less gradual ways and some even thought it progressed through revolutions.[5] William James did indeed hold that science was fallible and in this respect he differed from the 'scientific absolutists' like Clifford. But he was writing before Einstein and his scientific interests were in psychology and not in physics anyway.

I have mentioned Einstein to explain why the scientific community has abandoned the ideal of scientists as detached observers who wait till the evidence forces them to accept something before they believe it. But Einstein was not the first successful scientist who departed from the method of verification. The revolution in the philosophy of science has led historians of science to look quite differently at the successful scientists of the past and to tell their stories differently. There were counter-examples – Darwin himself may have been one[6]– which James might have pressed against Clifford. But it seems not to have occurred to him to challenge Clifford on this ground. As things stand he needs to make a great deal out of a vague and unsatisfactory dichotomy between our passional and our intellectual natures, allowing scientific method the supremacy over the latter but claiming the freer method for morality and religion. Clifford might have countered that this was special pleading and would certainly have waxed eloquent on the harm done by religious prejudices and on the particular reason not to be less intellectually rigorous in such matters.

There are other respects in which James's criticisms of Clifford are less effective than they might have been. One problem is that, whereas Clifford really is concerned with the *ethics* of belief, James is at best concerned to defend the right to believe something for which there is insufficient evidence. He is more concerned to argue on the ground of *prudence* than duty, following Pascal's wager, and assumes, contrary to Clifford, that there are cases where the risk involved in believing on insufficient evidence is my own and has no implications for others.

We should pass on to consider James's positive claims in their own right. But, as we are about to leave Clifford behind, it may be useful to summarize where we have got to. Clifford is opposed to faith where this is understood as belief that goes beyond the evidence. He claims that we have a duty to humankind not to indulge in such belief. But he is not convincing in his claim that such belief is invariably harmful and calling the tendency to it *credulity* – an acknowledged intellectual vice – is using a persuader word. There seem, contrary to what he claims, to be examples where it is good to go beyond the evidence in what one believes. Clifford supposes that the same rigorous standards of evidence should be extended to other areas (including religious belief) as apply in science. But, even supposing that this is so, Clifford's view of the good scientist is open to counter-example. It is not even true in science that it is always wrong to go beyond the evidence in what is believed.

JAMES'S DEFENCE OF RELIGIOUS FAITH

It is time to complete our reading of James's lecture. He has already been developing his own views in his critical evaluation of Pascal and Clifford and the seven introductory sections prepare the ground for the remaining three.

Read sections VIII to X of James's lecture (Reading 9). James defends this thesis as applied to religious belief in section X, and so he fulfils his advertised aim of offering a justification of faith.

Reading
pp. 176–80

Then turn back to section IV where he states his thesis generally – it is in italics.

EXERCISE 7.10

JAMES'S ARGUMENT

What do you think of James's argument? Are there good points? Is it open to objection and criticism? Make a note of your responses.

DISCUSSION

I have criticized James's vague dichotomy between our passional and intellectual natures. And there is much about his language that, however appropriate for a popular lecture, is too loose to be satisfactory in a written text. There is too much rhetoric and not enough close argument. None the less he often seems to be pointing in the right direction. His notion of a 'forced option', for instance, is an original contribution. There are cases where we need to make up our minds what to believe even though there simply is not enough evidence to settle the matter. However, I am not convinced about its application to religion. Not so many people nowadays would share his perception of religion as a '*momentous*' option. James himself appreciated that Pascal's wager was not a 'living option' for a Muslim or a

Protestant. He even acknowledged that there might be those in his audience for whom the religious hypothesis 'cannot, by any living possibility be true'. They, he suggested, 'need go no farther'. It is not recorded how many, if any, left his lecture at this point. But I imagine that in an average university audience nowadays there would be a number who would, or who would be sorely tempted to do so. Even those who might consider the truth of a particular religion a possibility may not perceive that it was a 'forced option'.

The root of the difficulty seems to be that the choice is not seen as one between 'the religious hypothesis' and 'the field'. James seems to have thought that, at bottom, there is only one religion and that the choice was between 'taking the world religiously' and not doing so. But this seems to be over-simple. The field is full of religions, many of which warn us of the dire consequences of not backing them and require big sacrifices if we do. People need to put up what might be a high stake for what, looked at in betting terms, is the very remote chance that they are on what James calls 'the winning side'. There is a problem as to whether it really is, in his own terms, prudent and rational for him to back whatever choice he makes.

James argues that people should have the right to do this. He seems to have regarded it as a matter of toleration or perhaps even respect: we should be free to believe (or do) in matters of religion, since the risk is ours alone. Others ought to respect our beliefs even if they cannot share them and we ought to respect their beliefs even though they are not 'options' for us. People should not be pressured in matters of religious belief by those (such as Clifford) who want to deny anyone the right to hold beliefs that are not wholly supported by the evidence.

I think there is an even more serious problem arising from James's dichotomy between our passional and intellectual natures. Even if it is granted that our passional natures come more to the fore in questions of human relations and religion than they do in science, James goes too far in the direction of denying that our intellectual natures have any business in determining questions of faith. Faith would not be faith if it were entirely determined by reason. But reason usually plays some part in predisposing us to hold those beliefs which involve going beyond the evidence in their favour.

FAITH, SCEPTICISM AND TOLERATION

In this book we have considered a few of the fundamental religious questions people ask. Some philosophers have thought that there were conclusive answers to some of these questions. Some have thought, for instance, that the immortality of the soul or the existence of God can be proved. That would mean that it was unreasonable to doubt the immortality of the soul or the existence of God. Others have thought, on the other hand, that there was conclusive evidence that the soul did not survive death or against believing that there was a wholly good and omnipotent God. That would mean that it was unreasonable to believe in immortality or in God and that such faith, held in the teeth of this evidence, would be contrary to reason. These bold strategies to eliminate doubt at one extreme or faith at the other do not, in my opinion, succeed. My own view is that belief in immortality or in a good God can be more or less reasonable but, at the end of the day, such beliefs are *matters of faith*. They are matters where we should not be indifferent to reason but where, in the end, we go beyond reason; and about which reasonable people can agree to differ and to concede that they might be wrong.

These conclusions, though disappointing in some respects, provide a support for toleration about beliefs one way or the other. James, as we saw, was concerned to oppose the dogmatic extension of the scientific way of forming beliefs to areas such as religion. But Clifford is not a typical example of intolerance against religion, if he is correctly identified as intolerant at all. More typical have been the actions of some Marxist governments to suppress religious groups. Such actions have commonly been defended partly on the ground that religion has a negative role in society (as 'opiate of the people') on a Marxist analysis and partly on the cognitive superiority of Marxism as a science. Scepticism about the claims of Marxism to be scientific has some role to play – though it cannot hope to be a decisive one – in promoting greater toleration.

The same can be said also about religious authoritarianism. It has been common, wherever a particular religion is established in a country, for there to be a problem as to whether those who are not of that religion are to be tolerated. Though tolerance is nowadays widely professed by Christian denominations, few of them until relatively recently had a good record of toleration where they enjoyed the upper hand. Here too they have often thought they had a right to impose their religion on others because they took themselves to have a privileged possession of religious truth.

A clear example is to be found in the writing of a seventeenth-century French Catholic bishop, who defended the use of force in the attempt to convert or at least ensure the religious conformity of Protestants, on the ground that the Church had been given the truth and had been charged with protecting it. Jacques-Bénigne Bossuet (1627–1704) believed that there was a truth which God had revealed to humankind, which was contained in the Gospels, and was attested to by miracles. (This is the kind of view criticized by Hume in his essay 'Of Miracles', as we saw in Chapter 6.) The task of the Church was to be the custodian of this truth and it is in virtue of the faithful discharge of this task that the Church had the right, according to Bossuet, to expect people to believe and worship in accordance with its teachings. The Church was given this task by Christ himself, when he gave the keys of the Kingdom of God to Peter. And the Church has, according to Bossuet, carried out this task:

> The Church of Jesus Christ, watchful guardian of the dogmas committed to its charge, makes no change in them; she adds not, neither does she take away, robbing them of nought that is essential, adding to them nought that is superfluous.[7]
>
> (Quoted in Hazard (1964), p. 233)

Protestants do not, of course, and cannot consistently, accept this account of the basis of the Catholic Church's authority. But Bossuet, believing not only that 'The truth that came from God was perfect in the beginning', but that the Church had been the faithful guardian of this truth, could only see the Protestant alternative of relying on private judgement as to the teaching of the Bible as a sure route to error, heresy and perdition. With such a belief he thought he could justify the use of force, if necessary, to bring Protestants back into line.

Not surprisingly there were Protestant writers who vigorously disputed this claim to possess the truth and so to have the right to impose on those who did not. The French Protestant refugee and philosopher Pierre Bayle[8] (1647–1706) is a noted example. Bayle became a keen opponent of every kind of dogmatism and, particularly through his *Critical and Historical Dictionary* (1697), was an influential exponent of philosophical scepticism. He established for many thinkers of the eighteenth-century *Enlightenment* a link between authoritarianism and dogmatism, on the one hand, and tolerance and scepticism on the other. An authoritarian, like Bossuet, who seeks to put his position on a rational basis, needs to claim the privilege of a knowledge not available to others. Bossuet did not claim this just for himself, of course, but for the (Catholic) Church as a whole. The sceptic, like Bayle, by seeking to subvert dogmatic claims to knowledge is thereby seeking to deprive authoritarianism of any rational basis. Though the effect of such philosophical defences of tolerance in religious matters is hard to assess it was arguably one of the more important contributions by philosophers to modern civilization. If James was right it is a role philosophers should continue to play.

SUMMARY

Two opposing views of religious faith have been considered in this chapter. One is that of Clifford, that faith is a kind of credulity, that to believe anything on insufficient evidence always does harm and so is wrong. The other is the view of James, who argues that, in religious matters, we cannot avoid taking a stand and that we need to risk error in order to achieve truth. James argues that it is more important to achieve truth than to avoid error and that therefore we have a right to believe in the truth of religion. James effectively offers an amended version of Pascal's wager but his version is open to the same objection, namely that he understates the odds against being right in the particular religious hypothesis someone bets on. He also plays down the amount an individual might have to stake. Thus it is less clear than he supposed that someone who chooses to back a particular religious hypothesis is acting prudently.

FURTHER READING

A fuller account of the diversity of views about religious belief can be found in P. Helm's *The Varieties of Belief* (Allen & Unwin, 1973). L. P. Pojman's *Religious Belief and the Will* (Routledge & Kegan Paul, 1986) offers a helpful review of the debate, historical (including Pascal, Clifford and James) and contemporary, as to the role of the will in religious belief. For a fuller critical treatment of fideism, see S. Brown's 'Christian Averroism, Fideism and the "Two-fold Truth"', in *The Philosophy in Christianity*, ed. Godfrey Vesey (Cambridge University Press, 1989), pp. 207–23. For a defence of religious belief consistent with views of rationality appropriate to science, see B. Mitchell's *The Justification of Religious Belief* (Oxford University Press, 1981). Recommended contributions to modern debates about faith and reason include: R. M. Adams's *The Virtue of Faith and Other Essays in Philosophical Theology* (Oxford University Press, 1987), A. Kenny's *What is Faith?* (Oxford University Press, 1992), T. Penelhum's *Reason and Religious Faith* (Westview Press, 1995), *Faith and Rationality*, ed. A. Plantinga and N. Wolterstorff (University of Notre Dame Press, 1983) and R. Swinburne's *Faith and Reason* (Oxford University Press, 1984). There is an excellent collection of readings, both historical and contemporary, edited by P. Helm, *Faith and Reason* (Oxford University Press, 1999).

NOTES

1   William Clifford was a Cambridge mathematician who became Professor of Applied Mathematics at University College, London. Though brought up a Christian he was converted to an anti-religious Darwinism. He died young (from consumption) but a number of works by him were published posthumously, including *The Commonsense of the Exact Sciences* (1885) and a book *Seeing and Thinking* (1879). The collected *Lectures and Essays* (1879) included his best known piece, 'The Ethics of Belief'. For an account of Clifford see Edwards (1967).
2   William James (1842–1910), an important American philosopher, was Professor of Psychology at Harvard from 1889 to 1897 and then Professor of Philosophy from 1897 till 1907. His books include *The Principles of Psychology* (1890), the collection of essays *The Will to Believe* (1897), *The Varieties of Religious Experience* (1902) and *Pragmatism* (1907). Bird (1987) provides a good critical introduction to his philosophy.
3   No consideration is given here to how far James was correct in the account of Pascal. For a fuller treatment, see Metzer (1967). For a more recent defence of Pascal's wager, see Brown (1984).
4   *Letter Concerning Toleration*, in Horton and Mendus (1991, p. 41).
5   See Kuhn (1970) and Radcliffe Richards (2000).
6   If, as is commonly said, he was inspired to his vision of nature as a struggle for survival by reading a book by the economist Malthus. See Desmond and Moore (1991).
7   These remarks were made in the *First Warning to Protestants* (1689).
8   For an excellent introduction to Bayle's life and thought, see Labrousse (1983).

Readings

1 | 'Problems about the Resurrection of the Body'

Linda Badham

In this article* Linda Badham argues that those who believe that the very same body will live again face serious problems, particularly arising from the fact that the atoms that constitute our bodies are changing all the time and that resurrected bodies, if the very same, will be liable to decay and dissolution. Those who hold, on the other hand, that people will be resurrected with quite new bodies have to face the problem of distinguishing them from replicas which are not the same people.

It is a popularly held view that science and religion are antithetical. And this view is supported by the sociological fact that leading scholars and scientists are significantly less likely to be Christian than other groups in society.[1] Yet even so, there are a number of very eminent scientists, and particularly physicists, who claim that there is no real conflict between their scientific and religious beliefs.[2] And many Christian apologists have drawn comfort from such claims in an age where the tide of secularism threatens to engulf the ancient citadel of Christian belief.[3] However, I have my doubts as to whether or not Christianity is secure from attack by science in general on some of its most crucial tenets. And, in particular, what I want to argue in this chapter is that the implications of modern science are far more damaging to doctrines of life after death than many Christian writers have supposed.

RESURRECTION OF THE BODY (THIS FLESH)

Although many might think that belief in the resurrection of this flesh at the end of time is now unthinkable, it has to be recognized that this is the form that orthodox Christian belief took from at least the second century onwards. Thus the Apostles' Creed affirms belief in the resurrection of the flesh;[4] the Nicene

Creed looks for the 'upstanding of the dead bodies';[5] and the Christian Fathers were utterly explicit that the resurrection was definitely a physical reconstitution.[6] Moreover, such belief is still Catholic orthodoxy: a recent *Catholic Catechism for Adults* declares that each one of us will rise one day 'the same person he was, in the same flesh made living by the same spirit'.[7] Hence it seems reasonable to suppose that this form of resurrection belief is still held among Christians. Yet a minimal knowledge of modern science seems sufficient to undermine it completely.

First, there is the problem that 'this flesh' is only temporarily mine. I am not like a machine or artefact, which keeps its atoms and molecules intact throughout its existence, save for those lost by damage or replaced during repair. Rather, I am a biological system in dynamic equilibrium (more or less) with my environment, in that I exchange matter with that environment continually. As J. D. Bernal writes, 'It is probable that none of us have more than a few atoms with which we started life, and that even as adults we probably change most of the material of our bodies in a matter of a few months'.[8] Thus it might prove an extremely difficult business to resurrect 'this' flesh at the end of time, for the atoms that will constitute me at the moment of death will return to the environment and will doubtless become part of innumerable other individuals. Augustine discussed the case of cannibals having to restore the flesh they had 'borrowed' as an exception.[9] But in the light of our current knowledge, shared atoms would seem the rule rather than the exception.

Moreover, there is the further problem that even if the exact atoms that constituted me at death could all be reassembled without leaving some other people bereft of vital parts, then the reconstituted body would promptly expire again. For whatever caused the systems' failure in my body, which led to my death originally, would presumably still obtain if the body exactly as it was prior to death were remade. But perhaps we can overcome this problem with a fairly simple proviso: the resurrection body should be identical to the body that died, malfunctions apart. After all, it might be said, we have no difficulty in accepting our television set returned in good working order from the repair shop after a breakdown as one and the same television set that we took to be repaired, even though some or even several of its components have been replaced. But people are not television sets. What counts as malfunction? Increasing age usually brings some diminution in physical and mental powers. Are all these to be mended too? How much change can a body take and still be the same person? Nor is it possible to suggest that the resurrection environment might be such as to reverse the effects of ageing and disease. For this move implies such a great change in the properties of the matter that is 'this flesh' as to make it dubious whether 'this' flesh really had been resurrected. The more one actually fills out the vague notion of the resurrection of the same flesh that perished, the more problems arise.

And even if the problem of reconstituting each one of us to the same (healthy) flesh he was (or might have been) could be overcome, there would remain the question of where we could all be resurrected. There is a space problem. If the countless millions of human beings who have ever lived and may live in the future were all to be resurrected on this earth, then the overcrowding would be acute. Now there are at least two theological manoeuvres that we could make to circumvent this embarrassment. If we want to retain resurrection on this earth, then we might say that only the chosen will be resurrected and thereby limit the numbers. But that solution raises insuperable problems about the morality of a God who would behave in such a way.[10] Alternatively, it might be argued that the resurrection will be to a new life in heaven and not to eternal life on earth. But in that case it has to be noted that resurrected bodies would need a biological environment markedly similar to the one we now live in. This leads to the implication that heaven would have to be a planet, or series of planets, all suitable for human life. The further one pushes this picture, the more bizarre and religiously unsatisfying it becomes.[11]

In sum, then, a little knowledge of the biochemistry of living organisms together with a brief consideration of the physicochemical conditions that such organisms require if they are to live, ought to have rendered the traditional notion of literal bodily resurrection unthinkable.

RESURRECTION OF THE BODY (TRANSFORMED)

It might be argued, as John Polkinghorne claims, that all this is irrelevant: 'We know that there is nothing significant about the material which at any one time constitutes our body ... It is the pattern they [the atoms] form which persists and evolves. We are liberated, therefore, from the quaint medieval picture of the reassembly of the body from its scattered components. In very general terms it is not difficult to imagine the pattern recreated (the body resurrected) in some other world.'[12]

At this point we should note that the doctrine being proposed here has shifted in a very significant way. The old doctrine of resurrection of the flesh guaranteed personal survival because the resurrected body was physically identical with the one laid in the grave. Physical continuity supplied the link between the person who died and the one who was resurrected. But Polkinghorne's version of the resurrection envisages recreation of a *pattern* in some other world. This is open to a host of philosophical problems about the sense in which the recreation of a replica can count as the survival of the person who died.[13]

What would we say, for example, if the replica were created *before* my death? Would I then die happily knowing that someone was around to carry on, as it were, in my place? Would I think to myself that the replica really was me? Consider the possibility of cloning. Let us imagine that science reaches a stage where a whole adult human individual can be regenerated from a few cells of a person in such a way that the original – Jones I – and the copy – Jones II – are genetically identical, and that the clone knows everything that Jones I knows. We may imagine that the purpose of doing this is to give a healthy body to house the thoughts of the physically ailing, but brilliant, Jones I. Now does Jones I die secure in the knowledge that he will live again? I would suggest that he might feel relieved to know that his life's work would carry on, and that his project would be entrusted to one incomparably suited to continue with it. He might also feel exceptionally close to Jones II and be deeply concerned for his welfare. But the other would not *be* him. In the end, Jones I would be dead and the other, Jones II, would carry on in his place. As far as Jones I was concerned, he himself would not live again, even though most other people would treat Jones II as if he were Jones I rejuvenated.

If these intuitions are correct, then they suggest that whatever it is that we count as essential for being one and the same person, it is not a 'pattern'. And I would suggest that all theories of resurrection that speak of our rising with new and transformed bodies fall foul of what I term the replica problem. For without some principle of continuity between the person who died and the one who was resurrected, then what was resurrected would only be something very similar to the one who died, a replica, and not a continuation of the dead person.

NOTES

* Taken from Badham (1987) 'Problems with accounts of life and death', in Badham, P. and Badham, L. (eds) (1987).

1 A sociological survey quoted by Daniel C. Batson and W. Larry Ventis in *The Religious Experience: A Social-Psychological Perspective* (Oxford: Oxford University Press, 1982), p. 225.

2 See, for example, John Polkinghorne, *The Way the World Is* (London: SPCK, 1983); and Russell Stannard, *Science and the Renewal of Belief* (London: SCM, 1982).

3 See, for example, Richard and Anthony Hanson, *Reasonable Belief* (Oxford: Oxford University Press, 1980), pp. 13ff.

4 It is to Cranmer's credit that he made the recitation of this creed easier for the English-speaking world by his deliberate mistranslation of 'resurrectio carnis' as 'resurrection of the body'.

5 In more idiomatic English we usually say 'resurrection of the dead'.

6 Paul Badham, *Christian Beliefs about Life after Death* (London: SPCK, 1978), pp. 47ff.

7 R. Lawler, D. W. Whuerl and T. C. Lawler, *The Teaching of Christ: A Catholic Catechism for Adults* (Dublin: Veritas, 1976), p. 544.

8 J. D. Bernal, *Science in History*, Vol. 3 (Harmondsworth: Penguin, 1969), p. 902.

9 Augustine, *City of God*, Book 22, Ch. 20.

10 Cf. Paul and Linda Badham, *Immortality or Extinction?* (London: SPCK, 1984), pp. 58ff.

11 Cf. Paul Badham, *Christian Beliefs about Life after Death*, Ch. 4.

12 John Polkinghorne, *The Way the World Is*, p. 93.

13 Cf. Bernard Williams, *Problems of the Self* (Cambridge: Cambridge University Press, 1978).

2 'Darwinism and the argument from design'

Richard Dawkins

In this extract from *The Blind Watchmaker* (Penguin, 1988), the author argues that the supposed theological alternatives to the theory of natural selection are not, on closer inspection, serious alternatives at all.

We have dealt with all the alleged alternatives to the theory of natural selection except the oldest one. This is the theory that life was created, or its evolution master-minded, by a conscious designer. It would obviously be unfairly easy to demolish some particular version of this theory such as the one (or it may be two) spelled out in Genesis. Nearly all peoples have developed their own creation myth, and the Genesis story is just the one that happened to have been adopted by one particular tribe of Middle Eastern herders. It has no more special status than the belief of a particular West African tribe that the world was created from the excrement of ants. All these myths have in common that they depend upon the deliberate intentions of some kind of supernatural being.

At first sight there is an important distinction to be made between what might be called 'instantaneous creation' and 'guided evolution'. Modern theologians of any sophistication have given up believing in instantaneous creation. The evidence for some sort of evolution has become too overwhelming. But many theologians who call themselves evolutionists ... smuggle God in by the back door: they allow him some sort of supervisory role over the course that evolution has taken, either influencing key moments in evolutionary history (especially, of course, *human* evolutionary history), or even meddling more comprehensively in the day-to-day events that add up to evolutionary change.

We cannot disprove beliefs like these, especially if it is assumed that God took care that his interventions always closely mimicked what would be expected from evolution by natural selection. All that we can say about such beliefs is, firstly, that they are superfluous and, secondly, that they *assume* the existence of the main thing we want to *explain*, namely organized complexity. The one thing that makes evolution such a neat theory is that it explains how organized complexity can arise out of primeval simplicity.

If we want to postulate a deity capable of engineering all the organized complexity in the world, either instantaneously or by guiding evolution, that deity must already have been vastly complex in the first place. The creationist, whether a naive Bible-thumper or an educated bishop, simply *postulates* an already existing being of prodigious intelligence and complexity. If we are going to allow ourselves the luxury of postulating organized complexity without offering an explanation, we might as well make a job of it and simply postulate the existence of life as we know it! In short, divine creation, whether instantaneous or in the form of guided evolution, joins the list of other theories we have considered in this chapter. All give some superficial appearance of being alternatives to Darwinism, whose merits might be tested by an appeal to evidence. All turn out, on closer inspection, not to be rivals of Darwinism at all. The theory of evolution by cumulative natural selection is the only theory we know of that is in principle *capable* of explaining the existence of organized complexity. Even if the evidence did not favour it, it would *still* be the best theory available! In fact the evidence does favour it. But that is another story.

3 'A modern argument for design'

Russell Stannard

Russell Stannard is Emeritus Professor of Physics at the Open University. In this extract* he summarizes the reasons why the traditional argument from design is now found unconvincing by scientifically educated people but argues that recent developments have provided the basis for a new argument. Life as we know it could only have come into existence if the conditions had been exactly right. Were these conditions only slightly different, a quite different universe would have resulted in which there was no life. Professor Stannard suggests that these conditions did not come about by chance though he thinks caution is needed about inferring that there must have been a designer of the universe.

What of the Argument for Design? The components of the animal and plant worlds fulfil their functions so well it is hard to resist the idea that someone must have designed them for those purposes. Just as the discovery of a watch on a beach would point to the existence of a watchmaker, so, it would appear, the discovery of the wonderful mechanisms at work in our bodies and elsewhere points to a mind that designed them.

This once popular argument no longer convinces. The Theory of Evolution by Natural Selection provides a satisfactory alternative. According to this theory, the physical characteristics and behaviour of animals are to some extent governed by genetic make-up. The genes are inherited from the parents, thus explaining why off-spring largely resemble their parents. But off-spring are not identical; though resembling their parents and each other, they show variations. Some will be able to run faster than average, or have a thicker protective hide, or sharper claw, or greater intelligence. Others will be less well endowed. The former have an advantage when it comes to surviving to an age when they can mate. Those that succeed in mating are, therefore, not truly representative of their generation as a whole; they will include more of those that happen by chance to have a genetic make-up that confers some advantage on its owner in terms of being well-adapted to survival within the particular environment. As a consequence, this type of genetic make-up has a greater than average chance of being passed on to the next generation. As generation succeeds generation the species become better and better adapted. The end result is animals that appear to have been deliberately designed for life in this environment. But the impression is false. These animals, ourselves included, have arisen through a process of natural selection.

The mechanism by which all this is carried out is now rather well understood. The genetic coding is to be found in the DNA molecule. This is shaped like a double helix, consisting of long chains of smaller constituent molecules. It is the specific sequences of these smaller molecules that make up the genetic codes that determine the physical characteristics and behaviour. Novel codes come into existence through mistakes in the copying process whereby DNA molecules are produced for the new off-spring. Mutations can also be caused by radiation impact, and possibly other accidental occurrences. These novel codes give rise to the random variations upon which the process of natural selection gets to work. There is no need for a designer to help this process along; it happens automatically. So again, by Ockham's Razor, the God hypothesis is eliminated as unnecessary.

The Argument from Design, having in this way seemingly been delivered a mortal blow, has in recent years suddenly and unexpectedly received a shot in the arm. Just when religious believers had come to accept that evolutionary biologists had pulled the rug from under the argument, astronomers and physicists have lately come up with indications that appear, on the surface at least, to argue towards a Mind that has fixed things. The new-style Argument from Design centres upon a consideration of those characteristics of the physical world that are the prerequisites for producing the right conditions under which life – any kind of life – can come into existence. Of course, in one sense the world we inhabit must be one in which life can evolve; otherwise we would not be here to observe it. But when one examines the conditions that the universe had to satisfy in order for life to put in an appearance, it is found that the constraints were exceedingly narrow. If one of a number of factors had been out by very much, life could not have got started.

In the first place, the conditions of the Big Bang had to be just right. If the violence of the explosion had been greater, the matter of the universe would have dispersed before the stars and planets could have condensed. If on the other hand it had been less violent, the universe would have re-collapsed into a Big Crunch before life on the planets could have developed to the point at which human beings could have put in an appearance. Between these extremes there lies a narrow band of conditions conducive to the eventual production of life, and that is where our universe happens to lie.

Secondly there needs to be a very careful balance between the values of the constants that determine physical behaviour – constants that govern, for instance, the strength of the gravitational attraction between objects and of the force between electric charges. If these had not been just right, stars of a size conducive to the formation of planets hospitable to life would not have formed. Not only that, but no carbon nuclei would have been produced. Carbon is the essential raw material out of which the basic building blocks of living matter are constructed. But on studying what came out of the Big Bang, we find only the two lightest chemical elements, hydrogen and helium. To produce carbon, these light elements had to be fused together. This is done in the fiery interior of a star. The carbon having been manufactured in this way, the star explodes spewing out the newly synthesised material. This later collects together under the influence of gravity and recondenses to form a second generation star (like our Sun) and accompanying planets (such as the Earth). The carbon on the surface of the planets is then ready to be incorporated into living tissue. It is when astrophysicists examine the conditions under which the carbon synthesis had to take place they discover just what a knife-edge situation it was. Had the fundamental constants been slightly different, no carbon would have formed, or had they been slightly different in another way, the carbon once formed would have been used up in the formation of other elements. The conditions had to be right with remarkable precision.

Thus, in a variety of apparently unconnected ways, there seems to have been a conspiracy to fix the conditions. Hence the temptation to resuscitate the Argument from Design. Not this time the design of living creatures – that much has been conceded to the evolutionary biologists – but the design of the fundamental fabric of the universe. However, before anyone jumps to the conclusion that here indeed is proof of God's existence, let me advise caution. Recently a theory has been put forward which, if correct, would account for the rate of expansion of the universe being right. I will not go into the details. Sufficient to say that it is a candidate theory for explaining the expansion rate of the universe as a natural and inevitable outcome of physical processes, rather than something happening fortuitously. As to why the fundamental physical constants should be arranged the way they are, no-one has yet come up with a proposal. But I think it premature to conclude that there will never be a solution. There might in the future be some discovery that forges unexpected links between these constants and gives us new insight into why they relate to each other in the way they do.

But even in the absence of such a development, one is still not justified in regarding this latest version of the Argument from Design as conclusive. A counter-proposal already advanced is that our universe is only one of an infinite number of universes. Each has its own set of physical constants, and only a small proportion of the universes are such as can lead to the production of life. Our own existence as living creatures dictates that our universe belongs to the latter class.

The first worry one has about this suggestion is that there appears to be no way to test it – the universes do not interact with each other. This means we are dealing with a metaphysical speculation rather than a proper scientific hypothesis. Secondly, the invocation of an infinite number of universes is, of course, the last word in extravagance! What of Ockham's Razor now? Would not the acceptance of the existence of God be a simpler alternative? Many of us might think so. A sceptic, however, could still prefer to settle for the infinite number of universes.

NOTE

* From Russell Stannard's *Grounds for Reasonable Belief* (Edinburgh: Scottish Academic Press, 1989).

4 'The argument from conscience'

John Henry Newman

In this extract* Newman argues that our moral experience, in particular of the workings of our consciences, provides sufficient reason to believe in God, i.e. in the existence of a moral governor of the universe.

1 I assume ... that Conscience has a legitimate place among our mental acts; as really so, as the action of memory, of reasoning, of imagination, or as the sense of the beautiful; that, as there are objects which, when presented to the mind, cause it to feel grief, regret, joy, or desire, so there are things which excite in us approbation or blame, and which we in consequence call right or wrong; and which, experienced in ourselves, kindle in us that specific sense of pleasure or pain, which goes by the name of a good or bad conscience. This being taken for granted, I will attempt to show that in this special feeling, which follows on the commission of what we call right or wrong, lie the materials for the real apprehension of a Divine Sovereign and Judge.

2 The feeling of conscience (being, I repeat, a certain keen sensibility, pleasant or painful, – self-approval and hope, or compunction and fear, – attendant on certain of our actions, which in consequence we call right or wrong) is twofold: – it is a moral sense, and a sense of duty; a judgement of the reason and a magisterial dictate. Of course its act is indivisible; still it has these two aspects, distinct from each other, and admitting of a separate consideration. Though I lost my sense of the obligation which I lie under to abstain from acts of dishonesty, I should not in consequence lose my sense that such actions were an outrage offered to my moral nature. Again; though I lost my sense of their moral deformity, I should not therefore lose my sense that they were forbidden to me. Thus conscience has both a critical and a judicial office, and though its promptings, in the breasts of the millions of human beings to whom it is given, are not in all cases correct, that does not necessarily interfere with the force of its testimony and of its sanction: its testimony that there is a right and a wrong, and its sanction to that testimony conveyed in the feelings which attend on right or wrong conduct. Here I have to speak of conscience in the latter point of view, not as

supplying us, by means of its various acts, with the elements of morals, such as
may be developed by the intellect into an ethical code, but simply as the dictate of
an authoritative monitor bearing upon the details of conduct as they come before
us, and complete in its several acts, one by one.

3 Let us then thus consider conscience, not as a rule of right conduct, but as a
sanction of right conduct. This is its primary and most authoritative aspect; it is
the ordinary sense of the word. Half the world would be puzzled to know what
was meant by the moral sense; but every one knows what is meant by a good or
bad conscience. Conscience is ever forcing on us by threats and by promises that
we must follow the right and avoid the wrong; so far it is one and the same in the
mind of every one, whatever be its particular errors in particular minds as to the
acts which it orders to be done or to be avoided; and in this respect it corre-
sponds to our perception of the beautiful and deformed. As we have naturally a
sense of the beautiful and graceful in nature and art, though tastes proverbially
differ, so we have a sense of duty and obligation, whether we all associate it with
the same certain actions in particular or not. Here, however, Taste and
Conscience part company: for the sense of beautifulness, as indeed the Moral
Sense, has no special relations to persons, but contemplates objects in themselves; conscience, on the other hand, is concerned with persons primarily, and
with actions mainly as viewed in their doers, or rather with self alone and one's
own actions, and with others only indirectly and as if in association with self. And
further, taste is its own evidence, appealing to nothing beyond its own sense of
the beautiful or the ugly, and enjoying the specimens of the beautiful simply for
their own sake; but conscience does not repose on itself, but vaguely reaches
forward to something beyond self, and dimly discerns a sanction higher than self
for its decisions, as is evidenced in that keen sense of obligation and responsibility
which informs them. And hence it is that we are accustomed to speak of
conscience as a voice, a term which we should never think of applying to the
sense of the beautiful; and moreover a voice, or the echo of a voice, imperative
and constraining, like no other dictate in the whole of our experience.

4 And again, in consequence of this prerogative of dictating and commanding,
which is of its essence, Conscience has an intimate bearing on our affections and
emotions, leading us to reverence and awe, hope and fear, especially fear, a feeling
which is foreign for the most part, not only to Taste, but even to the Moral Sense,
except in consequence of accidental associations. No fear is felt by any one who
recognizes that his conduct has not been betrayed into any kind of immorality, he
has a lively sense of responsibility and guilt, though the act be no offence against
society, – of distress and apprehension, even though it may be of present service
to him, – of compunction and regret, though in itself it be most pleasurable, – of
confusion of face, though it may have no witnesses. These various perturbations of
mind which are characteristic of a bad conscience, and may be very considerable,
– self-reproach, poignant shame, haunting remorse, chill dismay at the prospect
of the future, – and their contraries, when the conscience is good, as real though
less forcible, self-approval, inward peace, lightness of heart, and the like, – these
emotions constitute a specific difference between conscience and our other intellectual senses, – common sense, good sense, sense of expedience, taste, sense of
honour, and the like.

5 If, as is the case, we feel responsibility, are ashamed, are frightened, at transgressing the voice of conscience, this implies that there is One to whom we are responsible, before whom we are ashamed, whose claims upon us we fear. If, on doing wrong, we feel the same tearful, broken-hearted sorrow which overwhelms us on hurting a mother; if, on doing right, we enjoy the same sunny serenity of mind, the same soothing, satisfactory delight which follows on our receiving praise from a father, we certainly have within us the image of some person, to whom our love and veneration look, in whose smile we find our happiness, for whom we yearn, towards whom we direct our pleadings, in whose anger we are troubled and waste away. These feelings in us are such as require for their exciting cause an intelligent being: we are not affectionate towards a stone, nor do we feel shame before a horse or a dog; we have no remorse or compunction on breaking mere human law: yet, so it is, conscience excites all these painful emotions, confusion, foreboding, self-condemnation; and on the other hand it sheds upon us a deep peace, a sense of security, a resignation, and a hope, which there is no sensible, no earthly object to elicit. 'The wicked flees, when no one pursueth'; then why does he flee? Whence his terror? Who is it that he sees in solitude, in darkness, in the hidden chambers of his heart? If the cause of these emotions does not belong to this visible world, the Object to which his perception is directed must be Supernatural and Divine; and thus the phenomena of Conscience, as a dictate, avail to impress the imagination with the picture of a Supreme governor, a Judge, holy, just, powerful, all-seeing, retributive...

NOTE

* From John Henry Newman's *An Essay in Aid of a Grammar of Assent* (Tunbridge Wells: Burns & Oates, 1870), pp. 105–10.

5 'The problem of evil: the free-will defence'

John Hick

In this extract* Hick seeks to sustain the 'free-will defence' of belief in a wholly good and omnipotent God in the face of evil, i.e. the line of defence according to which God has to allow evil in a world in which it is important that people freely choose to do good. In this passage he is particularly concerned to reply to those who claim that God need not have allowed evil since he could have created humankind so that all would freely choose to do good.

To this question the Christian answer, both in the Augustinian and in the Irenaean types of theodicy, has always centred upon man's freedom and responsibility as a finite personal being. This answer has recently been critically discussed in the philosophical journals under the name of the free-will defence.[1] The discussion has been of great value in clarifying the issues involved, and as a result it is evident that, fully stated, the free-will defence falls into three stages.

The first stage establishes a conception of divine omnipotence. It is argued that God's all-power does not mean that He can do anything, if 'anything' is held to include self-contradictions such as making a round square, or a horse that has none of the characteristics of a horse, or an object whose surface both is and is not red all over at the same time. The self-contradictory, or logically absurd, does not fall within the scope of God's omnipotence; for a self-contradiction, being a logically meaningless form of words, does not describe anything that might be either done or not done. As Aquinas comments, 'it is more appropriate to say that such things cannot be done, than that God cannot do them'.[2] Thus, for example, God will never make a four-sided triangle. However, this is not because He cannot make figures with four or any other number of sides, but merely because the meaning of the word 'triangle' is such that it would never be correct to call a four-sided figure a triangle. Clearly this does not involve any limitation upon God's power such that if He had greater power He would be able to accomplish these logical absurdities. Not even infinite might can adopt a meaningless form of words as a programme for action.

The first phase of the argument is, I think, clearly sound, and since it is also accepted by the recent philosophical critics of the free-will defence[3] I will not defend it further here.

The second phase of the argument claims that there is a necessary connection between personality and moral freedom such that the idea of the creation of personal beings who are not free to choose wrongly as well as to choose rightly is self-contradictory and therefore does not fall within the scope of the divine omnipotence. If man is to be a being capable of entering into personal relationship with his Maker, and not a mere puppet, he must be endowed with the uncontrollable gift of freedom. For freedom, including moral freedom, is an essential element in what we know as personal as distinct from non-personal life. In order to be a person man must be free to choose right or wrong. He must be a morally responsible agent with a real power of moral choice. No doubt God could instead have created some other kind of being, with no freedom of choice and therefore no possibility of making wrong choices. But in fact He has chosen to create persons, and we can only accept this decision as basic to our existence and treat it as a premise of our thinking.[4]

This second phase of the argument, like the first, seems to be clearly sound and is likewise not challenged by the contemporary philosophical critics of the free-will defence. I will therefore not elaborate or defend it further.

3 THE RECENT CRITIQUE OF THE FREE-WILL DEFENCE

It is upon the third phase that discussion centres. Granted that God is going to make finite persons and not mere puppets or automata; and granted that persons must be genuinely free; could not God nevertheless have so made men that they would always freely do what is right? For human persons, though all endowed with some degree of freedom and responsibility, nevertheless vary markedly in their liability to sin. The saint, at one end of the scale, of whom we can say that it is logically possible but morally impossible for him to sin, and the depraved and perverted human monster at the other extreme, of whom we can say that it is logically possible but morally impossible for him not to sin, are both persons. They both, we are supposing, possess the freedom which is the ground of moral responsibility and the basis of liability to praise or blame. And accordingly it would be true of a morally perfect person that it is logically possible for him to sin and yet that he will never in fact do so, either because he has no inclination to sin or because he is so strongly oriented towards the good that he always masters such temptations as he meets. His whole nature would be perfect (even though it might contain the tension of temptations overcome), and accordingly the actions flowing from that nature would constitute perfect responses to his environment. That moral perfection is compatible with liability to temptation is established, for Christian belief, by the fact of Christ, who 'in every respect has been tempted as we are, yet without sinning'.[5] It would therefore seem that an omnipotent deity, creating *ex nihilo*, and determining solely by His own sovereign will both the nature of the beings whom He creates and the character of the environment in which He places them, could if He wished produce perfect persons who, while free to sin and even perhaps tempted to sin, remain for ever sinless.

...if God had so fashioned men's natures that they always freely act rightly, He would be in a relationship to His human creatures comparable with that of the hypnotist to his patient. That is to say, He would have pre-selected our responses to our environment, to one another, and to Himself in such a way that although these responses would from our own point of view be free and spontaneous, they would from God's point of view be unfree. He alone would know that our actions and attitudes, whilst flowing from our own nature, have in fact been determined by His initial fashioning of that nature and its environment. So long as we think of God's purpose for man, as Mackie does, exclusively in terms of man's performance in relation to his fellows, as a moral agent within human society, there is no contradiction in the idea of God's so making human beings that they will always freely act rightly. But if we proceed instead from the Christian view that God is seeking man's free response to Himself in faith, trust, and obedience, we see the necessity for our fourth question and for a negative answer to it. It would not be logically possible for God so to make men that they could be guaranteed freely to respond to Himself in genuine trust and love. The nature of these personal attitudes precludes their being caused in such a way. Just as the patient's trust in, and devotion to, the hypnotist would lack for the latter the value of a freely given trust and devotion, so our human worship and obedience to God would lack for Him the value of a freely offered worship and obedience. We should, in relation to God, be mere puppets, precluded from entering into any truly personal relationship with Him.

There might, indeed, be very great value in a universe of created beings who respond to God in a freely given love and trust and worship which He has Himself caused to occur by His initial formation of their nature. But if human analogies entitle us to speak about God at all, we must insist that such a universe could be only a poor second-best to one in which created beings, whose responses to Himself God has not thus 'fixed' in advance, come freely to love, trust, and worship Him. And if we attribute the latter and higher aim to God, we must declare to be self-contradictory the idea of God's so creating men that they will inevitably respond positively to Him.[6]

To summarize this proposed rebuttal of the Flew–Mackie challenge: God can without contradiction be conceived to have so constituted men that they could be guaranteed always freely to act rightly in relation to one another. But He cannot without contradiction be conceived to have so constituted men that they could be guaranteed freely to respond to Himself in authentic faith and love and worship. The contradiction involved here would be a contradiction between the idea of A loving and devoting him/herself to B, and of B valuing this love as a genuine and free response to himself whilst knowing that he has so constructed or manipulated A's mind as to produce it. The imagined hypnosis case reveals this contradiction as regards the relations between two human beings, and by analogy we apply the same logic of personal attitudes to the relation between God and man.

NOTES

*   From J. Hick, *Evil and the God of Love* (London: Macmillan, 1966).

1   J. L. Mackie, 'Evil and Omnipotence', *Mind* (April, 1955); Antony Flew, 'Divine Omnipotence and Human Freedom', *New Essays on Philosophical Theology*, ed. A. G. N. Flew and A. C. MacIntyre (London: SCM Press, 1955); S. A. Grave, 'On Evil and Omnipotence', *Mind* (April, 1956); P. M. Farrell, 'Evil and Omnipotence', *Mind* (July, 1958); Ninian Smart, 'Omnipotence, Evil and Supermen', *Philosophy* (April/July, 1961); and replies in this last journal by Flew (January, 1962) and Mackie (April, 1962). Mackie's 'Evil and Omnipotence' and Smart's 'Omnipotence, Evil and Supermen' are reprinted in Nelson Pike (ed.), *God and Evil* (Englewood Cliffs, NJ: Prentice Hall, 1964).

2   Aquinas (1259–64), Part i, Q. xxv, art. 3. Aquinas's entire discussion of this point is classic and definitive.

3   See J. L. Mackie, 'Evil and Omnipotence', *Mind,* p. 203, and Antony Flew, 'Divine Omnipotence and Human Freedom', *New Essays on Philosophical Theology*, p. 145.

4   Few would, after reflecting on the matter, be willing to follow T. H. Huxley: 'I protest that if some great Power would agree to make me always think what is true and do what is right, on condition of being turned into a sort of clocke ... I should instantly close with the offer' (*Collected Essays*, Vol. i (London: Macmillan, 1894), pp. 192–3).

5   Hebrews iv: 15.

6   W. D. Hudson argues along essentially the same lines in 'An Attempt to Defend Theism', *Philosophy* Vol. xxxix, No. 147 (January, 1964), p. 20. For a different response to the Flew–Mackie challenge, claiming that the notion of beings who are so created that they always freely act rightly is a logically incoherent notion, see Alvin Plantinga, 'The Free Will Defence', *Philosophy in America*, ed. Max Black (London: Allen & Unwin, 1965).

6 'The problem of animal suffering'

John Hick

In this passage* the author considers the objection that if God were wholly good and omnipotent there would not be the suffering there is amongst animals.

5 ANIMAL PAIN

To some, the pain suffered in the animal kingdom beneath the human level has constituted the most baffling aspect of the problem of evil.[1] For the considerations that may lighten the problem as it affects mankind – the positive value of moral freedom despite its risks; and the necessity that a world which is to be the scene of soul-making should contain real challenges, hardships, defeats, and mysteries – do not apply in the case of the lower animals. These are not moral personalities who might profit from the hazards of freedom or from the challenges of a rough environment. Why, then, we have to ask, does an all-powerful and infinitely loving Creator permit the pain and carnage of animal life? 'If there are any marks at all of special design in creation', said John Stuart Mill, 'one of the things most evidently designed is that a large proportion of animals should pass their existence in tormenting and devouring other animals. They have been lavishly fitted out with the instruments necessary for that purpose; their strongest instincts impel them to it, and many of them seem to have been constructed incapable of supporting themselves by any other food. If a tenth part of the pains which have been expended in finding benevolent adaptations in all nature, had been employed in collecting evidence to blacken the character of the Creator, what scope for comment would not have been found in the entire existence of the lower animals, divided, with scarcely an exception, into devourers and devoured, and a prey to a thousand ills from which they are denied the faculties necessary for protecting themselves!'[2]

The subject of pain in animals must, of course, remain largely a field for speculation and theoretical interpretation. We cannot enter into the consciousness of the lower species, or even prove demonstratively that they have consciousness. There is, however, sufficient evidence for the presence of some degree of consciousness, and some kind of experience of pain, at least throughout the vertebrate kingdom, to prohibit us from denying that there is any problem of animal suffering.[3] (1) The evidence for man's continuity with other forms of life within a common evolutionary process suggests that man's brain and consciousness differ in degree rather than absolutely from those of the animals;[4] and it would therefore be altogether surprising if man alone experienced pain. (2) We observe that when one of the higher mammals is in a situation in which a human would feel intense pain – for example, the situation of being burned – it behaves in ways characteristically similar to those in which a human would behave: it cries out and struggles violently to escape from the source of heat. This suggests that it is undergoing an experience of pain analogous to our own. Indeed, there is evidence that some of the higher animals not only experience physical pain but also a degree of non-physical suffering, in forms analogous to loneliness, fear, jealousy, and even bereavement. (3) The physical structure – especially the sensory and nervous systems – of the other vertebrates is basically similar to that of man. 'Mammals have all the physical structures which seem to be involved in the production of sensations of pain, and, as far as the physiological evidence goes, these structures seem to work in the same way in other mammals as in man.'[5] (4) The higher vertebrates can be taught by means of their reaction to the pleasure–pain dichotomy. In experimental situations they learn to perform actions that bring a reward and to avoid those which are answered by, say, an electric shock. Indeed, it is the part that pain plays in the learning process, and thus in adaptation to the environment, that constitutes its biological justification. For everything said above about the survival value of the pain mechanism in man applies to those of the lower animals that have a sufficiently developed nervous system to be able to feel pain. Neither the human nor the sub-human animal could survive if it did not quickly learn, under the insistent tutorship of pain, how to guide itself as a vulnerable bodily creature moving about in a relatively hard and rigid world of matter. Given that there are animal organisms with a degree of individual spontaneity, and inhabiting a common environment governed by causal regularities, the liability to pain must be a part of their equipment for survival.

What, however, of the lower vertebrates, such as the fishes and insects? Do they feel pain? Very different answers have been given to this question. At one extreme there is the assumption that

> The poor beetle, that we tread upon,
> In corporal sufferance finds a pang as great
> As when a giant dies.[6]

At the other extreme we are told that the squashed beetle feels no more than we do when our nails are pared or our hair cut. The naturalist Theodore Wood wrote:

When a crab will calmly continue its meal upon a smaller crab while being itself leisurely devoured by a larger and stronger; when a lobster will voluntarily and spontaneously divest itself of its great claws if a heavy gun be fired over the water in which it is lying; when a dragon-fly will devour fly after fly immediately after its abdomen has been torn from the rest of its body, and a wasp sip syrup while labouring – I will not say suffering – under a similar mutilation; it is quite clear that pain must practically be almost or altogether unknown.[7]

However, these instances, although accurate, may be misleading. The crab, for instance, has a built-in apparatus for divesting itself of its claws as an escape mechanism; but it does not follow that it is not capable of feeling pain in other circumstances. Again, insects may be insensitive to what is happening to them whilst they are intently carrying out some instinctive operation, such as eating or carrying food, and yet may perhaps not be similarly insensitive at other times. It is thus unsafe to conclude that even these relatively primitive creatures have no sensations of pain, however dim or fleeting. On the other hand, there are lower invertebrates, such as the sea anemone, which have no central nervous system at all, and it is therefore extremely improbable that they have conscious experiences.

I conclude thus far that a realistic response to the problem of pain in the lower vertebrates and higher invertebrates will not deny that there is any such problem, but will claim that in so far as these lower animals do feel pain this occurs within the general system whereby organic life is able to survive, namely by reacting to its environment through a nervous system which steers the individual away from danger by means of pain sensations.

There are, however, two important respects in which the animal's situation, as a being liable to pain, differs from man's. Whereas most human beings die through the eventual wearing out of their bodily fabric and its functions, most animals are violently killed and devoured by other species which, in the economy of nature, live by preying upon them. The animal kingdom forms a vast self-sustaining organism in which every part becomes, directly or indirectly, food for another part. And if we project ourselves imaginatively into this process, and see each creature as a self-conscious individual, its situation must seem agonizing indeed. But to do this is to miss the animal's proper good whilst feeling evils of which it is not conscious. Each individual – or at least each healthy individual – has its own fulfilment in the natural activity of its species, uncomplicated by knowledge of the future or a sense of the passage of time; and its momentary appreciation of its own physical impressions and activities are totally unaffected by the fact that after this thin thread of consciousness has snapped some other creature will devour the carcass. Death is not a problem to the animals, as it is to us; and herein lies the second major difference between the quality of human and animal experience. They do not wonder, 'in that sleep of death what dreams may come, When we have shuffled off this mortal coil',[8] or dread 'To lie in cold obstruction and to rot, This sensible warm motion to become, A kneaded clot'.[9] We may indeed say of them that 'Death is not an injury, but rather life a privilege'.[10] Not only is the animal's experience not shadowed by any anticipation of death or by any sense of its awesome finality; it is likewise simplified, in comparison with human consciousness, by a happy blindness to the dangers and pains that may lie between the present moment and this inevitable termination; and again by a similar oblivion to the past. Although possibly not total at every level of animal life, these restrictions must render all but the occasional animal genius immune to the distinctively human forms of suffering, which depend upon our capacity imaginatively to anticipate the future. The animal's goods and evils are exclusively those of the present moment, and in general it lives from instant to instant either in healthy and presumably pleasurable activity, or in a pleasant state of torpor. The picture, then, of animal life as a dark ocean of agonizing fear and pain is quite gratuitous, and arises from the mistake of projecting our distinctively human quality of experience into creatures of a much lower and simpler order.

NOTES

*   From J. Hick, *Evil and the God of Love* (London: Macmillan, 1966).

1   See, for example, C. C. J. Webb, *Problems in the Relations of God and Man* (London: James Nisbet, 1911), p. 268.

2   J. S. Mill, 'Nature', *Three Essays on Religion* (London: Longmans, Green, Reader & Dyer, 1875).

3   Such a denial is made, for example, by Dom Illtyd Trethowan in *An Essay in Christian Philosophy* (London: Longmans, Green, 1954), pp. 41 and 92.

4   For a discussion of the evidence for animal consciousness see W. H. Thorpe, 'Ethology and Consciousness', *Brain and Conscious Experience*, ed. J. Eccles (Berlin: Springer-Verlag, 1966).

5   G. C. Grindley, *The Sense of Pain in Animals* (London: The Universities Federation for Animal Welfare, 1959), p. 6.

6   Shakespeare, *Measure for Measure*, III. i. 89–91.

7   Theodore Wood, quoted by C. E. Raven, *The Creator Spirit* (London: Martin, Hopkinson, 1927), p. 120.

8   Shakespeare, *Hamlet*, III. i. 66–7.

9   Shakespeare, *Measure for Measure*, III. i. 119–20.

10   Lord Samuel, *Memoirs* (London: Cresset Press, 1945), p. 297.

7 'Miracles and Revelation'

David Hume

This extract is taken from David Hume's essay 'Of Miracles', published in his *Enquiry Concerning Human Understanding* (1748). Hume's argument in the essay is that there is no evidence sufficient to establish that any of the claimed historical miracles actually occurred. Indeed by the very nature of the case – a miracle being contrary to the uniform experience of humankind – it is unlikely that the initial evidence against a miracle will ever be outweighed by the evidence in favour of it. It is possible to imagine a case where this does happen but, in such a case, the miracle would not serve as a foundation for any particular system of religion. Christianity is, therefore, only founded on miracles in the sense that it requires a miracle of faith for anyone to believe it.

3 Though experience be our only guide in reasoning concerning matters of fact; it must be acknowledged, that this guide is not altogether infallible, but in some cases is apt to lead us into errors. One, who in our climate, should expect better weather in any week of June than in one of December, would reason justly, and conformably to experience; but it is certain, that he may happen, in the event, to find himself mistaken. However, we may observe, that, in such a case, he would have no cause to complain of experience; because it commonly informs us beforehand of the uncertainty, by that contrariety of events, which we may learn from a diligent observation. All effects follow not with like certainty from their supposed causes. Some events are found, in all countries and all ages, to have been constantly conjoined together: Others are found to have been more variable, and sometimes to disappoint our expectations; so that, in our reasonings concerning matter of fact, there are all imaginable degrees of assurance, from the highest certainty to the lowest species of moral evidence.

4 A wise man, therefore, proportions his belief to the evidence. In such conclusions as are founded on an infallible experience, he expects the event with the last degree of assurance, and regards his past experience as a full proof of the future existence of that event. In other cases, he proceeds with more caution: He weighs the opposite experiments: He considers which side is supported by the

greater number of experiments: to that side he inclines, with doubt and hesitation; and when at last he fixes his judgement, the evidence exceeds not what we properly call probability. All probability, then, supposes an opposition of experiments and observations, where the one side is found to overbalance the other, and to produce a degree of evidence, proportioned to the superiority. A hundred instances or experiments on one side, and fifty on another, afford a doubtful expectation of any event; though a hundred uniform experiments, with only one that is contradictory, reasonably beget a pretty strong degree of assurance. In all cases, we must balance the opposite experiments, where they are opposite, and deduct the smaller number from the greater, in order to know the exact force of the superior evidence.

5 To apply these principles to a particular instance; we may observe, that there is no species of reasoning more common, more useful, and even necessary to human life, than that which is derived from the testimony of men, and the reports of eye-witnesses and spectators. This species of reasoning, perhaps, one may deny to be founded on the relation of cause and effect. I shall not dispute about a word. It will be sufficient to observe that our assurance in any argument of this kind is derived from no other principle than our observation of the veracity of human testimony, and of the usual conformity of facts to the reports of witnesses. It being a general maxim, that no objects have any discoverable connexion together, and that all the inferences, which we can draw from one to another, are founded merely on our experience of their constant and regular conjunction; it is evident, that we ought not to make an exception to this maxim in favour of human testimony, whose connexion with any event seems, in itself, as little necessary as any other. Were not the memory tenacious to a certain degree; had not men commonly an inclination to truth and a principle of probity; were they not sensible to shame, when detected in a falsehood: Were not these, I say, discovered by experience to be qualities, inherent in human nature, we should never repose the least confidence in human testimony. A man delirious, or noted for falsehood and villainy, has no manner of authority with us.

6 And as the evidence, derived from witnesses and human testimony, is founded on past experience, so it varies with the experience, and is regarded either as a proof or a probability, according as the conjunction between any particular kind of report and any kind of object has been found to be constant or variable. There are a number of circumstances to be taken into consideration in all judgements of this kind; and the ultimate standard, by which we determine all disputes, that may arise concerning them, is always derived from experience and observation. Where this experience is not entirely uniform on any side, it is attended with an unavoidable contrariety in our judgements, and with the same opposition and mutual destruction of argument as in every other kind of evidence. We frequently hesitate concerning the reports of others. We balance the opposite circumstances, which cause any doubt or uncertainty; and when we discover a superiority on any side, we incline to it; but still with a diminution of assurance, in proportion to the force of its antagonist.

7 This contrariety of evidence, in the present case, may be derived from several different causes; from the opposition of contrary testimony; from the character or number of the witnesses; from the manner of their delivering their

testimony; or from the union of all these circumstances. We entertain a suspicion concerning any matter of fact, when the witnesses contradict each other; when they are but few, or of a doubtful character; when they have an interest in what they affirm; when they deliver their testimony with hesitation, or on the contrary, with too violent asseverations. There are many other particulars of the same kind, which may diminish or destroy the force of any argument, derived from human testimony.

8 Suppose, for instance, that the fact, which the testimony endeavours to establish, partakes of the extraordinary and the marvellous; in that case, the evidence, resulting from the testimony, admits of a diminution, greater or less, in proportion as the fact is more or less unusual. The reason why we place any credit in witnesses and historians, is not derived from any connexion, which we perceive a priori, between testimony and reality, but because we are accustomed to find a conformity between them. But when the fact attested is such a one as has seldom fallen under our observation, here is a contest of two opposite experiences; of which the one destroys the other, as far as its force goes, and the superior can only operate on the mind by the force, which remains. The very same principle of experience, which gives us a certain degree of assurance in the testimony of witnesses, gives us also, in this case, another degree of assurance against the fact, which they endeavour to establish; from which contradiction there necessarily arises a counterpoise, and mutual destruction of belief and authority.

9 I should not believe such a story were it told me by Cato, was a proverbial saying in Rome, even during the lifetime of that philosophical patriot.[1] The incredibility of a fact, it was allowed, might invalidate so great an authority.

10 The Indian prince, who refused to believe the first relations concerning the effects of frost, reasoned justly; and it naturally required very strong testimony to engage his assent to facts, that arose from a state of nature, with which he was unacquainted, and which bore so little analogy to those events, of which he had had constant and uniform experience. Though they were not contrary to his experience, they were not conformable to it.[2]

11 But in order to increase the probability against the testimony of witnesses, let us suppose, that the fact, which they affirm, instead of being only marvellous, is really miraculous; and suppose also, that the testimony considered apart and in itself, amounts to an entire proof; in that case, there is proof against proof, of which the strongest must prevail, but still with a diminution of its force, in proportion to that of its antagonist.

12 A miracle is a violation of the laws of nature; and as a firm and unalterable experience has established these laws, the proof against a miracle, from the very nature of the fact, is as entire as any argument from experience can possibly be imagined. Why is it more than probable, that all men must die; that lead cannot, of itself, remain suspended in the air; that fire consumes wood, and is extinguished by water; unless it be, that these events are found agreeable to the laws of nature, and there is required a violation of these laws, or in other words, a miracle to prevent them? Nothing is esteemed a miracle, if it ever happen in the common course of nature. It is no miracle that a man, seemingly in good health, should die on a sudden: because such a kind of death, though more unusual than

any other, has yet been frequently observed to happen. But it is a miracle, that a dead man should come to life; because that has never been observed in any age or country. There must, therefore, be a uniform experience against every miraculous event, otherwise the event would not merit that appellation. And as a uniform experience amounts to a proof, there is here a direct and full *proof*, from the nature of the fact, against the existence of any miracle; nor can such a proof be destroyed, or the miracle rendered credible, but by an opposite proof, which is superior.[3]

13 The plain consequence is (and it is a general maxim worthy of our attention), 'That no testimony is sufficient to establish a miracle, unless the testimony be of such a kind, that its falsehood would be more miraculous, than the fact, which it endeavours to establish; and even in that case there is a mutual destruction of arguments, and the superior only gives us an assurance suitable to that degree of force, which remains, after deducting the inferior.' When anyone tells me, that he saw a dead man restored to life, I immediately consider with myself, whether it be more probable, that this person should either deceive or be deceived, or that the fact, which he relates, should really have happened. I weigh the one miracle against the other; and according to the superiority, which I discover, I pronounce my decision, and always reject the greater miracle. If the falsehood of his testimony would be more miraculous, than the event which he relates; then, and not till then, can he pretend to command my belief or opinion.

. . .

PART II

24 I may add as a *fourth* reason, which diminishes the authority of prodigies, that there is no testimony for any, even those which have not been expressly detected, that is not opposed by an infinite number of witnesses; so that not only the miracle destroys the credit of testimony, but the testimony destroys itself. To make this the better understood, let us consider, that, in matters of religion, whatever is different is contrary; and that it is impossible the religions of ancient Rome, of Turkey, of Siam, and of China should, all of them, be established on any solid foundation. Every miracle, therefore, pretended to have been wrought in any of these religions (and all of them abound in miracles), as its direct scope is to establish the particular system to which it is attributed; so has it the same force, though more indirectly, to overthrow every other system. In destroying a rival system, it likewise destroys the credit of those miracles, on which that system was established; so that all the prodigies of different religions are to be regarded as contrary facts, and the evidences of these prodigies, whether weak or strong, as opposite to each other. According to this method of reasoning, when we believe any miracle of Mahomet or his successors, we have for our warrant the testimony of a few barbarous Arabians: And on the other hand, we are to regard the authority of Titus Livius; Plutarch, Tacitus, and, in short, of all the authors and witnesses, Grecian, Chinese, and Roman Catholic, who have related any miracle in their particular religion; I say, we are to regard their testimony in the same light as if they had mentioned that Mahometan miracle, and had in express terms contradicted it, with the same certainty as they have for the miracle they relate.

This argument may appear over subtle and refined; but is not in reality different from the reasoning of a judge, who supposes, that the credit of two witnesses, maintaining a crime against any one, is destroyed by the testimony of two others, who affirm him to have been two hundred leagues distant, at the same instant when the crime is said to have been committed.

...

35 Upon the whole, then, it appears, that no testimony for any kind of miracle has ever amounted to a probability, much less to a proof; and that, even supposing it amounted to a proof, it would be opposed by another proof; derived from the very nature of the fact, which it would endeavour to establish. It is experience only, which gives authority to human testimony; and it is the same experience, which assures us of the laws of nature. When, therefore, these two kinds of experience are contrary, we have nothing to do but subtract the one from the other, and embrace an opinion, either on one side or the other, with that assurance which arises from the remainder. But according to the principle here explained, this subtraction, with regard to all popular religions, amounts to an entire annihilation; and therefore we may establish it as a maxim, that no human testimony can have such force as to prove a miracle, and make it a just foundation for any such system of religion.

36 I beg the limitations here made may be remarked, when I say, that a miracle can never be proved, so as to be the foundation of a system of religion. For I own, that otherwise, there may possibly be miracles, or violations of the usual course of nature, of such a kind as to admit of proof from human testimony; though, perhaps, it will be impossible to find any such in all the records of history. Thus, suppose, all authors, in all languages, agree, that, from the first of January 1600, there was a total darkness over the whole earth for eight days: suppose that the tradition of this extraordinary event is still strong and lively among the people: that all travellers, who return from foreign countries, bring us accounts of the same tradition, without the least variation or contradiction: it is evident, that our present philosophers, instead of doubting the fact, ought to receive it as certain, and ought to search for the causes whence it might be derived. The decay, corruption, and dissolution of nature, is an event rendered probable by so many analogies, that any phenomenon, which seems to have a tendency towards that catastrophe, comes within the reach of human testimony, if that testimony be very extensive and uniform.

37 But suppose, that all the historians who treat of England, should agree, that, on the first of January 1600, Queen Elizabeth died; that both before and after her death she was seen by her physicians and the whole court, as is usual with persons of her rank; that her successor was acknowledged and proclaimed by the parliament; and that, after being interred a month, she again appeared, resumed the throne, and governed England for three years: I must confess that I should be surprised at the concurrence of so many odd circumstances, but should not have the least inclination to believe so miraculous an event. I should not doubt of her pretended death, and of those other public circumstances that followed it: I should only assert it to have been pretended, and that it neither was, nor possibly could be real. You would in vain object to me the difficulty, and almost impossibility of deceiving the world in an affair of such consequence; the

wisdom and solid judgement of that renowned queen; with the little or no advantage which she could reap from so poor an artifice: All this might astonish me; but I would still reply, that the knavery and folly of men are such common phenomena, that I should rather believe the most extraordinary events to arise from their concurrence, than admit of so signal a violation of the laws of nature.

38 But should this miracle be ascribed to any new system of religion; men, in all ages, have been so much imposed on by ridiculous stories of that kind, that this very circumstance would be a full proof of a cheat, and sufficient, with all men of sense, not only to make them reject the fact, but even reject it without farther examination. Though the Being to whom the miracle is ascribed, be, in this case, Almighty, it does not, upon that account, become a whit more probable; since it is impossible for us to know the attributes or actions of such a Being, otherwise than from the experience which we have of his productions, in the usual course of nature. This still reduces us to past observation, and obliges us to compare the instances of the violation of truth in the testimony of men, with those of the violation of the laws of nature by miracles, in order to judge which of them is most likely and probable. As the violations of truth are more common in the testimony concerning religious miracles, than in that concerning any other matter of fact; this must diminish very much the authority of the former testimony, and make us form a general resolution, never to lend any attention to it, with whatever specious pretence it may be covered.

. . .

40 I am the better pleased with the method of reasoning here delivered, as I think it may serve to confound those dangerous friends or disguised enemies to the *Christian Religion*, who have undertaken to defend it by the principles of human reason. Our most holy religion is founded on *Faith*, not on reason; and it is a sure method of exposing it to put it to such a trial as it is, by no means, fitted to endure. To make this more evident, let us examine those miracles, related in scripture; and not to lose ourselves in too wide a field, let us confine ourselves to such as we find in the *Pentateuch*, which we shall examine, according to the principles of these pretended Christians, not as the word or testimony of God himself, but as the production of a mere human writer and historian. Here then we are first to consider a book, presented to us by a barbarous and ignorant people, written in an age when they were still more barbarous, and in all probability long after the facts which it relates, corroborated by no concurring testimony, and resembling those fabulous accounts, which every nation gives of its origin. Upon reading this book, we find it full of prodigies and miracles. It gives an account of a state of the world and of human nature entirely different from the present: Of our fall from that state: Of the age of man, extended to near a thousand years: Of the destruction of the world by a deluge: Of the arbitrary choice of one people, as the favourites of heaven; and that people the countrymen of the author: Of their deliverance from bondage by prodigies the most astonishing imaginable: I desire any one to lay his hand upon his heart, and after a serious consideration declare, whether he thinks that the falsehood of such a book, supported by such a testimony, would be more extraordinary and miraculous than all the miracles it relates; which is, however, necessary to make it be received, according to the measures of probability above established.

41 What we have said of miracles may be applied, without any variation to prophecies; and indeed, all prophecies are real miracles, and as such only, can be admitted as proofs of any revelation. If it did not exceed the capacity of human nature to foretell future events, it would be absurd to employ any prophecy as an argument for a divine mission or authority from heaven. So that, upon the whole, we may conclude, that the *Christian Religion* not only was at first attended with miracles, but even at this day cannot be believed by any reasonable person without one. Mere reason is insufficient to convince us of its veracity; And whoever is moved by *Faith* to assent to it, is conscious of a continued miracle in his own person, which subverts all the principles of his understanding, and gives him a determination to believe what is most contrary to custom and experience.

NOTES

1 Plutarch, in *vita Catonis*.
2 No Indian, it is evident, could have experienced that water did not freeze in cold climates. This is placing nature in a situation quite unknown to him; and it is impossible for him to tell a priori what will result from it. It is making a new experiment, the consequence of which is always uncertain. One may sometimes conjecture from analogy what will follow; but still this is but conjecture. And it must be confessed, that, in the present case of freezing, the event follows contrary to the rules of analogy, and is such as a rational Indian would not look for. The operations of cold upon water are not gradual, according to the degrees of cold; but whenever it comes to the freezing point, the water passes in a moment, from the utmost liquidity to perfect hardness. Such an event, therefore, may be denominated extraordinary, and requires a pretty strong testimony, to render it credible to people in a warm climate: But still it is not miraculous, not contrary to uniform experience of the course of nature in cases where all the circumstances are the same. The inhabitants of Sumatra have always seen water fluid in their own climate, and the freezing of their rivers ought to be deemed a prodigy: But they never saw water in Muscovy during the winter; and therefore they cannot reasonably be positive what would there be the consequence.
3 Sometimes an event may not, in itself, seem to be contrary to the laws of nature, and yet, if it were real, it might, by reason of some circumstances, be denominated a miracle; because, in fact, it is contrary to these laws. Thus if a person, claiming a divine authority, should command a sick person to be well, a healthful man to fall down dead, the clouds to pour rain, the winds to blow, in short, should order many natural events, which immediately follow upon his command; these might justly be esteemed miracles, because they are really, in this case, contrary to the laws of nature. For if any suspicion remain, that the event and command concurred by accident, there is no miracle and no transgression of the laws of nature. If this suspicion be removed, there is evidently a miracle, and a transgression of these laws; because nothing can be more contrary to nature than that the voice or command of a man should have such an influence. A miracle may be accurately defined, a transgression of a law of nature by a particular volition of the Deity, or, by the interposition of some invisible agent. A miracle may either be discoverable by men or not. This alters not its nature and essence. The raising of a house or ship into the air is a visible miracle. The raising of a feather, when the wind wants ever so little of a force requisite for that purpose, is as real a miracle, though not so sensible with regard to us.

8 'The Ethics of Belief'

William K. Clifford

In this well-known article,* Clifford sought to uphold the view that 'it is wrong always, everywhere, and for anyone, to believe anything upon insufficient evidence'. Clifford uses examples to suggest that all beliefs, however trivial and however insignificant those who hold them, have some effect on 'the fate of mankind'. Credulity thus has its risks not just for the believer but for society.

1 THE DUTY OF INQUIRY

1

A shipowner was about to send to sea an emigrant-ship. He knew that she was old, and not over-well built at the first; and she had seen many seas and climes, and often had needed repairs. Doubts had been suggested to him that possibly she was not seaworthy. These doubts preyed upon his mind, and made him unhappy; he thought that perhaps he ought to have her thoroughly overhauled and refitted, even though this should put him to great expense. Before the ship sailed, however, he succeeded in overcoming these melancholy reflections. He said to himself that she had gone safely through so many voyages and weathered so many storms that it was idle to suppose she would not come safely home from this trip also. He would put his trust in Providence, which could hardly fail to protect all these unhappy families that were leaving their fatherland to seek for better times elsewhere. He would dismiss from his mind all ungenerous suspicions about the honesty of builders and contractors. In such ways he acquired a sincere and comfortable conviction that his vessel was thoroughly safe and seaworthy; he watched her departure with a light heart, and benevolent wishes for the success of the exiles in their strange new home that was to be; and he got his insurance-money when she went down in mid-ocean and told no tales.

2

What shall we say of him? Surely this, that he was verily guilty of the death of those men. It is admitted that he did sincerely believe in the soundness of his ship; but the sincerity of his conviction can in no wise help him, because *he had no right to believe on such evidence as was before him*. He had acquired his belief not by honestly earning it in patient investigation, but by stifling his doubts. And although in the end he may have felt so sure about it that he could not think otherwise, yet inasmuch as he had knowingly and willingly worked himself into the frame of mind, he must be held responsible for it.

3

Let us alter the case a little, and suppose that the ship was not unsound after all; that she made her voyage safely, and many others after it. Will that diminish the guilt of her owner? Not one jot. When an action is once done, it is right or wrong for ever; no accidental failure of its good or evil fruits can possibly alter that. The man would not have been innocent, he would only have been not found out. The question of right or wrong has to do with the origin of his belief, not the matter of it; not what it was, but how he got it; not whether it turned out to be true or false, but whether he had a right to believe on such evidence as was before him.

4

There was once an island in which some of the inhabitants professed a religion teaching neither the doctrine of original sin nor that of eternal punishment. A suspicion got abroad that the professors of this religion had made use of unfair means to get their doctrines taught to children. They were accused of wresting the laws of their country in such a way as to remove children from the care of their natural and legal guardians; and even of stealing them away and keeping them concealed from their friends and relations. A certain number of men formed themselves into a society for the purpose of agitating the public about this matter. They published grave accusations against individual citizens of the highest position and character, and did all in their power to injure these citizens in the exercise of their professions. So great was the noise they made, that a Commission was appointed to investigate the facts; but after the Commission had carefully inquired into all the evidence that could be got, it appeared that the accused were innocent. Not only had they been accused on insufficient evidence, but the evidence of their innocence was such as the agitators might easily have obtained, if they had attempted a fair inquiry. After these disclosures the inhabitants of that country looked upon the members of the agitating society, not only as persons whose judgement was to be distrusted, but also as no longer to be counted honourable men. For although they had sincerely and conscientiously believed in the charges they had made, yet *they had no right to believe on such evidence as was before them*. Their sincere convictions, instead of being honestly earned by patient inquiring, were stolen by listening to the voice of prejudice and passion.

5

Let us vary this case also, and suppose, other things remaining as before, that a still more accurate investigation proved the accused to have been really guilty. Would this make any difference in the guilt of the accusers? Clearly not; the question is not whether their belief was true or false, but whether they entertained it on wrong grounds. They would no doubt say, 'Now you see that we were right after all; next time perhaps you will believe us.' And they might be believed, but they would not thereby become honourable men. They would not be innocent, they would only be not found out. Every one of them, if he chose to examine himself *in foro conscientiae*, would know that he had acquired and nourished a belief, when he had no right to believe on such evidence as was before him; and therein he would know that he had done a wrong thing.

6

It may be said, however, that in both of these supposed cases it is not the belief which is judged to be wrong, but the action following upon it. The shipowner might say, 'I am perfectly certain that my ship is sound, but still I feel it my duty to have her examined, before trusting the lives of so many people to her.' And it might be said to the agitator, 'However convinced you were of the justice of your cause and the truth of your convictions, you ought not to have made a public attack upon any man's character until you had examined the evidence on both sides with the utmost patience and care.'

7

In the first place, let us admit that, so far as it goes, this view of the case is right and necessary; right, because even when a man's belief is so fixed that he cannot think otherwise, he still has a choice in regard to the action suggested by it, and so cannot escape the duty of investigating on the ground of the strength of his convictions; and necessary, because those who are not yet capable of controlling their feelings and thoughts must have a plain rule dealing with overt acts.

8

But this being premised as necessary, it becomes clear that it is not sufficient, and that our previous judgement is required to supplement it. For it is not possible so to sever the belief from the action it suggests as to condemn the one without condemning the other. No man holding a strong belief on one side of a question, or even wishing to hold a belief on one side, can investigate it with such fairness and completeness as if he were really in doubt and unbiased; so that the existence of a belief not founded on fair inquiry unfits a man for the performance of this necessary duty.

9

Nor is that truly a belief at all which has not some influence upon the actions of him who holds it. He who truly believes that which prompts him to an action has looked upon the action to lust after it, he has committed it already in his heart. If a belief is not realized immediately in open deeds, it is stored up for the guidance of the future. It goes to make a part of that aggregate of beliefs which is the link between sensation and action at every moment of all our lives, and which is so organized and compacted together that no part of it can be isolated from the rest, but every new edition modifies the structure of the whole. No real belief, however trifling and fragmentary it may seem, is ever truly insignificant; it prepares us to receive more of its like, confirms those which resembled it before, and weakens others; and so gradually it lays a stealthy train in our inmost thoughts, which may some day explode into overt action, and leave its stamp upon our character for ever.

10

And no one man's belief is in any case a private matter which concerns himself alone. Our lives are guided by that general conception of the course of things which has been created by society for social purposes. Our words, our phrases, our forms, and processes and modes of thought, are common property, fashioned and perfected from age to age; an heirloom which every succeeding generation inherits as a precious deposit and a sacred trust to be handed on to the next one, not unchanged but enlarged and purified, with some clear marks of its proper handiwork. Into this, for good or ill, is woven every belief of every man who has speech of his fellows. An awful privilege, and an awful responsibility, that we should help to create the world in which posterity will live.

11

In the two supposed cases which have been considered, it has been judged wrong to believe on insufficient evidence, or to nourish belief by suppressing doubts and avoiding investigation. The reason of this judgement is not far to seek: it is that in both these cases the belief held by one man was of great importance to other men. But for as much as no belief held by one man, however seemingly trivial the belief, and however obscure the believer, is ever actually insignificant or without its effect on the fate of mankind, we have no choice but to extend our judgement to all cases of belief whatever. Belief, that sacred faculty which prompts the decisions of our will, and knits into harmonious working all the compacted energies of our being, is ours not for ourselves, but for humanity. It is rightly used on truths which have been established by long experience and waiting toil, and which have stood in the fierce light of free and fearless questioning. Then it helps to bind men together, and to strengthen and direct their common action. It is desecrated when given to unproved and unquestioned statements, for the solace and private pleasure of the believer; to add a tinsel splendour to the plain straight road of our life and display a bright mirage beyond it; or even to drown the common sorrows of our kind by a self-deception which allows them not only to cast down, but also to degrade us. Whoso would deserve well of his fellows in this matter will guard the purity of his belief with a very fanaticism of jealous care, lest at any time it should rest on an unworthy object, and catch a stain which can never be wiped away.

It is not only the leader of men, statesmen, philosopher, or poet, that owes this bounden duty to mankind. Every rustic who delivers in the village alehouse his slow, infrequent sentences, may help to kill or keep alive the fatal superstitions which clog his race. Every hard-worked wife of an artisan may transmit to her children beliefs which shall knit society together, or rend it in pieces. No simplicity of mind, no obscurity of station, can escape the universal duty of questioning all that we believe.

It is true that this duty is a hard one, and the doubt which comes out of it is often a very bitter thing. It leaves us bare and powerless where we thought that we were safe and strong. To know all about anything is to know how to deal with it under all circumstances. We feel much happier and more secure when we think we know precisely what to do, no matter what happens, than when we have lost our way and do not know where to turn. And if we have supposed ourselves to know all about anything, and to be capable of doing what is fit in regard to it, we naturally do not like to find that we are really ignorant and powerless, that we have to begin again at the beginning, and try to learn what the thing is and how it is to be dealt with — if indeed anything can be learnt about it. It is the sense of power attached to a sense of knowledge that makes men desirous of believing, and afraid of doubting.

This sense of power is the highest and best of pleasures when the belief on which it is founded is a true belief, and has been fairly earned by investigation. For then we may justly feel that it is common property, and holds good for others as well as for ourselves. Then we may be glad, not that I have learned secrets by which I am safer and stronger, but that we men have got mastery over more of the world; and we shall be strong, not for ourselves, but in the name of Man and in his strength. But if the belief has been accepted on insufficient evidence, the pleasure is a stolen one. Not only does it deceive ourselves by giving us a sense of power which we do not really possess, but it is sinful because it is stolen in defiance of our duty to mankind. That duty is to guard ourselves from such beliefs as from a pestilence, which may shortly master our own body and then spread to the rest of the town. What would be thought of one who, for the sake of a sweet fruit, should deliberately run the risk of bringing a plague upon his family and his neighbours?

And, as in other such cases, it is not the risk only which has to be considered; for a bad action is always bad at the time when it is done, no matter what happens afterwards. Every time we let ourselves believe for unworthy reasons, we weaken our powers of self-control, of doubting, of judicially and fairly weighting evidence. We all suffer severely enough from the maintenance and support of false beliefs and the fatally wrong actions which they lead to, and the evil born when one such belief is entertained is great and wide. But a greater and wider evil arises when the credulous character is maintained and supported, when a habit of believing for unworthy reasons is fostered and made permanent. If I steal money from any person, there may be no harm done by the mere transfer of possession; he may not feel the loss, or it may prevent him from using the money badly. But I cannot help doing this great wrong towards Man, that I make myself dishonest. What hurts society is not that it should lose its property, but that it should become a den of thieves; for then it must cease to be society. This is why we ought not to do evil that good may come; for at any rate this great evil has come, that we have done evil and are made wicked thereby. In like manner, if I let myself believe anything on insufficient evidence, there may be no great harm done by the mere belief; it may be true after all, or I may never have occasion to exhibit it in outward acts. But I cannot help doing this great wrong towards Man, that I make myself credulous. The danger to society is not merely that it should believe wrong things, though that is great enough; but that it should become credulous, and lose the habit of testing things and inquiring into them; for then it must sink back into savagery.

The harm which is done by credulity in a man is not confined to the fostering of a credulous character in others, and consequent support of false beliefs. Habitual want of care about what I believe leads to habitual want of care in others about the truth of what is told to me. Men speak the truth to one another when each reveres the truth in his own mind and in the other's mind; but how shall my friend revere the truth in my mind when I myself am careless about it, when I believe things because I want to believe them, and because they are comforting and pleasant: Will he not learn to cry, 'Peace,' to me, when there is no peace? By such a course I shall surround myself with a thick atmosphere of falsehood and fraud, and in that I must live. It may matter little to me, in my cloud-castle of sweet illusions and darling lies; but it matters much to Man that I have made my neighbours ready to deceive. The credulous man is father to the liar and the cheat; he lives in the bosom of this his family, and it is no marvel if he should become even as they are. So closely are our duties knit together, that whoso shall keep the whole law, and yet offend in one point, he is guilty of all.

To sum up: it is wrong always, everywhere, and for anyone, to believe anything upon insufficient evidence […].

NOTE

* From Clifford's 'The Ethics of Belief', *Contemporary Review* (1877).

9 'The Will to Believe'

William James

> This extract is from a lecture entitled 'The Will to Believe', given by William
> James at Harvard in 1896 and published in *The Will to Believe and Other Essays*
> (1897). James distinguishes between different kinds of options with which we
> may be faced, particularly between 'forced' and 'avoidable' options and between
> 'living' and 'dead' ones, and denies that in the case of 'forced' options we can
> simply suspend judgement where we do not have sufficient evidence. He argues
> that Clifford's ethics of belief, though a good recipe for avoiding error, will not
> lead us to the truth. In the case of 'forced' options we are quite right to go
> beyond the objective evidence. James claims that religious questions are
> amongst those where we have a 'forced' option.

I have brought with me to-night something like a sermon on justification by faith
to read to you – I mean an essay in justification *of* faith, a defence of our right to
adopt a believing attitude in religious matters, in spite of the fact that our merely
logical intellect may not have been coerced. 'The Will to Believe', accordingly, is
the title of my paper.

I have long defended to my own students the lawfulness of voluntarily adopted
faith; but as soon as they have got well imbued with the logical spirit, they have as
a rule refused to admit my contention to be lawful philosophically, even though
in point of fact they were personally all the time chock-full of some faith or other
themselves. I am all the while, however, so profoundly convinced that my own
position is correct, that your invitation has seemed to me a good occasion to
make my statements more clear. Perhaps your minds will be more open than
those with which I have hitherto had to deal. I will be as little technical as I can,
though I must begin by setting up some technical distinctions that will help us in
the end.

I

Let us give the name of *hypothesis* to anything that may be proposed to our belief;

and just as the electricians speak of live and dead wires, let us speak of any hypothesis as either *live* or *dead*. A live hypothesis is one which appeals as a real possibility to him to whom it is proposed. If I ask you to believe in the Mahdi, the notion makes no electric connection with your nature — it refuses to scintillate with any credibility at all. As an hypothesis it is completely dead. To an Arab, however (even if he be not one of the Mahdi's followers), the hypothesis is among the mind's possibilities: it is alive. This shows that deadness and liveness in an hypothesis are not intrinsic properties, but relations to the individual thinker. They are measured by his willingness to act. The maximum of liveness in an hypothesis means willingness to act irrevocably. Practically, that means belief; but there is some believing tendency wherever there is willingness to act at all.

Next, let us call the decision between two hypotheses an *option*. Options may be of several kinds. They may be — 1, *living* or *dead*; 2, *forced* or *avoidable*; 3, *momentous* or *trivial*; and for our purposes we may call an option a *genuine* option when it is of the forced, living and momentous kind.

1 A living option is one in which both hypotheses are live ones. If I say to you: 'Be a theosophist or be a mahomedan,' it is probably a dead option, because for you neither hypothesis is likely to be alive. But if I say 'Be an agnostic or be a Christian,' it is otherwise: trained as you are, each hypothesis makes some appeal, however small, to your belief.

2 Next, if I say to you: 'Choose between going out with your umbrella or without it,' I do not offer you a genuine option, for it is not forced. You can easily avoid it by not going out at all. Similarly, if I say 'Either love me or hate me,' 'Either call my theory true or call it false,' your option is avoidable. You may remain indifferent to me, neither loving nor hating, and you may decline to offer any judgement as to my theory. But if I say 'Either accept this truth or go without it,' I put on you a forced option, for there is no standing place outside of the alternative. Every dilemma based on a complete logical disjunction, with no possibility of not choosing, is an option of this forced kind.

3 Finally, if I were Dr Nansen and proposed to you to join my North Pole expedition, your option would be momentous; for this would probably be your only similar opportunity, and your choice now would either exclude you from the North Pole sort of immortality altogether or put at least the chance of it into your hands. He who refuses to embrace a unique opportunity loses the prize as surely as if he tried and failed. *Per contra*, the option is trivial when the opportunity is not unique, when the stake is insignificant, or when the decision is reversible if it later prove unwise. Such trivial options abound in the scientific life. A chemist finds an hypothesis live enough to spend a year in its verification: he believes in it to that extent. But if his experiments prove inconclusive either way, he is quit for his loss of time, no vital harm being done.

It will facilitate our discussion if we keep all these distinctions well in mind.

II

The next matter to consider is the actual psychology of human opinion. When we look at certain facts, it seems as if our passional and volitional nature lay at the root of all our convictions. When we look at others, it seems as if they could do nothing when the intellect had once said its say. Let us take the latter facts up first.

Does it not seem preposterous on the very face of it to talk of our opinions being modifiable at will? Can our will either help or hinder our intellect in its perceptions of truth? Can we, by just willing it, believe that Abraham Lincoln's existence is a myth, and that the portraits of him in *McClure's Magazine* are all of someone else? Can we, by any effort of our will, or by any strength of wish that it were true, believe ourselves well and about when we are roaring with rheumatism in bed, or feel certain that the sum of the two one-dollar bills in our pocket must be a hundred dollars? We can *say* any of these things, but we are absolutely impotent to believe them …

In Pascal's *Thoughts* there is a celebrated passage known in literature as Pascal's wager. In it he tries to force us into Christianity by reasoning as if our concern with truth resembled our concern with the stakes in a game of chance. Translated freely his words are these: You must either believe or not believe that God is – which will you do? Your human reason cannot say. A game is going on between you and the nature of things which at the day of judgement will bring out either heads or tails. Weigh what your gains and your losses would be if you should stake all you have on heads, or God's existence: If you win in such case, you gain eternal beatitude; if you lose, you lose nothing at all. If there were an infinity of chances, and only one for God in this wager, still you ought to stake your all on God; for though you surely risk a finite loss by this procedure, a finite loss is reasonable, even a certain one is reasonable, if there is but the possibility of infinite gain. Go, then, and take holy water, and have masses said; belief will come and stupefy your scruples. Why should you not? At bottom, what have you to lose?

You probably feel that when religious faith expresses itself thus, in the language of the gaming-table, it is put to its last trumps. Surely Pascal's own personal belief in masses and holy water had far other springs; and this celebrated page of his is but an argument for others, a last desperate snatch at a weapon against the hardness of the unbelieving heart. We feel that a faith in masses and holy water adopted wilfully after such a mechanical calculation would lack the inner soul of faith's reality; and if we were ourselves in the place of the Deity, we should probably take particular pleasure in cutting off believers of this pattern from their infinite reward. It is evident that unless there be some pre-existing tendency to believe in masses and holy water, the option offered to the will by Pascal is not a living option. Certainly no Turk ever took to masses and holy water on its account; and even to us Protestants these means of salvation seem such foregone impossibilities that Pascal's logic, invoked for them specifically, leaves us unmoved. As well might the Mahdi write to us, saying 'I am the Expected One whom God has created in his effulgence. You shall be infinitely happy if you confess me; otherwise you shall be cut off from the light of the sun.

Weigh, then, your infinite gain if I am genuine against your finite sacrifice if I am not!' His logic would be that of Pascal; but he would vainly use it on us, for the hypothesis he offers us is dead. No tendency to act on it exists in us to any degree.

The talk of believing by our volition seems, then, from one point of view, simply silly. From another point of view it is worse than silly, it is vile. When one turns to the magnificent edifice of the physical sciences, and sees how it was reared; what thousands of disinterested moral lives of men lie buried in its mere foundations; what patience and postponement, what choking down of preference, what submission to the icy laws of outer fact are wrought into its very stones and mortar; how absolutely impersonal it stands in its vast augustness – then how besotted and contemptible seems every little sentimentalist who comes blowing his voluntary smoke wreaths, and pretending to decide things from out of his private dream! Can we wonder if those bred in the rugged and manly school of science should feel like spewing such subjectivism out of their mouths? The whole system of loyalties which grow up in the schools of science go dead against its toleration; so that it is only natural that those who have caught the scientific fever should pass over to the opposite extreme, and write sometimes as if the incorruptibly truthful intellect ought positively to prefer bitterness and unacceptableness to the heart in its cup.

> 'It fortifies my soul to know
> That, though I perish, Truth is so –'

sings Clough, whilst Huxley exclaims: 'My only consolation lies in the reflection that, however bad our posterity may become, so long as they hold by the plain rule of not pretending to believe what they have no reason to believe because it may be to their advantage so to pretend [the word 'pretend' is surely here redundant], they will not have reached the lowest depths of immorality.' And that delicious *enfant terrible* Clifford writes: 'Belief is desecrated when given to unproved and unquestioned statements, for the solace and private pleasure of the believer … Whoso would deserve well of his fellows in this matter will guard the purity of his belief with a very fanaticism of jealous care, lest at any time it should rest on an unworthy object, and catch a stain which can never be wiped away … If [a] belief has been accepted on insufficient evidence [even though the belief be true, as Clifford on the same page explains], the pleasure is a stolen one … It is sinful, because it is stolen in defiance of our duty to mankind. That duty is to guard ourselves from such beliefs as from a pestilence, which may shortly master our own body and then spread to the rest of the town … It is wrong always, everywhere, and for anyone, to believe anything upon insufficient evidence.'

III

All this strikes one as healthy, even when expressed, as by Clifford, with somewhat too much of robustious pathos in the voice. Free-will and simple wishing do seem, in the matter of our credence, to be only fifth wheels to the coach. Yet if anyone should thereupon assume that intellectual insight is what remains after wish and will and sentimental preference have taken wing, or that pure reason is what then settles our opinions, he would fly quite as directly in the teeth of the facts.

It is only our already dead hypotheses that our willing nature is unable to bring to life again. But what has made them dead for us is for the most part a previous action of our willing nature of an antagonistic kind. When I say 'willing nature,' I do not mean only such deliberate volition as may have set up habits of belief that we cannot now escape from – I mean all such factors of belief as fear and hope, prejudice and passion, imitation and partisanship, the circumpressure of our caste and set. ... Our reason is quite satisfied, in nine hundred and ninety-nine cases out of every thousand of us, if it can find a few arguments that will do to recite in case our credulity is criticized by someone else. Our faith is faith in someone else's faith, and in the greatest matters this is most the case. Our belief in truth itself, for instance, that there is a truth, and that our minds and it are made for each other – what is it but a passionate affirmation of desire, in which our social system backs us up? We want to have a truth; we want to believe that our experiments and studies and discussions must put us in a continually better and better position towards it; and on this line we agree to fight out our thinking lives. But if a pyrrhonistic sceptic asks us *how we know* all this, can our logic find a reply? No! Certainly it cannot. It is just one volition against another – we willing to go in for life upon a trust or assumption which he, for his part, does not care to make ...

As a rule we disbelieve all facts and theories for which we have no use ... Why do so few 'scientists' even look at the evidence for telepathy, so called? Because they think, as a leading biologist, now dead, once said to me, that even if such a thing were true, scientists ought to band together to keep it suppressed and concealed. It would undo the uniformity of Nature and all sorts of other things without which scientists cannot carry on their pursuits. But if this very man had been shown something which as a scientist he might *do* with telepathy, he might not only have examined the evidence, but even have found it good enough. This very law which the logicians would impose upon us – if I may give the name of logicians to those who would rule out our willing nature here – is based on nothing but their own natural wish to exclude all elements for which they, in their professional quality of logicians, can find no use.

Evidently, then, our non-intellectual nature does influence our convictions. There are passional tendencies and volitions which run before and others which come after belief, and it is only the latter that are too late for the fair; and they are not too late when the previous passional work has been already in their own direction. Pascal's argument, instead of being powerless, then seems a regular clincher, and is the last stroke needed to make our faith in masses and holy water complete. The state of things is evidently far from simple; and pure insight and logic, whatever they might do ideally, are not the only things that really do produce our creeds.

IV

Our next duty, having recognized this mixed-up state of affairs, is to ask whether it be simply reprehensible and pathological, or whether, on the contrary, we must treat it as a normal element in making up our minds. The thesis I defend is, briefly stated, this: *Our passional nature not only lawfully may, but must, decide an option between propositions, whenever it is a genuine option that cannot by its nature be decided on intellectual grounds; for to say, under such circumstances, 'Do not decide, but leave the question open,' is itself a passional decision — just like deciding yes or no — and is attended with the same risk of losing the truth.* The thesis thus abstractly expressed will, I trust, soon become quite clear. But I must first indulge in a bit more of preliminary work.

V

It will be observed that for the purposes of this discussion we are on 'dogmatic' ground — ground, I mean, which leaves systematic philosophical scepticism altogether out of account. The postulate that there is truth, and that it is the destiny of our minds to attain it, we are deliberately resolving to make, though the sceptic will not make it. We part company with him, therefore, absolutely, at this point. But the faith that truth exists, and that our minds can find it, may be held in two ways. We may talk of the *empiricist* way and of the *absolutist* way of believing in truth. The absolutists in this matter say that we not only can attain to knowing truth, but we can *know when* we have attained to knowing it; whilst the empiricists think that although we may attain it, we cannot infallibly know when. To *know* is one thing, and to know for certain *that* we know is another. One may hold to the first being possible without the second; hence the empiricists and the absolutists, although neither of them is a sceptic in the usual philosophic sense of the term, show very different degrees of dogmatism in their lives.

If we look at the history of opinions, we see that the empiricist tendency has largely prevailed in science, whilst in philosophy the absolutist tendency has had everything its own way ...

When the Cliffords tell us how sinful it is to be Christians on such 'insufficient evidence,' insufficiency is really the last thing they have in mind. For them the evidence is absolutely sufficient, only it makes the other way. They believe so completely in an anti-christian order of the universe that there is no living option: Christianity is a dead hypothesis from the start.

VI

But now, since we are all such absolutists by instinct, what in our quality of students of philosophy ought we to do about the fact? Shall we espouse and indorse it? Or shall we treat it as a weakness of our nature from which we must free ourselves, if we can?

I sincerely believe that the latter course is the only one we can follow as reflective men. Objective evidence and certitude are doubtless very fine ideals to play with, but where on this moonlit and dream-visited planet are they found? I am, therefore, myself a complete empiricist so far as my theory of human knowledge goes. I live, to be sure, by the practical faith that we must go on experiencing and thinking over our experience, for only thus can our opinions grow more true; but to hold any one of them – I absolutely do not care which – as if it never could be re-interpretable or corrigible, I believe to be a tremendously mistaken attitude, and I think that the whole history of philosophy will bear me out ...

VII

One more point, small but important, and our preliminaries are done. There are two ways of looking at our duty in the matter of opinion – ways entirely different, and yet ways about whose difference the theory of knowledge seems hitherto to have shown very little concern. *We must know the truth*; and *we must avoid error* – these are our first and great commandments as would-be knowers; but they are not two ways of stating an identical commandment, they are two separable laws. Although it may indeed happen that when we believe the truth *A*, we escape as an incidental consequence from believing the falsehood *B*, it hardly ever happens that by merely disbelieving *B* we necessarily believe *A*. We may in escaping *B* fall into believing other falsehoods, *C* or *D*, just as bad as *B*; or we may escape *B* by not believing anything at all, not even *A*.

Believe truth! Shun error! – these, we see, are two materially different laws; and by choosing between them we may end by colouring differently our whole intellectual life. We may regard the chase for truth as paramount, and the avoidance of error as secondary; or we may, on the other hand, treat the avoidance of error as more imperative, and let truth take its chance. Clifford, in the instructive passage which I have quoted, exhorts us to the latter course. Believe nothing, he tells us, keep your mind in suspense forever, rather than by closing it on insufficient evidence incur the awful risk of believing lies. You, on the other hand, may think that the risk of being in error is a very small matter when compared with the blessings of real knowledge, and be ready to be duped many times in your investigation rather than postpone indefinitely the chance of guessing true. I myself find it impossible to go with Clifford. We must remember that these feelings of our duty about either truth or error are in any case only expressions of our passional life. Biologically considered, our minds are as ready to grind out falsehood as veracity, and he who says 'Better go without belief forever than believe a lie!' merely shows his own preponderant private horror of becoming a dupe. He may be critical of many of his desires and fears, but this fear he slavishly obeys. He cannot imagine anyone questioning its binding force. For my own part, I have also a horror of being duped; but I can believe that worse things than being duped may happen to a man in this world: so Clifford's exhortation has to my ears a thoroughly fantastic sound. It is like a general informing his soldiers that it is better to keep out of battle forever than to risk a single wound. Not so are victories either over enemies or over nature gained. Our errors are surely not such awfully solemn things. In a world where we are so certain to incur them in spite of all our caution, a certain lightness of heart seems healthier than this excessive nervousness on their behalf. At any rate, it seems the fittest thing for the empiricist philosopher.

VIII

And now, after all this introduction, let us go straight at our question. I have said, and now repeat it, that not only as a matter of fact do we find our passional nature influencing us in our options, but that there are some options between opinions in which this influence must be regarded both as an inevitable and as a lawful determinant of our choice.

I fear here that some of you my hearers will begin to scent danger, and lend an inhospitable ear. Two first steps of passion you have indeed had to admit as necessary – we must think so as to avoid dupery, and we must think so as to gain truth; but the surest path to those ideal consummations, you will probably consider, is from now onwards to take no farther passional step.

Well, of course I agree as far as the facts will allow. Wherever the option between losing truth and gaining it is not momentous, we can throw the chance of *gaining truth* away, and at any rate save ourselves from any chance of *believing falsehood*, by not making up our minds at all till objective evidence has come. In scientific questions, this is almost always the case; and even in human affairs in general, the need of acting is seldom so urgent that a false belief to act on is better than no belief at all. Law courts, indeed, have to decide on the best evidence attainable for the moment, because a judge's duty is to make law as well as to ascertain it, and (as a learned judge once said to me) few cases are worth spending much time over: the great thing is to have them decided on *any* acceptable principle, and got out of the way. But in our dealings with objective nature we obviously are recorders, not makers, of the truth; and decisions for the mere sake of deciding promptly and getting on to the next business would be wholly out of place. Throughout the breadth of physical nature facts are what they are quite independently of us, and seldom is there any such hurry about them that the risks of being duped by believing a premature theory need be faced. The questions here are always trivial options, the hypotheses are hardly living (at any rate not living for us spectators), the choice between believing truth or falsehood is seldom forced. The attitude of sceptical balance is therefore the absolutely wise one if we would escape mistakes. What difference, indeed, does it make to most of us whether we have or have not a theory of the Röntgen rays, whether we believe or not in mind-stuff, or have a conviction about the causality of conscious states? It makes no difference. Such options are not forced on us. On every account it is better not to make them, but still keep weighting reasons *pro et contra* with an indifferent hand.

I speak, of course, here of the purely judging mind. For purposes of discovery such indifference is to be less highly recommended, and science would be far less advanced than she is if the passionate desires of individuals to get their own faiths confirmed had been kept out of the game ... On the other hand, if you want an absolute duffer in an investigation, you must, after all, take the man who has no interest whatever in its results: he is the warranted incapable, the positive fool. The most useful investigator, because the most sensitive observer, is always he whose eager interest in one side of the question is balanced by an equally keen nervousness lest he become deceived. Science has organized this nervousness into a regular *technique*, her so-called method of verification; and she has fallen so deeply in love with the method that one may even say she has ceased to care for truth by itself at all. It is only truth as technically verified that interests her. The truth of truths might come in merely affirmative form, and she would decline to touch it. Such truth as that, she might repeat with Clifford, would be stolen in defiance of her duty to mankind. Human passions, however, are stronger than technical rules. 'Le coeur a ses raisons,' as Pascal says, 'que la raison ne connait point'; and however indifferent to all but the bare rules of the game the umpire, the abstract intellect, may be, the concrete players who furnish him the materials to judge of are usually, each one of them, in love with some pet 'live hypothesis' of his own. Let us agree, however, that wherever there is no forced option, the dispassionately judicial intellect with no pet hypothesis, saving us, as it does, from dupery at any rate, ought to be our ideal.

The question next arises: Are there not somewhere forced options in our speculative questions, and can we (as men who may be interested at least as much in positively gaining truth as in merely escaping dupery) always wait with impunity till the coercive evidence shall have arrived? It seems *a priori* improbable that the truth should be so nicely adjusted to our needs and powers as that. In the great boarding-house of nature, the cakes and the butter and the syrup seldom come out so even and leave the plates so clean. Indeed, we should view them with scientific suspicion if they did.

IX

Turn now ... to a certain class of questions of fact, questions concerning personal relations, states of mind between one man and another. *Do you like me or not?* – for example. Whether you do or not depends, in countless instances, on whether I meet you half-way, am willing to assume that you must like me, and show you trust and expectation. The previous faith on my part in your liking's existence is in such cases what makes your liking come. But if I stand aloof, and refuse to budge an inch until I have objective evidence, until you shall have done something apt ... The desire for a certain kind of truth here brings about that special truth's existence; and so it is in innumerable cases of other sorts. Who gains promotions, boons, appointments, but the man in whose life they are seen to play the part of live hypotheses, who discounts them, sacrifices other things for their sake before they have come, and takes risks for them in advance? His faith acts on the powers above him as a claim, and creates its own verification.

A social organism of any sort whatever, large or small, is what it is because each member proceeds to his own duty with a trust that the other members will simultaneously do theirs. Wherever a desired result is achieved by the co-operation of many independent persons, its existence as a fact is a pure consequence of the percussive faith in one another of those immediately concerned. A government, an army, a commercial system, a ship, a college, an athletic team, all exist on this condition, without which not only is nothing achieved, but nothing is even attempted. A whole train of passengers (individually brave enough) will be looted by a few highwaymen, simply because the latter can count on one another, while each passenger fears that if he makes a movement of resistance, he will be shot before anyone else backs him up. If we believed that the whole car-full would rise at once with us, we should each severally rise, and train-robbing would never even be attempted. There are, then, cases where a fact cannot come at all unless a preliminary faith exists in its coming. *And where faith in a fact can help create the fact*, that would be an insane logic which should say that faith running ahead of scientific evidence is the 'lowest kind of immorality' into which a thinking being can fall. Yet such is the logic by which our scientific absolutists pretend to regulate our lives!

X

In truths dependent on our personal action, then, faith based on desire is certainly a lawful and possibly an indispensable thing.

But now, it will be said, these are all childish human cases, and have nothing to do with great cosmical matters, like the question of religious faith. Let us then pass on to that ...

If we are to discuss the question at all, it must involve a living option. If for any of you religion be a hypothesis that cannot, by any living possibility be true, then you need go no farther. So proceeding, we see, first, that religion offers itself as a *momentous* option. We are supposed to gain, even now, by our belief, and to lose by our non-belief, a certain vital good. Secondly, religion is a *forced* option, so far as that good goes. We cannot escape the issue by remaining sceptical and waiting for more light, because, although we do avoid error in that way *if religion be untrue*, we lose the good, *if it be true*, just as certainly as if we positively chose to disbelieve ... Scepticism, then, is not avoidance of option; it is option of a certain particular kind of risk. *Better risk loss of truth than chance of error* — that is your faith-vetoer's exact position. He is actively playing his stake as much as the believer is; he is backing the field against the religious hypothesis, just as the believer is backing the religious hypothesis against the field. To preach scepticism to us as a duty until 'sufficient evidence' for religion be found, is tantamount therefore to telling us, when in presence of the religious hypothesis, that to yield to our fear of its being error is wiser and better than to yield to our hope that it may be true. It is not intellect against all passions, then; it is only intellect with one passion laying down its law. And by what, forsooth, is the supreme wisdom of this passion warranted? Dupery for dupery, what proof is there that dupery through hope is so much worse than dupery through fear? I, for one, can see no proof; and I simply refuse obedience to the scientist's command to imitate his kind of option, in a case where my own stake is important enough to give me the right to choose my own form of risk. If religion be true and the evidence for it be still insufficient, I do not wish, by putting your extinguisher upon my nature (which feels to me as if it had after all some business in this matter), to forfeit my sole chance in life of getting upon the winning side — that chance depending, of course, on my willingness to run the risk of acting as if my passional need of taking the world religiously might be prophetic and right.

All this is on the supposition that it really may be prophetic and right, and that, even to us who are discussing the matter, religion is a live hypothesis which may be true. Now to most of us religion comes in a still farther way that makes a veto on our active faith even more illogical. The more perfect and more eternal aspect of the universe is represented in our religions as having personal form. The universe is no longer a mere *It* to us, but a *Thou*, if we are religious; and any relation that may be possible from person to person might be possible here ... This feeling, forced on us we know not whence, that by obstinately believing that there are gods (although not to do so would be so easy both for our logic and our life) we are doing the universe the deepest service we can, seems part of the living essence of the religious hypothesis. If the hypothesis *were* true in all its parts, including this one, then pure intellectualism, with its veto on our making willing advances, would be an absurdity; and some participation of our sympathetic nature would be logically required. I, therefore, for one, cannot see my way to accepting the agnostic rules for truth-seeking, or wilfully agree to keep my willing nature out of the game. I cannot do so for this plain reason, that *a rule of thinking which would absolutely prevent me from acknowledging certain kinds of truth if those kinds of truth were really there, would be an irrational rule*. That for me is the long and short of the formal logic of the situation, no matter what the kinds of truth might materially be.

I confess I do not see how this logic can be escaped. But sad experience makes me fear that some of you may still shrink from radically saying with me, *in abstracto*, that we have the right to believe at our own risk any hypothesis that is live enough to tempt our will. I suspect, however, that if this is so, it is because you have got away from the abstract logical point of view altogether, and are thinking (perhaps without realizing it) of some particular religious hypothesis which for you is dead. The freedom to 'believe what we will' you apply to the case of some patent superstition; and the faith you think of is the faith defined by the schoolboy when he said, 'Faith is when you believe something that you know ain't true.' I can only repeat that this is misapprehension. *In concreto*, the freedom to believe can only cover living options which the intellect of the individual cannot by itself resolve; and living options never seem absurdities to him who has them to consider. When I look at the religious question as it really puts itself to concrete men, and when I think of all the possibilities which both practically and theoretically it involves, then this command that we shall put a stopper on our heart, instincts and courage, and *wait* – acting of course meanwhile more or less as if religion were *not* true – till doomsday, or till such time as our intellect and senses working together may have raked in evidence enough – this command, I say, seems to me the queerest idol ever manufactured in the philosophic cave. Were we scholastic absolutists, there might be more excuse. If we had an infallible intellect with its objective certitudes, we might feel ourselves disloyal to such a perfect organ of knowledge in not trusting to it exclusively, in not waiting for its releasing word. But if we are empiricists, if we believe that no bell in us tolls to let us know for certain when truth is in our grasp, then it seems a piece of idle fantasticality to preach so solemnly our duty of waiting for the bell. Indeed we *may* wait if we will – I hope you do not think that I am denying that – but if we do so, we do so at our peril as much as if we believed. In either case we *act*, taking our life in our hands. No one of us ought to issue vetoes to the other, nor should we bandy words of abuse. We ought, on the contrary, delicately and profoundly to respect one another's mental freedom – then only shall we bring about the intellectual republic; then only shall we have that spirit of inner tolerance without which all our outer tolerance is soulless, and which is empiricism's glory; then only shall we live and let live, in speculative as well as in practical things.

Revision test

The following exercises are designed to enable you to test whether you have absorbed some of the key ideas from the foregoing material and whether you have achieved the relevant chapter objectives.

CHAPTER 1

1 Which of the following are pertinent objections to the Platonic argument for immortality based upon the simplicity of the soul?

   (a) There are other ways for things to cease to exist than being broken into parts.
   (b) Dualism is not a tenable theory of the mind–body relationship.
   (c) Souls are not substances in their own right.

2 Which of the following are pertinent objections to believing that people have substantial souls that persist after the destruction of their bodies?

   (a) There is no good reason to believe that souls can exist as separate entities.
   (b) No one wants to live for ever.
   (c) An account of human immortality needs to be accompanied by an explanation of how animals that have some consciousness fit in.
   (d) The belief in immortality is simply wishful thinking.
   (e) Even if there are disembodied beings it is not clear how they can be said to be identical with some person who lived in our world.

3 Idealism is the view that:

   (a) Hope should always triumph over experience.
   (b) The only things that exist are minds and their contents.
   (c) Ideas are all important.

CHAPTER 2

4 If materialism is true then what follows for belief in an afterlife?

   (a) An afterlife is absolutely impossible.
   (b) An afterlife is very improbable.
   (c) It is likely that our bodies will be resurrected.

5 According to Peter Van Inwagen, which of the following claims needs to be defended by a materialist theory of the resurrection?

   (a) God brings back together all the atoms that formerly constituted each individual resurrected.
   (b) God preserves the physical core of a person after death.
   (c) God substitutes a new body for the one that has been destroyed.

6 Which of the following are offered by Linda Badham as objections to believing in the resurrection of the same body?

   (a) We are constantly losing our atoms to others and it would be impossible to restore all atoms to their rightful owners.
   (b) Resurrected bodies would be just as much subject to decay and death as those they replaced.
   (c) If everyone were resurrected then the afterlife would be too crowded.

7 Which of the following must be true if Darwinism is true?

   (a) The human race came from the dust and to the dust it will return.
   (b) God created each individual human soul at the moment of conception.

CHAPTER 3

8 Which of the following are implications of Darwinism?

   (a) The universe was not designed.
   (b) The argument from design is shown to be inconclusive.
   (c) We do not need to assume intelligence in order to explain the presence of order in the universe that serves a purpose.

9 According to Occam's Razor, which of the following maxims should be observed?

   (a) A theory should not contain more abstract entities than is strictly necessary.

(b) The simpler a theory is the better.

(c) The shorter a book is the better.

(d) If in doubt, cut it out.

10 Which of the following must someone who believes in natural theology as a basis for religious belief subscribe to?

(a) What you read in the Bible is not necessarily true.

(b) There are no divinely revealed truths.

(c) Religious belief can be given a basis in reason.

(d) We should follow nature in forming our religious beliefs.

CHAPTER 4

11 Which of the following assumptions did J. H. Newman use in his 'moral' argument for the existence of God?

(a) Conscience is the only reliable guide as to our duties.

(b) Conscience points to a higher sanction.

(c) Conscience makes cowards of us all.

12 Which of the following assumptions did Kant use in his 'moral' argument for the existence of God?

(a) People have a duty to promote the highest good.

(b) If we *ought* to achieve something, this implies we *are able to* achieve it.

(c) Morality is a matter of our long-term interest.

13 Which of the following assumptions did Rashdall use in his 'moral' argument for the existence of God?

(a) Statements of moral duties are categorical imperatives.

(b) Moral standards are in no way material.

(c) There is a mental world quite separate from the material.

(d) Moral standards exist independently of human minds.

CHAPTER 5

14 Does John Hick either subscribe to or deny any of the following in his discussion of 'the free-will defence'?

(a) God can do anything even if it involves a contradiction.

(b) There is no inconsistency in the claim that God could have made us so that we would all freely act in the ways he wanted all of the time.

  (c) A universe in which people freely choose the good is better than a
      universe of robots.
  (d) The devil does not exist.

15 Does John Hick either subscribe to or deny any of the following in his discussion of the problem of animal suffering?

  (a) Animals do not feel pain.
  (b) Animals do not worry about the future.
  (c) Pain helps animals to survive.

CHAPTER 6

16 Which of the following qualify as a miracle, in accordance with Hume's definitions?

  (a) A violation of a law of nature.
  (b) An amazing coincidence.
  (c) A marvel.
  (d) Any departure from the usual course of nature.
  (e) A transgression of a law of nature by the particular volition of a deity.

17 Which of the following is implied by Hume's injunction that we should
   always reject the greater miracle?

  (a) Only believe minor miracles.
  (b) Always believe the more probable of two conflicting accounts.
  (c) The taller the story the more likely it is that someone is lying.

18 For which of the following reasons did Hume claim that miracles could never
   be the foundation of any system of religion?

  (a) There are no violations of laws of nature.
  (b) The evidence for the miracles of any one religion is contradicted by the
      evidence for the miracles favouring all others.
  (c) Religious beliefs have no rational foundation.

CHAPTER 7

19 Why did Clifford hold that it is always wrong to believe on insufficient
   evidence?

  (a) The belief held is bound to be false.
  (b) The belief will, on balance, cause more unhappiness than happiness.
  (c) The belief is bound to have a harmful effect on the destiny of mankind.

20 Which of the following expresses Pascal's wager?

    (a) Believing in God is a safe bet.

    (b) If you stake your life on the Catholic religion you have a better than even chance of being right.

    (c) If you stake your life on the Catholic religion you have only an even chance of being right but you lose little if you are wrong compared with what you gain if you are right.

21 Which of the following are pertinent criticisms of Pascal's wager?

    (a) There is much less chance of being right, whatever we believe about religion, than Pascal assumed.

    (b) Gambling is wrong and doubly wrong in religious matters.

    (c) The wager falsely assumes that we can decide whether or not to believe in God.

    (d) The choice is not a 'living option' except for lapsed Catholics.

Answers to exercises

EXERCISE 1.1

Premise 1   Anything that cannot be dispersed is immortal.
Premise 2   Anything that does not have parts cannot be dispersed.
Premise 3   The soul does not have parts.

Therefore,

Conclusion 1   The soul cannot be dispersed. (Sub-conclusion from premises 2 and 3.)

Therefore,

Conclusion 2   The soul is immortal. (Conclusion from premise 1 and conclusion 1.)

EXERCISE 1.3

1   One assumption is that memory is a *necessary condition* of personal identity. In the language Reid himself used – which seems to echo that of Locke – it is necessary for 'the general's consciousness to reach as far back as his flogging' if he is to be identified with the boy who was flogged. This means that if his consciousness did not reach that far back, if (that is to say) he cannot recall the flogging, 'he is not the person who was flogged'.
2   The other assumption is a logical principle regarding identity: If X is identical with Y and Y is identical with Z, then X is identical with Z.

EXERCISE 1.5

1   Basically Berkeley's argument is an abridged version of the Platonic argu-

ment from the simplicity of the soul. (There is one complication, namely that Berkeley also implies that the active nature of the soul is a reason for thinking it is immortal. But he does not expand on this, so we will need to pass it over.) His main point is that the soul is an 'indivisible', 'simple, uncompounded' substance and is therefore 'incorruptible' and 'indissoluble' by natural forces. The argument appears to be that only extended, compound things are liable to be dissolved or corrupted. This is so of corporeal things. Souls, however, are simple and uncompounded and so not liable to be dissolved or corrupted, at least by natural means.

2 The objections that have been raised to the Platonic argument from the simplicity of the soul also apply to Berkeley's argument.

EXERCISE 2.2

The three objections are:

(a) The atoms that constitute our body are continually being lost by us to our environment and to other individuals and we are constantly acquiring 'borrowed' atoms from our environment, including other individuals. The project of restoring the atoms to their proper owners is fraught with difficulty.

(b) Even if our body could be reconstituted it would still be subject to decay and indeed would be liable to malfunction and to perish again. If it were mended as much as was needed to avoid this, it is doubtful whether it could be called the 'same flesh' any more or whether the person could be called the same person.

(c) Even if these problems could be surmounted, there are simply too many people who will have lived at one time or another. The afterlife would be hopelessly overcrowded if they were all made immortal.

EXERCISE 3.2

1 He appears to mean that creationism (etc.) are alleged to be serious 'rivals' of natural selection, whose claims are based upon evidence, but that, on inspection, they are not serious rivals at all. Hence his remark that all 'give some superficial appearance of being alternatives to Darwinism', but they are not really so because, unlike the theory of natural selection, they don't really explain organized complexity at all.

2 He specifically acknowledges that it is not possible to disprove either creationism or the guided evolution theory, so long as they do not make claims about the phenomena which might turn out to be wrong. (Then it would be possible, he seems to think, to give a scientific refutation of them.)

3 The doomed rivals are not, then, views that science has disproved but rather, or so Dawkins claims, ones that turn out not to provide the kind of explanation that we need – which is, according to him, an explanation of the organized complexity that exists in the universe. According to Dawkins only

the theory of natural selection does this. It has no serious rivals and its apparent rivals are doomed to be dismissed as 'superfluous'.

EXERCISE 3.3

The modern argument for design is, fundamentally, that it is too much of a coincidence that the conditions are exactly right for life to have evolved and hence that those conditions did not arise by mere chance.

The two reservations are:

1 There may be a scientific explanation of these constants which would explain why they are as they are. One has been suggested for the expansion rate of the universe.
2 If our universe were one of an infinite number of universes, then we could imagine that in the vast majority the conditions are wrong for the emergence of life as we know it – so, for instance, no stars formed or the planets did not last long enough (and so on). In that context it would be unsurprising that the conditions were just right in at least one case.

EXERCISE 3.5

It is a *valid* argument. This means that if we accept the premises 1–3 then we must accept the conclusion. Or, put another way, if the premises 1–3 are true then truth of the conclusion is guaranteed. Despite being valid, however, the argument does not take us where we want. For while many others would accept premises 2 and 3, only a Muslim would accept premise 1. The argument only works for Muslims who do not already believe that the good will be rewarded and wicked punished. But they may be hard to find. And in any case we want an argument that will convince non-Muslims as well.

EXERCISE 4.2

The author begins by claiming that conscience has a 'legitimate' place amongst our mental acts (paragraph 1). Conscience both tells us what duties are and enjoins us to perform them (paragraph 2). Unlike taste, conscience points beyond self to a 'higher' sanction (paragraph 3). It is, moreover, associated with emotions such as fear and reverence (paragraph 4). These can only be aroused in us by another intelligent being (paragraph 5). But they are not aroused by an 'earthly object'. Therefore they must be aroused by an object that is 'Supernatural and Divine'.

EXERCISE 4.5

Premise 1   People have a duty to promote the highest good (*summum bonum*) (second statement in passage).

Premise 2   People cannot attain the highest good unaided (first statement in passage).

But

Premise 3   People only have a duty to achieve goals that they can achieve
                   (suppressed premise, drawn from ought–implies–can principle).

So

Conclusion 1   People can achieve the highest good through superhuman aid.

Hence

Conclusion 2   There is a superhuman agency enabling people to achieve the
                   highest good.

EXERCISE 5.1

The argument can be continued as follows:

Conclusion 1   God will prevent all the evil he can (from premises 2 and 5).
Conclusion 2   Evil does not exist (from premise 3 and conclusion 1).
Conclusion 3   Therefore, evil both exists and does not exist (from premise 4
                   and conclusion 2).

EXERCISE 5.3

1 In the first phase Hick points out that, although God is omnipotent, that
  does not mean that he can accomplish what is self-contradictory. It would
  only be a limitation of God's power if it was possible to describe some
  outcome that he could not bring about. But what is logically impossible
  cannot be described. In the second phase Hick puts forward the claim that it
  would be a self-contradiction to speak of personal beings who were not free
  to choose to do wrong as well as to do right.
2 The objection is that there is no self-contradiction in the idea that persons
  are created by God who are free to choose wrong but always choose to do
  what is right. Thus there need not be evil in the world, i.e. it was logically
  possible for God to have created a world without evil if only he had wanted
  to. Hence the free-will defence does not succeed and the logical problem of
  evil remains. Hick's reply is that there is a contradiction in the idea that God
  should value the love of humans freely given to him when he realizes all
  along that he had constructed them just so that they would. So the objection
  to the free-will defence, he argues, does not stand.

EXERCISE 6.1

1 Hume begins by enunciating the principle that experience is our only guide
  in matters of fact. The more our own experience has been of a particular
  kind (such as not having seen frost in July) the more we will be inclined to

expect it to continue in the same way (no frost in July). But experience also teaches us ways in which, if we are wise, we will qualify our beliefs. Our own experience teaches us how far and when we can rely upon the testimony of others. We know it is more likely to be reliable if, for instance, it is confirmed by many witnesses or if they are of known integrity. We should not accept it, however, if, for instance, it is contradictory or if the witnesses have a vested interest in getting others to believe their story. We should consider the intrinsic likelihood of the story itself as well as the credibility of the witnesses who testify to it. In an extreme case, Hume says, the 'incredibility of a fact' may be sufficient to outweigh the evidence of witnesses, no matter how reliable.

2 Hume says that the Indian prince 'reasoned justly', since his own experience was uniformly so different from that reported by travellers. He had more reason to doubt the reliability of those who told him stories about how water froze when it became very cold than he had to believe the stories. (It requires quite a bit of imagination for us to appreciate that, without television or film to give indirect experience of polar regions or winter weather far from the Equator and without freezers to give direct experience of frozen water, the existence of ice might be harder to accept than the existence of dragons or giants. Hume's point can be put by saying that, whereas experience prepares us for remarkable variations in species and significant variations in the size of humans, the prince's experience did not prepare him for variations in water between a liquid and a solid state.)

EXERCISE 6.3

1 A 'law of nature' is an invariable conjunction or separation of two kinds of phenomena. Being mortal, to give one of Hume's examples, is invariably conjoined with being human. All humans are mortal. Being lead, to give another example, is invariably separated from being unsupported in the air. Laws of nature are known through experience which Hume refers to as 'firm and unalterable' and as 'uniform'. They admit of no exception.

2 Hume states that a miracle is 'a violation of a law of nature'. He refines this definition in a note, saying that a miracle is 'a transgression of a law of nature by a particular volition of the Deity, or by the interposition of some invisible agent'. But the fuller definition is not needed in the context of Hume's argument since he is concerned with the question whether it can ever be reasonable to believe that events occur which are contrary to laws of nature. The further question as to how such events are to be understood does not arise except for those who concede that they actually take place.

3 Hume's argument is that the evidence that establishes a law of nature, namely the uniform experience of humankind, establishes it as universal and as holding therefore without exception. Whatever evidence there is in favour of a law of nature is at the same time evidence *against* any exceptions. Miracles are exceptions. Thus, by the nature of the case (i.e. of what miracles are), miracles are events of whose non-occurrence we have the strongest evidence possible, this evidence being the uniform experience of humankind.

EXERCISE 6.4

1 The general maxim Hume enunciates is that a testimony could only establish the fact of a miracle if it were more miraculous for the testimony to be false than for the alleged miraculous events to have actually occurred. He puts it even more succinctly in the injunction: 'always reject the greater miracle'.

2 Hume does not think it is absolutely impossible that miracles do occur. His point is that, to be a miracle, it would need to be the kind of event which human experience (as so far known) overwhelmingly rules out. But experience is limited and so it is not absolutely impossible that such events do occur. Like the Indian prince we may yet discover that things do happen that are exceptions to what we take to be laws of nature.

EXERCISE 6.7

Hume seems to have two kinds of argument. First, as he argues in paragraph 24, different systems of religion are mutually incompatible. Thus any evidence that supports a miracle wrought in any one system is destructive of those of rival systems, and vice versa. The total evidence is thus contradictory and no conclusion favouring any particular system of religion can be reached. The second line of argument is the one he gives in paragraph 38. Here his point is that fraud is so commonplace in such matters as to ensure that the probability of the testimony being true will never be high enough to offset the improbability of the event.

EXERCISE 7.1

Clifford begins by offering two examples where he expects us all to agree that someone is blameworthy for believing something on insufficient evidence. He then tries to generalize from these two examples.

EXERCISE 7.3

It is not a valid argument, since there is no inconsistency in admitting that people have a particular biological urge and believing that they should not follow it. The argument can, of course, be made valid by adding an extra premise to the effect that people always ought to follow their biological urges.

EXERCISE 7.6

INTRODUCTION

James begins by announcing that he is going to defend holding a believing attitude in matters of religion.

I He distinguishes between different kinds of *option*: living versus dead; forced versus avoidable; momentous versus trivial; giving examples of each.

II There is a problem whether our 'passional and volitional' nature can influence our opinions, and, if it can, whether it should.

III James argues that, in certain circumstances, it not only can but should, but he thinks that in others it cannot and should not.

IV The thesis of the lecture is formally stated.

V A distinction is drawn between 'empiricism' and 'absolutism'.

VI Absolutism is held to be a weakness in our nature from which we should try to free ourselves.

VII Faced with the choice between seeking truth and avoiding error Clifford wrongly chooses to avoid error where an empiricist will choose to seek truth.

VIII Where there are no forced options, however, the ideal would be not to go beyond the objective evidence.

IX Questions to do with personal relations are among those where we do have forced options.

X So are religious questions and hence we are entitled, in religious matters, to go beyond the evidence in what we believe.

EXERCISE 7.7

James thinks that Pascal's wager takes for granted that the choice between believing in God and not believing is a 'living option'. It would make no impression on a Turk or even a Protestant or anyone else in whom there did not already exist some tendency to act on it. (James here assumes Turks are Muslims. He includes Protestants as those he assumes will have no inclination to believe in the efficacy of masses.) Both examples could be confusing. In the case of a 'living option' there is already some inclination to believe, however small. Where there is already some inclination to believe in the efficacy of masses etc., according to James: 'Pascal's argument, instead of being powerless, then seems a regular clincher, and is the last stroke needed to make our faith in masses and holy water complete.'

EXERCISE 7.8

1 James draws a distinction between dogmatic *absolutists*, who believe they know for certain when they have attained the truth, and *empiricists*, like himself, who are not dogmatic in this way. Absolutists will have a closed mind on certain topics and so certain options will be dead for them that are still alive for more open-minded empiricists. James objects to Clifford partly because he seemed to him to be an absolutist about Christianity, i.e. assumes throughout that there is no question of its being true. He also objects to Clifford's claim that it is always wrong to believe something which is not entirely supported by the evidence.

2 James's dichotomy between the dogmatic absolutist and the open-minded empiricist is clearly intended to imply that Clifford has a wrong attitude. The suggestion seems to be that absolutism is a characteristic intellectual vice of philosophers and that they would do better to be empiricists and adopt the more open-minded attitudes that tend to prevail amongst scientists. (See section V.)

He also objects, in section VII (paragraph 2), that Clifford insists, in effect, on the principle that we must avoid error at all costs and that Clifford does not attach sufficient weight to the principle ('law') that we must seek truth. Errors, James suggests, are 'not such awfully solemn things' and it is wrong to be so nervous about making them that we miss out on the 'paramount' goal, which is to arrive at truth. James likens Clifford to the general who tells his soldiers that it is better to keep out of battle than to risk a single wound. But, just as this is no way to advance a war, so making avoidance of error paramount is no way to advance the frontiers of science.

Answers to revision test

1	(a) and (c)
2	(a), (c) and (e)
3	(b)
4	(b)
5	(b)
6	(a), (b) and (c)
7	Neither
8	(b) and (c)
9	(a) and (b)
10	(c)
11	(b)
12	(a) and (b)
13	(b), (c) and (d)
14	Hick denies (a) and (b) but subscribes to (c)
15	Hick denies (a) but subscribes to (b) and (c)
16	(a) and (e)
17	(b) and (c)
18	(b)
19	(c)
20	(c)
21	(a), (c) and (d)

Bibliography

Aquinas, Thomas, *Summa de Veritate Catholicae Fidei Contra Gentiles* (1259–64), trans. A. C. Pegis and others as *On the Truth of the Catholic Faith*, 5 vols, Garden City, NY: Doubleday, 1955–7.

Badham, P. and Badham, L. (eds) (1987) *Death and Immortality in the Religions of the World*, Oxford: Pergamon Press.

Bayle, P. (1686) *Commentaire philosophique sur les paroles de Jésus-Christ 'Constrains-les d'entrer'* (Philosophical Commentary on the words of Jesus 'Compel them to come in'), Rotterdam.

Bayle, P. (1695–7) *Dictionnaire historique et critique*, Rotterdam. Partially translated in *Historical and Critical Dictionary: Selections*, trans. R. H. Popkin, Indianapolis: Hackett, 1991.

Berkeley, G. (1710) *The Principles of Human Knowledge*, Dublin.

Berkeley, G. (1975) *Philosophical Works*, ed. M. R. Ayers, London: Dent.

Berman, D. (1994) *George Berkeley: Idealism and the Man*, Oxford: Clarendon Press.

Bird, G. (1987) *William James*, London: Routledge & Kegan Paul.

Brown, G. (1984) 'A Defence of Pascal's Wager', *Religious Studies* 20: 465–80.

Brown, S. (1989) 'Christian Averroism, Fideism and the "Two-fold Truth"', in *The Philosophy in Christianity*, ed. G. Vesey, Cambridge: Cambridge University Press, pp. 207–23.

Brown, S. (1996) 'John Locke as Secret Spinozist: The Perspective of William Carroll', in *Disguised and Overt Spinozism around 1700*, ed. W. van Bunge and W. Klever, Leiden: Brill.

Brown, S. (1997) 'F. M. van Helmont: His Philosophical Connections and the Reception of his Later Cabbalistic Philosophy', in *Studies in Seventeenth-Century European Philosophy*, ed. M. A. Stewart, Oxford: Clarendon Press, pp. 97–116.

Brown, S. (1998) 'Soul, Body and Natural Immortality', *Monist* 81: 573–90.

Brown, S., Collinson, D. and Wilkinson, R. (eds) (1996) *Biographical Dictionary of Twentieth-Century Philosophers*, London: Routledge.

Carr, B. J. and Rees, M. J. (1979) 'The Anthropic Principle and the Structure of the Physical World', *Nature* 12 (April).

Carroll, L. (1960) *The Annotated Alice*, London: Anthony Blond.

Catholic University of America (Editorial Staff) (1967) *New Catholic Encyclopedia*, New York: McGraw-Hill.

Churchland, P. (1984) *Matter and Consciousness: A Contemporary Introduction to the Philosophy of Mind*, Cambridge, MA: Bradford Books/MIT Press.

Clark, M. (1974) *Paley*, Toronto: University of Toronto Press.

Clifford, W. K. (1875) 'Right and Wrong: The Scientific Ground of their Distinction', *Fortnightly Review*. Reprinted in *The Ethics of Belief and Other Essays*, ed. L. Stephen and F. Pollock, London: Watts (*The Thinker's Library*), 1947.

Clifford, W. K. (1877a) 'The Ethics of Belief', *Contemporary Review*. Reprinted in *Lectures and Essays*, London: Macmillan, 1879.

Clifford, W. K. (1877b) 'The Ethics of Religion', *Fortnightly Review*. Reprinted in *The Ethics of Belief and Other Essays*, ed. L. Stephen and F. Pollock, London: Watts (*The Thinker's Library*), 1947.

Corey, M. A. (1993) *God and the New Cosmology: The Anthropic Design Argument*, New York: Rowman & Littlefield.

Cottingham, J. (1986) *Descartes*, Oxford: Blackwell.

Cottingham, J. (ed.) (1992) *The Cambridge Companion to Descartes*, Cambridge: Cambridge University Press.

Craig, E. (ed.) (1998) *Routledge Encyclopedia of Philosophy*, London: Routledge.

Crowe, C. J. (1984) *Plato*, Brighton: Harvester Press.

Cullmann, O. (1958) *Immortality of the Soul or Resurrection of the Dead?*, London: Epworth.

Darwin, F. (ed.) (1887) *Life and Letters of Charles Darwin*, London: Murray.

Davies, B. (1993) *An Introduction to the Philosophy of Religion*, Oxford: Oxford University Press, 2nd edition. Available as Opus Paperback.

Davies, P. C. W. (1982) *The Accidental Universe*, Cambridge: Cambridge University Press.

Davis, S. T. (ed.) (1989) *Death and Afterlife*, London: Macmillan.

Dawkins, R. (1988) *The Blind Watchmaker*, Harmondsworth: Penguin.

de Beer, E. S. (ed.) (1974) *Charles Darwin and T.H. Huxley: Autobiographies*, Oxford: Oxford University Press.

Dennett, D. (1995) *Darwin's Dangerous Idea*, Harmondsworth: Penguin.

Descartes, R. (1964–76) *Oeuvres de Descartes*, ed. C. Adam and P. Tannery, revised edition, 12 vols, Paris: Vrin/CNRS.

Descartes, R. (1991) *The Philosophical Writings of Descartes*, trans. J. Cottingham, R. Stoothoff and D. Murdoch, Cambridge: Cambridge University Press.

Desmond, A. and Moore, J. (1991) *Darwin*, Harmondsworth: Michael Joseph.

Eddy, M. B. (1875) *Science and Health*, Boston: Christian Science Publishing; 1934 edition.

Edwards, P. (ed.) (1967) *The Encyclopedia of Philosophy*, New York: Macmillan.

Edwards, P. (ed.) (1997) *Immortality*, Amherst, NY: Prometheus Books.

Elliot-Binns, J. E. (1956) *English Thought 1860–1900. The Theological Argument*, Harlow: Longmans, Green.

Evans, C. S. (1997) 'Moral Arguments', in *The Blackwell Companion to the Philosophy of Religion*, ed. P. L. Quinn and C. Taliaferro, Oxford: Blackwell, pp. 345–51.

Gaskin, J. C. A. (1978) *Hume's Philosophy of Religion*, New York: Macmillan.

Hazard, P. (1964) *The European Mind 1680–1715*, trans. J. Lewis May, Harmondsworth: Penguin.

Helm, P. (1973) *The Varieties of Belief*, London: Allen & Unwin.

Helm, P. (1981) *Divine Commands and Morality*, Oxford: Oxford University Press.

Hick, J. (1966) *Evil and the God of Love*, London: Macmillan.

Holland, R. F. (1965) 'The Miraculous', *American Philosophical Quarterly* 2: 43–51.

Horton, J. and Mendus, S. (1991) *John Locke: A Letter Concerning Toleration in Focus*, London: Routledge.

Hume, D. (1748) 'Of Miracles', *Enquiry Concerning Human Understanding*, Sect. X. in *Hume's Enquiries: Concerning Human Understanding and Concerning the Principles of Morals*, ed. L. A. Selby-Bigge. Revised P. H. Nidditch, Oxford: Clarendon Press, 1975.

Hume, D. (1779) *Dialogues Concerning Natural Religion* (posth.), ed. J. C.A. Gaskin, Oxford: Oxford University Press, 1993.

James, W. (1896) 'The Will to Believe', in *The Will to Believe and Other Essays in Popular Philosophy*, ed. W. James, Harlow: Longman, 1897.

James, W. (1897) *The Will to Believe and Other Essays in Popular Philosophy*, Harlow: Longman.

Jolley, N. (1999) *Locke: His Philosophical Thought*, Oxford: Oxford University Press.

Kant, I. (1788) *Critique of Pure Reason*, trans. L. W. Beck, Riga: Bobbs-Merrill (Library of Liberal Arts), 1956.

Kant, I. (1793) *Religion within the Limits of Reason Alone*, trans. T. M. Greene and H. H. Hudson, Königsberg: Harper Torchbooks edition, 1960.

Kenny, A. (1969) *The Five Ways*, London: Routledge & Kegan Paul.

Ker, I. T. (1990) *The Achievement of John Henry Newman*, Notre Dame, IN: University of Notre Dame Press.

Kuhn, T. S. (1970) *The Structure of Scientific Revolutions*, Chicago: Chicago University Press, 2nd edition.

Labrousse, E. (1983) *Bayle*, Oxford: Oxford University Press (Past Master's Series).

Le Poidevin, R. (1996) *Arguing for Atheism: An Introduction to the Philosophy of Religion*, London: Routledge.

Leibniz, G. (1988) *Discourse on Metaphysics and Related Writings*, ed. and trans. R. N. D. Martin and Stuart Brown, Manchester: Manchester University Press.

Lewis, H. D. (1978) *Persons and Life after Death*, London: Macmillan.

Lewis, H. D. (1993) *The Self and Immortality*, London: Macmillan.

Locke, J. (1690) *An Essay Concerning Human Understanding*, ed. Peter H. Nidditch, Oxford: Clarendon Press, 1975.

Luria, Isaac, 'De Revolutionibus Animarum Tractatus', trans. from Hebrew by Christian Knorr von Rosenroth, in *Kabbala Denudata*, ed. C. K. von Rosenroth, Vol. 2, 1684, reprinted Hildesheim: Olms, 1974.

Lyons, W. (1980) *Gilbert Ryle: An Introduction to his Philosophy*, Brighton: Harvester Press.

MacDonald Ross, G. (1984) *Leibniz*, Oxford: Oxford University Press.

Mackie, J. L. (1955) 'Evil and Omnipotence', *Mind* LXIV.

Mackie, J. L. (1982) *The Miracle of Theism*, Oxford: Clarendon Press.

McCord Adams, M. and Adams, R. M. (1990) *The Problem of Evil*, Oxford: Oxford University Press.

McCord Adams, M. (1987) *William Ockham*, Notre Dame, IN: University of Notre Dame Press.

Metzer, S. E. (1967) *Discourses of the Fall: A Study of Pascal's Pensées*, Berkeley, CA: University of California Press.

Mitchell, B. (1981) *The Justification of Religious Belief*, Oxford: Oxford University Press.

Nadler, S. (ed.) (2000) *The Cambridge Companion to Malebranche*, Cambridge: Cambridge University Press.

Newman, J. H. (1870) *An Essay in Aid of a Grammar of Assent*, Burns & Oates. New edition: I. T. Ker (ed.), Oxford: Clarendon Press, 1985.

Owen, H. P. (1965) *The Moral Argument for Christian Theism*, London: Allen & Unwin.

Paley, W. (1838) *The Works of William Paley*, Harlow: Longman, Vol. I.

Pascal, B. (1973) *Blaise Pascal: Pensées: Notes on Religion and Other Subjects*, ed. Louis Lafuma, trans. John Warrington, London: J. M. Dent.

Penelhum, T. (1995) *Reason and Religious Faith*, Boulder, CO: Westview Press.

Perry, J. (1978) *A Dialogue on Personal Identity and Immortality*, Indianapolis: Hackett.

Peterson, M. *et al.* (eds) (1996) *Philosophy of Religion: Selected Readings*, Oxford: Oxford University Press.

Pojman, L. P. (1986) *Religious Belief and the Will*, London: Routledge & Kegan Paul.

Popper, K. R. (1965) *Conjectures and Refutations*, London: Routledge & Kegan Paul, 2nd edition.

Putnam, H. (1988) *Representation and Reality*, Reading, Ma: MIT Press.

Quinn, P. L. and Taliaferro, C. (eds) (1997) *The Blackwell Companion to the Philosophy of Religion*, Oxford: Blackwell.

Radcliffe Richards, J. (2000) *Human Nature after Darwin*, Milton Keynes: Open University and London: Routledge.

Rashdall, H. (1907) *Theory of Good and Evil*, Oxford: Oxford University Press.

Reid, T. (1785) *Essays on the Intellectual Powers of Man*, Edinburgh.

Richardson, A. (1947) *Christian Apologetics*, London: SCM Press.

Ryle, G. (1949) *The Concept of Mind*, London: Hutchinson.

Scholem, G. G. (1941) *Major Trends in Jewish Mysticism*, Jerusalem.

Smart, J. J. C. and Haldane, J. J. (1996) *Atheism and Theism*, Oxford: Blackwell.

Sober, E. (1994) 'Let's Razor Ockham's Razor', in E. Sober (ed.) *From a Biological Point of View*, Cambridge: Cambridge University Press, pp. 136–57.

Stannard, R. (1989) *Grounds for Reasonable Belief*, Edinburgh: Scottish Academic Press.

Swinburne, R. (1979) *The Existence of God*, Oxford: Clarendon Press.

Swinburne, R. (ed.) (1989) *Miracles*, New York: Macmillan.

Swinburne, R. (1997) *The Evolution of the Soul*, Oxford: Clarendon Press, revised edition.

Van Helmont, F. M. (1684), *Two Hundred Queries moderately propounded concerning the Doctrine of the Revolution of Humane Souls ...*, London.

Van Inwagen, P. (n.d.) 'Resurrection', posted at Website http://www.faithquest.com/philosophers/vaninwagen/res.html.

Van Inwagen, P. (1978) 'The Possibility of Resurrection', *International Journal for Philosophy of Religion* 9: 114–21. Reprinted in Edwards, Paul (ed.), *Immortality*, Amherst, NY: Prometheus Books, 1997, pp. 242–6.

Vesey, G. (ed.) (1989) *The Philosophy in Christianity*, Cambridge: Cambridge University Press.

Warburton, N. (1996) *Thinking from A to Z*, London: Routledge.

Warner, Richard and Szubka, Tadeusz (eds) (1994) *The Mind–Body Problem: A Guide to the Current Debate*, Oxford: Blackwell.

Wilkinson, R. (2000) *Minds and Bodies*, Milton Keynes: Open University and London: Routledge.

Wood, A. W. (1970) *Kant's Moral Religion*, Ithaca, NY: Cornell University Press.

Index